Transforming Leadership, Improving the Patient Experience

This book focuses on the patient experience as a leadership strategy. It explores the relationships between coordinated care, expert leadership, provider-patient communications, and the patient experience. When clinical and nonclinical staff collaborate effectively, healthcare teams can improve patient outcomes, prevent medical errors, improve efficiency, and increase patient satisfaction.

Surprisingly, however, healthcare leaders tend to prioritize specific metrics to improve hospital performance and patient satisfaction even though patient experience and provider-patient communications are intertwined. Determining the most effective strategy for achieving higher levels of service quality and patient satisfaction can prove elusive for providers.

Consider the evidence: a survey in 2012 of more than 17,000 healthcare leaders in North America, for example, found that leaders' perceptions did not always match the data, and many hospital leaders overestimated the performance of their hospitals. Over 75% of the hospital leaders reported "quality of care" was something their hospital did well, while their patients, on average, rated them lower on perceived service quality. Ten years later, in 2022, only a few providers integrated best practices to achieve high patient satisfaction which severely impacted CMS Hospital Star Rating. This has significant effects on profit margins since patients consider the star rating differentials in their choices of hospitals and are willing to pay upward of 17% extra for treatments in 5-star hospitals, a revenue generating source of income at times when hospitals have seen falling revenues (down 4.8%) and rising labor (up 37%) from pre-COVID-19 pandemic levels.

To reduce the gap between perception and reality, hospital leaders can consider the link between communication goals (e.g., responsiveness of hospital staff, pain management, communication about medicines) and outcomes (e.g., increased adherence and compliance, readmission, healthcare delivery costs, hospital overall ratings) as well as improve the patient experience.

When intentions and outcomes are aligned, they create a powerful medium by which healthcare leaders can evaluate the gaps that exist between patient care measures and best practices and mitigate organizational or technological factors relevant to improving the patient experience. When the alignment is optimal, care teams develop a better sense of shared purpose, become more committed and accountable, and work together to improve the patient experience. When accomplished, patients participate more fully and actively in the exchange and are discharged with an enhanced commitment to carry out care management requirements.

Key topics in this practical book include provider-patient communications; demonstrating the value of patient-focused care; how physician and nurse executives use synergy as a strategy; engaging board members in promoting quality and safety goals and in developing hospital community partnerships; building bridges between physicians, administrators, trustees, and hospital staff; and developing a leadership pipeline.

Transforming Leadership, Improving the Patient Experience

Communication Strategies for Driving Patient Satisfaction

Alan T. Belasen, Ph.D.
Barry Eisenberg, Ph.D.
Jill Borgos, Ph.D.

Routledge
Taylor & Francis Group

A PRODUCTIVITY PRESS BOOK

First published 2024
by Routledge
605 Third Avenue, New York, NY 10158

and by Routledge
4 Park Square, Milton Park, Abingdon, Oxon, OX14 4RN

Routledge is an imprint of the Taylor & Francis Group, an informa business

ISBN: 978-1-032-55516-4 (hbk)
ISBN: 978-1-032-55515-7 (pbk)
ISBN: 978-1-003-43107-7 (ebk)

DOI: 10.4324/9781003431077

Typeset in Garamond
by KnowledgeWorks Global Ltd.

Dedication

In early 2020, state and local governments in the United States implemented preventative measures to curb the transmission of SARS-CoV-2, the virus responsible for the COVID-19 pandemic. Despite these efforts, COVID-19 began to devastate densely populated urban centers, including New York City, by rapidly overwhelming hospitals. My daughter, Dr. Abigail Belasen, was completing her Internal Medicine Residency at the Icahn School of Medicine at Mount Sinai and was one of the front-line physicians at Elmhurst Hospital in Queens, NY, a predominantly Hispanic neighborhood. At the time, Elmhurst was considered the "epicenter of the epicenter" of the pandemic in the United States. Her heroic experience working under immense, unprecedented pressure due to shortages in ventilators, personal protective equipment (PPE), face shields, and testing kits and at a time when so much was unknown about COVID-19, has inspired me to explore tools and strategies for quality improvement and patient safety.

The pandemic quickly swept across the nation, disproportionally affecting urban areas with high racial and ethnic population density. In response, health leaders have been challenged to rethink their operating models within ambulatory care, hospitals, and post-acute care settings with a focus on expanding healthcare access and improving patient outcomes across the continuum of care. This book is a tribute to the COVID-19 warriors – the doctors, nurses, and other front-line providers for their courage and resiliency to put patients first in the face of a public health crisis.

Alan Belasen, Ph.D.

Contents

Contents

Foreword

Hospital leadership today has a dual role. While it strives to achieve patient satisfaction, it must also ensure excellent care. Yet the integration of satisfaction and quality care can prove an elusive goal. Do hospitals hold practitioners and staff to acceptable standards of both? Does hospital leadership specifically address this issue with all employees with whom patients and their families interact? Patient satisfaction and quality of care may be distinct in some ways, yet they are inextricably linked by complementary threads, and both must be consistently and continuously assessed and enforced.

Of principal importance is the question, does the board hold the CEO responsible for leading the quality development efforts in their hospital? In one incident, a surgeon began prepping his patient for surgery on the wrong side of the patient's body. Fortunately, the operating room nurses stopped the surgeon, albeit hesitantly, before he began the incision. He was reported to the Hospital's Quality Improvement Committee, which consisted solely of physicians. The surgeon testified that it was the fault of the nurses, claiming "They had my patient backwards in the suite. I'm a busy practicing surgeon and I expect them to have the patient properly set up so I can immediately begin."

The rumor mill cited the incident as just another among many in "The Good Ole Boy's Club." One nurse, off the record, stated that the Quality Improvement Committee members suggested that the surgeon should "Please just pay a little bit more attention when walking into the OR."

Unfortunately, such preventable errors occur, and such defensiveness can still prevail even in this era of comprehensive safeguards such as multiple pre-surgical checklists and mandatory training of physicians and hospital staff on safety as well as greater awareness about the importance of communication between patients and all levels of hospital personnel.

I believe the greatest challenge currently facing hospital executives is encouraging their boards to assume responsibility for patient quality while balancing corporate fiscal goals and objectives. Statutory requirements, regulatory expectations, along with case law, affirm that governing boards of hospitals are ultimately accountable for safety and overall quality of patient care. However, boards generally delegate these tasks to the CEO and/or the medical staff leadership, or seek advice from experts or subcommittees, and in my experience, it is not uncommon for the board to fall short in its oversight. A big part of the reason is that they do not evaluate quality so that it is measurable in relation to outcome standards.

What if a hospital in a large system has no local board or advisory board with whom the local hospital CEO can work? Does that local CEO have the support of the corporate executives to address quality improvement? When the local CEO establishes annual goals and objectives besides financial considerations, do they include measurable medical quality standards? For non-profits, how are finances (e.g., surplus revenue) and quality of care incorporated into goals and objectives to meet broader community needs? With respect to for-profit facilities, there is a much greater concern involving operating margins and ROI for investors.

Quality improvement must start with the local CEO in concert with corporate leadership. When dealing with boards, either local or corporate, these well-meaning board members venture into an area where they typically have little exposure or training. Physicians and nurses constitute one very qualified group who ought to be more fully recruited for board membership as they are familiar with the dynamics of hospitals and healthcare delivery. They have the experience and knowledge base for identifying measurable quality models for development and implementation. As such, the overall acceptance of measurable quality standards becomes less of a hospital cultural challenge. In addition, physicians and nurses are acutely aware that the success of any hospital lies in the provision of quality care.

By extension, CEOs who create a collaborative work culture have a greater opportunity to translate those standards into actual practice. Working together, nurses, the pharmacy department, physicians, informational technology specialists, and all others have brought about meaningful change. This is just one example of vertically integrated problem-solving that *Transforming Leadership, Improving the Patient Experience* embraces as the enlightened path forward for hospital systems and, specifically, for executive leadership. When employees participate in formulating goals, each employee becomes invested in achieving success. In fact, across the organization, every employee in some way is a vital participant in improving patient experience and reducing healthcare costs.

I became CEO of a hospital at a young age. What struck me most was the need on the part of patients for reassurance. It wasn't just a matter of being kind and sensitive, although of course, that is important. More deeply, patients want to trust that their welfare is first and foremost. When they do, they tend to participate more in their own care. Toward that end, I always made sure that department leaders had input into goal development from their employees. Going back to my early years as a CEO, those goals usually encompassed cost, efficiency, employee turnover, and employee satisfaction. The indicators for measuring quality were rarely included except for length of stay, falls, and medication errors.

But how we structured the organization was also important in achieving patient-centered goals. Back in the late 1970s, we created one of the first vertically integrated systems in New Jersey, consisting of acute, long-term, and primary care in which our patients could experience a full range of services under one umbrella. We supported these efforts with subsidiary companies that offered services such as marketing and communications to create a comprehensive outreach and patient education initiative.

Many years later, I had the good fortune to lead another health system, this one in Oregon. Laws and local culture may differ, but patients everywhere want the same thing: to believe the organization provides quality care and has their best interests in mind. This takes a lot of hard work along with a well-developed understanding of quality standards and the know-how for inspiring and mobilizing the organization to meet and exceed them.

In *Transforming Leadership, Improving the Patient Experience: Communication Strategies for Driving Patient Satisfaction*, Drs. Belasen, Eisenberg, and Borgos explore the complex relationship between leadership and the patient experience. They do so by making it plain and relatable, by untangling the complexities. You will gain insight into how to incorporate trust into the relationship between the healthcare organization and its patients.

Through this book, you will have the opportunity to build your leadership strengths, explore issues emerging in the deployment of quality strategies, and target key considerations and takeaways with the goal of fostering a better overall hospital experience for the patients and families whom they serve.

Victor Fresolone, M.H.S., FACHE
Chief Executive Officer (retired): Union Hospital,
Mercy Medical Center, ATRIO Health Plan

Acknowledgments

This book is the most recent of many projects that Alan and I have done together. He is as generous a collaborator as he is prolific, and it is always an absolute joy working with him. Bringing Jill onto this project added a dimension of expertise in nursing leadership that has been extraordinarily complementary. I am proud to call both friends as well as colleagues.

The healthcare world is indeed complex. But we have learned that when healthcare organizations genuinely and steadfastly place the patient at the center of their decision-making, quality of care improves. We sought to demonstrate that on every page in this book.

I am indebted to my wife, Dr. Amy Eisenberg, whose insights from her work with hospitals on patient satisfaction have been instrumental in strengthening my understanding of what it takes to fully address and meet patients' needs. Beyond that, I rely on her amazing writing skills for guidance. But mostly, I am grateful for her love and support, along with that of our wonderful children and their partners – Kerry and Nathan; Jesse, Anna, and our adorable grandson; and Hallie and Nullah.

Much gratitude goes to Victor Fresolone, M.H.S., FACHE, who wrote our Foreword. Victor was a pioneer in creating a vertically integrated, continuum-of-care hospital system in New Jersey. His record of accomplishment in hospital system leadership is outstanding.

Finally, I extend my deepest appreciation to the students in the MBA in Healthcare Leadership at SUNY Empire State University. Their passion for learning and commitment to ensuring high-quality healthcare for all is most inspiring.

Barry Eisenberg

It was an honor and privilege to work with my colleagues Alan and Barry in the writing of this book. Their collective experiences and the overall collaborative approach they brought to the development of this book were inspiring. In sharing a passion for improving the quality of care, patient safety, and the overall patient experience, we hope to advance the current discussions on the state of healthcare in the United States.

A special thanks to my husband William Borgos, M.D., Chief Medical Officer Hudson Headwaters Health Network, for his reflection, suggestions, and invaluable editorial insights that brought greater clarity and perspective to the ideas expressed in this book. As always, I am grateful to my children Maggie and Teddy who are always supportive and willing to patiently wait until that last sentence is written for the day.

Throughout my career as a nursing professional, I am beyond thankful for the many experiences and opportunities I have had over the last 30 years working with some of the most accomplished and amazingly dedicated health professionals. And special thanks and gratitude to my academic nursing colleagues at Empire State University, Dianne and Teresa, who are always there to offer words of encouragement and support. Their dedication to educating the next generation of nursing professionals is something to admire.

Jill Borgos

First and foremost, I would like to acknowledge the wonderful experience of writing this book with Barry Eisenberg and Jill Borgos, my two collaborators. Our diverse knowledge and complementary skills, positive feedback, and mutual encouragement are what made this book a true collaborative effort signified by mutual respect, trust, effective communication, and above all a joint commitment to meet the publisher's tight deadlines. Thanks Barry and Jill!

Many networks, governmental agencies, and resource centers, including the Centers for Medicare & Medicaid Services (CMS); the Johns Hopkins Coronavirus Resource Center; American College of Healthcare Executives (ACHE); and the American Hospital Directory (AHD), have provided access to sources of data for my research projects. The anonymous reviewers of many journals helped stimulate my thinking about new directions for managing the complexity of healthcare environments, especially at times of major disruptions. These include reviewers from the *International*

Journal for Quality in Health Care; *Journal of Health Organization and Management*; *Gender in Management, an International Journal*; *Journal of Racial and Ethnic Health Disparities*; and the *Academy of Management – Healthcare Management*.

Special thanks go to my research partners whose collaboration with me on many COVID-related research projects has sparked important insights into the qualities of healthcare leadership that are now infused throughout the book. Ari Belasen and Marlon Tracey, Department of Economics and Finance, Southern Illinois University Edwardsville; and Jane Oppenlander and Zhilan Feng, David D. Reh School of Business, Clarkson University, shaped my thoughts about the impact of COVID-19 on healthcare access and quality of patient care, hospital resource utilization, and provider-patient communication through lengthy discussions and exchanges.

Thanks to Kristine Mednansky, Acquisitions Editor, Taylor & Francis Group, who endorsed the aims and scope of this book project and was instrumental in moving this book project along the various stages of production.

My wife Susan provided the social and emotional support as well as the sounding board for many of my research projects. Being surrounded by my five A's has always been rewarding and intellectually stimulating. Ari, an SIUE professor, consultant, and a prolific researcher and my partner for many published articles and conference papers; Amy, an accomplished author, founder of ABD Creative, and a customer-focused business expert in the hospitality industry; Anat, NSF Postdoctoral Research Fellow in Biology, UT Austin, Dept of Integrative Biology; Amanda, a client service specialist in a global organization; and Abigail, a physician at Albany Medical Center. I am very grateful to them for their support and kindness.

Alan Belasen

About the Authors

Alan T. Belasen, Ph.D., has over 30 years of experience in professional, management, and leadership development. He led the design and implementation of the MBA programs in management, global leadership, and healthcare leadership at SUNY Empire State University. Many of Belasen's research articles on executive education, hospital leadership, improving healthcare access, provider-patient communication, and women in healthcare leadership have been published in peer-reviewed journals. Dr. Belasen has written numerous books, including *Resilience in Healthcare Leadership: Practical Strategies and Self-Assessment Tools for Identifying Strengths and Weaknesses* (Routledge, 2022); *Dyad Leadership and Clinical Integration: Driving Change, Aligning Strategies* (HAP, 2019); and *Women in Management: A Framework for Sustainable Work-life Integration* (Routledge, 2017). He is the recipient of the International Accreditation Council for Business Education's 2017 John L. Green Award for Excellence in Business Education, and the 2014–2015 SUNY Chancellor's Award for Scholarship and Creative Activities.

Barry Eisenberg, Ph.D., has 40 years of experience in healthcare management, consulting, and higher education. He established and directed a management development program at Memorial-Sloan Kettering Cancer Center in New York and later served as vice president of human resources and administration/operations in a New Jersey-based hospital. In addition to directing SUNY Empire State College's MBA in Healthcare Leadership, Dr. Eisenberg consults with healthcare organizations on strategic planning, mergers and acquisitions, market expansion, and board of directors' development. Dr. Eisenberg is co-author of *Mastering Leadership: A Vital Resource for Healthcare Organizations* as well as many articles and book chapters on healthcare management. He also maintains a blog which addresses health issues, among many others, with a wide distribution: https://barryeisenbergauthor.com/blog. Dr. Eisenberg serves on the boards of multiple nonprofit organizations dedicated to expanding access to scholarship, social justice, and promoting arts education.

Jill Borgos, Ph.D., M.S., R.N., is an assistant professor in SUNY Empire State University's MBA in Healthcare Leadership program. She holds a Ph.D. from the University at Albany in Educational Policy & Leadership, a Master of Science degree from the University of Michigan Rackham Graduate School in Nursing Administration & Patient Care Services, and a Bachelor of Science degree in Nursing from Boston College. Dr. Borgos has 30 years of combined academic, clinical, and leadership experience in healthcare. She has held academic appointments in Nursing undergraduate and graduate programs where she taught courses in Health Policy, Organizational Behavior, Nursing Leadership, and Population Health. With an interest in education as a determinate of health outcomes globally, Borgos' research spans the areas of nursing education, policy, and the internationalization of higher education. She has published and presented on cross-border medical and nursing education, organizational social network analysis, resource dependency across geopolitical borders, and distance learning. Borgos is the 2013 recipient of the University at Albany's Sanford H. Levin Fellowship for her work in educational leadership and a 2015 recipient of a Sigma Theta Tau International Chapter Recognition Award for Excellence in Nursing Research.

Chapter 1

Introduction – Bridging the Intention-Action Gap

This book focuses on assessing and improving patient experience as a leadership strategy. We set out to demonstrate the value of patient-focused care through effective provider-patient communications and explore collaboration strategies for maximizing the synergy between board members, hospital administrators, nurses, and physicians. When clinical and nonclinical staff collaborate effectively, healthcare teams can prevent medical errors, increase efficiency, and improve patient outcomes.

The book is written for aspiring healthcare leaders, senior-level executives in provider organizations, physicians and nurses targeted for administrative positions, and managers and professionals seeking to strengthen their competencies for improving the quality of patient satisfaction across the continuum of care. It is also geared toward hospital board members wishing to prepare themselves for their roles in the evolving value-based healthcare market and looking to adapt effectively in a patient-centered environment. Healthcare management consultants, educators, and graduate students of healthcare administration can use this book to update their knowledge and gain relevant skills for optimizing care coordination and for forging effective partnership between patients, families, caregivers, and primary care providers.

The book offers actionable ideas and best practices for examining critical needs of individuals, teams, and organizations to improve safety and quality and promote patient engagement. Methods for identifying executive strengths and weaknesses, increasing self-awareness, and guiding developmental needs for future training and skill building are also shared

DOI: 10.4324/9781003431077-1

with specific recommendations on how to hone those critical skills which facilitate meaningful relationships. Key features include the following:

- Concepts and tools from current research to address quality improvement in healthcare services
- Theory-based strategies and best practices for enhancing the patient experience
- Analytical frameworks to identify critical needs and bridge gaps between perception and reality of healthcare services
- Leadership roadmaps for personal development, self-assessments, and personal scorecards to track strengths and weaknesses
- Communication strategies to align executive roles with business strategies
- Proven models for co-leadership in healthcare
- Tools for promoting physician and nurse leaders and developing the leadership pipeline in hospitals
- Assessment instruments and actionable pathways for self-development and self-improvement

A common theme across the book centers on the need to reduce the gap that exists between patient care measures and best practices, as well as the need to mitigate and better understand the organizational or technological factors relevant to improving the patient experience. However, determining the most effective strategy for achieving higher levels of service quality and patient satisfaction can prove elusive for providers who tend to prioritize specific metrics to improve hospital performance and patient satisfaction even though patient experience and provider-patient communications are intertwined.

A survey in 2012 showed that leaders' perceptions did not always match the data, and many hospital leaders overestimate the performance of their hospitals. Over 75% of the hospital leaders reported "quality of care" was something their hospital did well, while their patients, on average, rated them lower on perceived service quality. Ten years later, in 2022, only a small number of healthcare settings, including inpatient hospitals, outpatient clinics, free-standing surgical centers, long-term care facilities, had adopted best practices to achieve high patient satisfaction.

Of the 3,094 hospitals in the 2022 CMS Hospital Star Ratings, only 429 hospitals, or 13.9%, received a 5-star rating; 28.8% received a 4-star rating; and 57.3% received a 3-star rating or lower. A star rating below 3 implies that hospital performance is below average compared to other hospitals. This has significant effects on profit margins since patients consider the star rating differentials in their choice of hospitals and are willing to pay upward of 17% extra for treatments in 5-star hospitals, a critical source of income at times when hospitals have seen falling revenues (down 4.8%) and rising labor costs (up 37%) compared to pre-COVID-19 pandemic levels.

When intentions and outcomes are aligned, they create a powerful medium by which healthcare leaders can evaluate the linkage between communication goals (e.g., responsiveness of hospital staff; pain management; communication about medicines) and patient outcomes (e.g., increased adherence and compliance; readmission; healthcare delivery costs; hospital overall ratings). Care teams develop a better sense of shared purpose, become more committed and accountable, and work together to improve the patient experience. When accomplished, patients participate more fully and actively in the exchange and are discharged with an enhanced commitment to carry out care management requirements.

The book promotes the proposition that patient experience is anchored in an organizational culture that values patient-focused care achieved through meaningful provider-patient communication. It is a leadership strategy. Leaders must clearly articulate a hospital's commitment to meet the unique needs of its patients and their families. Empowering and engaging patients actively in the decision-making process establishes an environment of trust, promotes patient centeredness, and ultimately increases patient satisfaction.

Healthcare leaders must ensure that respect for the patient's values, preferences, and expressed needs are prioritized; information and education are available; access to quality care is provided; emotional support to reduce fear and mitigate anxiety exists; engagement of family and friends is encouraged; and coordination of services after discharge are clearly communicated. Studies show that when patient satisfaction is high, compliance with medical directives increases; predisposition to follow up with questions to a provider strengthens; the inclination to initiate litigation against a provider decreases; and 30-day readmission rates are lower.

During the fight against the COVID-19 pandemic, with limited resources and a rise in demand for inpatient beds, 5-star hospitals continued to excel through patient-focused care and improved hospital operating efficiency as compared with low-quality hospitals. Evidence about their best practices and successful communication strategies infuse many chapters and sections in this book.

Book Chapters

Chapter 2. Provider-Patient Communication – Evidence from the Field

From a health policy standpoint, it is imperative that hospital leaders stress open and clear communication between providers and patients to avoid problems ranging from misdiagnosis to incorrect treatment. Understanding the context of patient safety and social environment through effective partnership with patients is empowering and correlates with positive clinical outcomes and higher hospital ratings. Thus, a critical factor in the effectiveness of healthcare delivery is sustaining patient centeredness through meaningful provider-patient communication.

However, gaps between actual and best possible Hospital Compare scores in U.S. hospitals appear to indicate that hospitals are not performing at their best possible level. This may be due to constraints on their resources or due to organizational-level factors, which in turn may affect patients' perceptions of the quality of care and their overall satisfaction.

Gaps in communication may also occur because of insufficient provider-patient interactions. In a study of 2,756 hospitals, no patients reported that physicians "sometimes or never" communicated well in the best performing hospitals, whereas 21% of patients in the worst performing hospitals reported that physicians "sometimes or never" communicated well. Stated another way, providers at the best performing hospitals appear to place greater emphasis on communicating with their patients, and this effort pays dividends in terms of an enhanced patient experience. By recognizing and addressing potential gaps, leaders in relatively low-quality hospitals can develop better relationships with patients, including paying close attention to patient-centered principles, communications with patients, and their effects on patients' perceived fairness of treatment.

Chapter 3. The Critical Nature of the Nurse-Patient Relationship

At the recent 72nd World Health Assembly, the *Pan American Health Organization* and the *World Health Organization* designated 2020 the *International Year of the Nurse and Midwife* to honor the importance of their respective work and contributions to the delivery of healthcare across the world. This designation predated the onslaught of the global COVID-19 pandemic, and the feature of emergency room nurse Amy O'Sullivan on the cover of *Time* magazine as one of the most influential people in 2020. O'Sullivan was the registered nurse who treated the first identified COVID patient in New York City. O'Sullivan's dedication and courage in the face of multiple unknowns and the overwhelming death rates that the pandemic brought highlight the role of the nurse in treating and caring for the patients who come through the doors of healthcare organizations in the United States and across the world. The skillful, compassionate care provided to COVID patients by nurses illustrates one of the core values of the role of the professional nurse – communicating with patients who are scared and vulnerable.

Given the unprecedented attention to the efforts of the nursing profession in the wake of COVID-19, it is no surprise that a *2022 Gallup* poll ranked registered nurses as the most "Honest and Ethical" profession for the 20th year in a row. Given these positive results, it is important to consider the implications of honesty and ethical behavior on effective nurse-patient communication in combination with trust as a contributing factor in the evaluation of patient satisfaction and the overall patient experience.

Measuring patient satisfaction and illuminating the effectiveness of nursing communication as a part of the patient experience is a complex endeavor. The optimal patient experience depends on several factors from the moment the patient or their family (caregivers) interacts with any given healthcare organization, but it can be argued that it hinges on the communication between the nurse and the patient as an essential element for building trust and relieving patient anxiety. This can be in settings, including hospice care, home care, nurse-led primary care community clinics, outpatient dialysis centers, or addiction treatment centers.

Chapter 4. Board Leadership and Stakeholder Engagement

The expansion of systems in the U.S. healthcare and life sciences industry has occurred on a relatively unrelenting basis in the past 30 years. In the ten-year period of 2010–2021 alone, there were 2,733 ownership change transactions in the industry, involving a staggering $2.4 trillion in assets. In recent years, the number of transactions has trended slightly downward, while the value per transaction has increased, suggesting that mergers and acquisition of hospital-based systems, as opposed to takeovers of individual hospitals, are occurring more frequently.

The corporatization of healthcare has accelerated the concentration of governance authority at the corporate level, with a concomitant diminishing of strategy development at the board level of the local hospital. Centralized policy and strategy oversight has benefits for the hospital system, for example, with respect to competition, market share development, and capitalization. But it does not occur without cost. In the specific case of stakeholder relationships, a marginalized local board would have a weaker capacity to maintain awareness of socio-cultural elements of the communities served by its hospital as well as a constrained aptitude for community advocacy at the boardroom table. Moreover, a corporate board viewed as light-years away from a member hospital's workers may find it challenging to sustain its credibility. As also described in this book, one of the great challenges for the boards of smaller, community hospitals remains whether to fight for continued independence versus seeking out like-minded partners for collaboration while looking for larger health system interested in acquiring them which may be seen as a potential financial lifeline.

A governance model with a more balanced distribution of lines of authority between central and local boards is needed to enhance the extent to which sensitivity to community and organizational culture are factored into corporate strategy, outreach, and program development.

Chapter 5. Communicating Quality – Hospital Leadership and Performance Outcomes

As the COVID-19 pandemic continued to disrupt hospitals' performance due to lockdown policies, a suspension of elective surgeries, implementation of stay-at-home orders, and increased demand for telemedicine, it also provided a unique lens through which acute care hospital utilization and patient satisfaction can be examined as a function of the leader's professional background and education.

Evidence presented in this chapter shows that physician-led hospitals experienced improved patient outcomes, enjoyed higher financial performance, and had 25% overall quality scores higher than those run by nonphysicians. Other findings showed a positive relationship between participation of physicians on boards and improved hospital performance, including higher quality ratings and lower morbidity rates, better performance by hospital management staff, and more effective utilization of clinical quality metrics on target settings and operations. Notably, physician executives are more likely to approach decisions based on the clinical delivery model with an increased emphasis on quality metrics and patient outcomes, thereby driving higher patient satisfaction.

Exploring the relationship between physician leadership and hospital ratings and identifying best practices could inform hospitals wishing to improve quality-of-care delivery. It could also lead to a more focused approach to leadership training and development and improve hospital succession planning. Further, it could also inform hospital CEO recruitment strategies and selection processes and potentially close the gap created by high CEO turnover rates in U.S. hospitals.

Chapter 6. Nursing Leadership and the Patient Experience

Nurse leaders have a unique role and responsibility to work collaboratively across the healthcare system to achieve optimal patient outcomes. The determination and measurement of patient outcomes varies tremendously depending on the healthcare setting, the patient population, and the treatment patients receive. Patient outcomes in a hospice setting are different than patient outcomes in an outpatient pediatric clinic; however, the roles executives play are similar across settings. Nursing leaders, like all leaders, should ideally collaborate to guide the overall direction of the organization based on its mission and vision using evidence-based data that draws on best leadership practices and clinical expertise.

Situated against the backdrop of the 50th anniversary of *Title IX*, the Me Too Movement, and the emphasis on building corporate culture embedded with diversity, equity, and inclusion policies and practices, the focus on women and leadership has never been more present in the media and academic literature. The overwhelming number of nurses are women, nearly 90% according to the *2021 BLS* census. Interestingly, according to the *AACN*, despite nursing professionals making up the largest segment of health professionals, very few nurses serve in the role of chief executive officers or presidents of health organizations.

A recent U.S. News & Report about the top 20 hospitals indicated that only two of the top 20 hospitals had CEOs who were women with a nursing background. This is not to say that nurses who identify as women are not in a variety of administrative positions throughout healthcare systems such as vice president, chief nursing officer, director of patient care services, director of quality and compliance, and unit managers throughout inpatient units and outpatient clinics, but they are not assuming CEO and president roles at the same rate as men nor are they serving on boards of healthcare organizations at the same rate as men.

Fittingly, a study in the *American Journal of Medical Quality found* that 44% of boards of high-performing hospitals included at least one nurse as a voting member as compared to 11% of low-performing hospitals, adding a level of significance to appointing women and nurses to governing boards.

Chapter 7. Engaging Hospital Boards in Patient Safety and Quality of Care

The primary issues facing boards of directors invariably constitute a priority framework for organizational leadership. For hospital boards, top concerns include the management of operations, finances, payers, and risk. It is not surprising that such matters would occupy board attention considering the significant industry challenges associated with worker shortages in such critical fields as medicine, nursing, and rehabilitation with weighted median operating margins at just 2% and narrowing.

Of course, this is not to suggest that other imperatives, particularly patient safety and quality of care, are neglected. But with institutional viability and market share as dominant attention draws, critical questions arise as to whether governing boards place sufficient emphasis on patient safety and quality of care and if board composition reflects an ability to adequately integrate safety and quality into the uppermost rungs of its priority ladder. With respect to the latter, the average board representation of physicians and nurses in the highest revenue hospital systems is just under 14%. As such, those with the most advanced knowledge of quality and safety have a relatively limited board presence.

This question is more complicated, influenced by trends that increasingly emphasize quality of care in emerging reimbursement models, but which occur in the context of pressures to expand patient volumes, institute efficiencies, and seek economies of scale. A more robust board engagement with safety and quality of care is critical to ensuring that attention to these from organizational leadership is unwavering and vigorous. It also requires participation in training and development. Moreover, the most effective board perspective is one which does not view operational and financial viability as mutually exclusive from safety and quality of care or in which the latter are primarily expenses on a profit and loss (P&L) statement. Rather, healthcare systems are far more likely to thrive when safety and quality of care are seen as investments and as priorities highly integrated with all others, unified by a commitment to serve those who come for care.

Chapter 8. Shared Leadership and the Patient Experience

In healthcare, the concept of shared leadership is emerging as a vital strategy for integrated health systems faced with increasing complexity, change, and interprofessional collaboration across the continuum of care. The shift to a shared leadership structure with greater involvement of clinicians can help reduce barriers to communication and enhance patient safety.

The outdated, but still common, command-and-control style, with a single authority line at the top or from the middle out, typically led by a nonclinical administrator, is insufficient for handling intricate tasks in health systems that are increasingly becoming more complex and matrixed. The entrenched solo leadership, which drives strategic planning and decision-making, creates unclear reporting lines and misalignments between system-level physician leaders and settings such as medical groups and clinically integrated networks.

Evidence in this chapter will show that more diverse and inclusive leadership teams make better decisions up to 87% of the time, are faster 50% of the time, and deliver 60% better results. At its core, shared leadership is a form of interprofessional cooperation between two or more individuals with complementary strengths and abilities. Shared leadership could operate in multiple locations in health systems, including upper echelon (e.g., CMO, CQO), divisions of care providers (e.g., RPCN, health centers), and service lines (e.g., cardiovascular, orthopedics, cancer care). In acute care hospitals, individuals in potentially shared leadership roles are board chairpersons and directors, CEOs, operations, nursing, and medical officers as well as unit managers. In nursing homes, such leadership can come from facility owners, administrators, directors of nursing, and managers.

One variant of this form of leadership is the dyad. In the dyad, the partners bring their unique perspectives to create win-win outcomes. For example, administrators bring business skills essential for managing productivity and cost-effective delivery of care to populations. Physicians bring clinical expertise for determining health initiatives, providing high-value patient care, assuring quality and patient safety, and assessing clinical outcomes.

Evidence from a survey of 868 Insights Council members by the *New England Journal of Medicine* showed that 72% of these members use a dyad leadership model in their organizations and 85% believe that dyad structures work effectively. Another by the *Medical Group Management Association* with 1,303 applicable responses found that 77% of the respondents indicate that their organizations utilize a physician and administrator (dyad) leadership team model.

Chapter 9. The Nurse Executive Professional Development

In 2010 the *Institute of Medicine* (IOM) released its report about the future of nursing focusing on the need for a more collaborative approach in healthcare leadership and the call for nurses to become full partners with physicians and other health professionals in redesigning healthcare. It was strongly suggested that patient outcomes and, by extension, the patient experience with the healthcare system would not change without a new style of leadership that breaks down traditional hierarchical silos and replaces them with a culture of collaboration in which nurses play an important role in shared leadership in key executive management positions.

By 2016 the IOM identified disappointing progress toward the advancement of nurses in the leadership triad model, a partnership between administrators, nurses, and physicians. It recommended a more focused approach to nursing education in the areas of leadership and policy, the full engagement of the *Champion Nursing Coalition Campaign for Action* to track nursing leadership data, and the advancement of Magnet recognition programs. Magnet designation, awarded by the *American Nurses Credentialing Center*, requires nursing to be full partners in hospital governance structures and participate in decision-making and strategic planning. More specifically, Magnet-designated hospitals must appoint a chief nursing officer which further aligns collaborative leadership and full partnership of nursing with other appointed leadership positions such as chief medical officers.

As of 2021, 171 additional hospitals have achieved Magnet designation for a total of 549, a mere 2% growth in the last ten years. Advancing a triad leadership approach in healthcare as a part of improving the patient experience requires more attention to action pathways and promotion of nurses to leadership positions.

Chapter 10. Conclusion: Leadership Practices to Improve the Patient Experience

This book began by highlighting a disconnect between how well healthcare leaders believe their organizations perform relative to the patient experience and what their patients report in surveys. We also sought to explain why this gap occurs and create a framework to help leaders narrow that gap.

Today's leaders face formidable challenges in an exceedingly complex healthcare environment. With system expansion, both horizontally and vertically, leadership is increasingly separated from front-line employees by ever more layers of senior and middle management. And yet, regulatory, financial, and policy trends demand that the patient experience occupies a central focus in the leadership decision-making culture. We need to look at only one example for insight – the shift from volume- to value-based care models which underscores the growing significance of quality of care and patient outcomes as key measures of institutional performance. Yet, it is the very leader who is organizationally furthest from those on the front line who must inspire and mobilize organizational resources to ensure that quality goals are realized.

The world of healthcare is not going to simplify. It is an industry with expenditures and a workforce size that dwarfs every other industry, including that of energy and the military. Health systems are high reliability organizations that must place a premium on performing flawlessly. At the same time, they are bound by forces that test even the highest functioning organization. Leadership success in such a labyrinth, in a sea of competing forces, is contingent on communication practice that engenders trust, clarifies the information environment and makes it accessible, and shows respect for all in the stakeholder spectrum.

Thus, we close by re-examining the aims and scope of effective internal and external communications. We may think of communication as the "process of creating shared meaning." Simple, for sure. But profound in its implications. According to this definition, communication does not require the parties to agree or coalesce around the same conclusion. Nor does it require the parties to forge a closer relationship. However, it does mean that the parties seek a common understanding, that is, they strive to have the other party feel seen, heard, and understood. This cannot occur without active listening. And, by extension, the term "shared" implies that communication is not one-way but rather a dynamic process in which all parties are engaged. Moreover, as a process, communication is shaped by context, history, culture, and motives.

While, as an industry, it is important to endeavor to create coherence and fairness, organizational leaders can use tools of communication and relationship management to bring continuous improvement to their domains, build institutional cultures of quality, promote transparency, and aim for higher levels of stakeholder input and satisfaction. If that is the framework they adopt, they will navigate their organizations so the experience of the patient is the single most significant determinant of organizational success.

The CEO who believes that communication is a matter exclusively of informing others may be satisfying one condition of communication, but they may miss the complexity, not to mention, the spirit, of the definition. Furthermore, trust is inextricable to communication effectiveness. It needs to be initiated and sustained. Establishing trust between patients and providers creates a partnership that helps sustain patient engagement. When trust is present, employees feel empowered to devote more energy, adapt to shifting circumstances and thereby exercise more resilience, and take pride in serving those for whom the organization exists – the patient.

Chapter 2

Provider-Patient Communication – Evidence from the Field

Introduction

A critical factor in the effectiveness of healthcare delivery is sustaining patient centeredness through meaningful provider-patient communication. When patient satisfaction is high, compliance with medical directives increases, behavioral tendencies to follow up with the provider are strengthened, the inclination to initiate litigation against providers diminishes, and 30-day readmission rates are lower. Broken communication, on the other hand, may contribute to medical nonadherence and other adverse events, including readmission and unnecessary health costs. Of the 2 million patients that were readmitted in 2022, with an estimated cost of $26 billion to Medicare, a whopping 65%, or $17 billion, was attributed to preventable readmissions.

Physicians often tend to overestimate their ability to communicate in interpersonal exchanges by considering the communication to be adequate or even effective, when in reality patients are dissatisfied. Belasen and Belasen (2018) report on studies of orthopedic surgeons in which 75% of the respondents believed that they communicated satisfactorily with their patients, while only 21% of their patients reported satisfactory communication with their doctors. In another study involving primary care physicians and surgeons, researchers reviewed audiotapes of informed decision-making and found that consultation about alternatives occurred in 5.5%–29.5% of the interactions, of pros and cons in 2.3%–26.3%, and of risk factors associated with the decision in 1.1%–16.6%. However, physicians rarely explored whether patients understood the decision (0.9%–6.9%).

Gaps in communication may also occur because of uneasiness or lack of interest. Studies show that while 63% of the patients expressed a need to talk with their physicians about out-of-pocket costs and 79% of the physicians felt these conversations were important, only 15% of patients and 35% of physicians reported having these conversations. Patients and physicians cited discomfort, insufficient time, patients' belief that their physicians did not have a viable solution, and concerns about the impact of the conversations on the quality of care. Thus, despite the mutual understanding that provider-patient communication about healthcare costs is important, little such communication occurred (Alexander et al., 2005)

From a health policy standpoint, it is imperative that hospital administrators stress open and clear communication between doctors and patients to avoid problems ranging from misdiagnoses to incorrectly followed treatment plans. Patients who report positive communication with their doctors are more likely to communicate pertinent information about their ailments more quickly and are more likely to adhere to treatment regimens. While this may require accommodation and training for doctors to alter their standard "script" when communicating with patients, it may increase the quality of care and improve patient satisfaction.

This chapter covers clinical and operational issues as well as costs associated with miscommunication and the need to use metrics such as the Hospital Consumer Assessment of Healthcare Providers and Systems (HCAHPS) that allow consumers to see how hospitals differ on specific characteristics. However, sometimes the perceptual gap between how healthcare leaders view the effectiveness of their organizations or how physicians believe they perform their communicative duties versus how actually patients feel is too wide to overcome. Next, we discuss the importance of developing effective partnership between physicians and their patients in both primary care practices and multi-specialty groups.

Measuring Patient Experience

Over 600,000 people are admitted to hospitals on any given day in the United States.

To promote consumer choice, public accountability, and greater transparency in healthcare delivery, the Centers for Medicare and Medicaid

Services (CMS) employs the Hospital Consumer Assessment of Healthcare Providers and Systems (HCAHPS) to measure patients' perceptions of their hospital experience based on common metrics.

Daily, more than 30,000 patients are surveyed about their recent hospital experience, and more than 8,400 patients complete the survey. The basic sampling procedure for HCAHPS is the drawing of a random sample of eligible discharges monthly. Data are collected from patients throughout each month of the 12-month reporting period and then aggregated quarterly to create a rolling four-quarter data file for each hospital. The most recent four quarters of data are used in public reporting. To ensure comparability, hospitals may not switch the type of sampling, the mode of survey administration, or the survey vendor within a calendar quarter.

HCAHPS elicit responses from discharged patients about their recent hospital stay. The 29-item survey includes 19 questions that encompass critical aspects of the hospital experience (communication with doctors, communication with nurses, responsiveness of hospital staff, cleanliness of the hospital environment, quietness of the hospital environment, pain management, communication about medicines, discharge information, overall rating of hospital, recommendation of hospital, and transition to post-hospital care); 3 items to direct patients to relevant questions; 5 items adjusting for the mix of patients across hospitals; and 2 items supporting congressionally mandated reports. The core set of HCAHPS questions can also be combined with customized, hospital-specific supplemental items to support internal customer service and quality-related activities. Supplemental items are placed after all HCAHPS questions (1–29) since CMS does not review, approve, or obtain data from supplemental items.

The survey response rate and the number of completed surveys are also publicly reported on the *Hospital Compare* website. The site allows consumers to select multiple hospitals and directly compare quality measures across five categories with predetermined weights: mortality (22%), patient safety (22%), readmission rates (22%), patient experience (22%), and timely and effective care (12%). For each hospital, a hospital summary score is calculated by taking the weighted average of the hospital's scores for each category. If a hospital has no measures in a certain measure group, the weighted percentage is redistributed proportionally to the other measure groups. For example, if a hospital had no measures in the timely and effective care category, the 12% weight would be redistributed evenly as 25% for each of the mortality, safety of care, readmission, and patient experience categories.

The inter-correlations of scores displayed in Table 2.1 are based on 2.9 million completed surveys from patients discharged between July 2018 and June 2019. All correlations are statistically significant at p-value of 0.1 (i.e., sufficiently rejecting the null hypothesis that there is no difference between the means). Hospitals can rely on these scores to predict global

Table 2.1   HCAHPS Patient-Level Correlations

	Communication with Nurses	Communication with Doctors	Responsiveness of Hosp. Staff	Comm. About Medicines	Cleanliness of Hospital Env.	Quietness of Hospital Env.	Discharge Information	Care Transition	Hospital Rating	Recommend the Hospital
Communication with nurses	1	0.54	0.56	0.51	0.38	0.33	0.28	0.45	0.64	0.58
Communication with doctors		1	0.39	0.44	0.28	0.27	0.29	0.42	0.53	0.48
Responsiveness of hospital staff			1	0.42	0.34	0.32	0.21	0.37	0.51	0.45
Comm. about medicines				1	0.33	0.29	0.36	0.47	0.49	0.43
Cleanliness of hospital env.					1	0.28	0.19	0.28	0.41	0.37
Quietness of hospital env.						1	0.13	0.26	0.36	0.30
Discharge information							1	0.32	0.31	0.29
Care transition								1	0.49	0.46
Hospital rating									1	0.77
Recommend the hospital										1

Source: CMS, https://www.hcahpsonline.org, April 22, 2020.

items, such as hospital overall ratings and the willingness to recommend as well as identify key areas for improvement in patient experience. Willingness to recommend is critical especially in large urban areas with highly heterogeneous patient populations since potentially lower ratings could affect hospitals' reimbursement and bottom line. Results from surveys of 934,800 patients in 3,907 hospitals in more than 3,100 counties were reviewed and it was found that lower HCAHPS scores tend to cluster in heterogeneous population-dense areas and that county-level factors accounted for 30% and 16% of the variability in patient satisfaction on the HCAHPS measures of doctor and nurse communication, respectively (McFarland et al., 2017).

Star Ratings

Since 2016, CMS has been displaying HCAHPS Star Ratings on *Hospital Compare,* which has driven hospitals to improve quality and reduce costs. Hospitals strive to sustain high ratings to leverage competition, lower costs, and improve care quality. Consumers and patient advocates point to *Hospital Compare* and its star ratings as important resources and rely on the latest data to make informed choices.

The overall *hospital rating* ranges from 1 to 5 *stars* and shows how well each *hospital* performs, on average, compared to other U.S. *hospitals.* The most common overall *hospital rating* is 3 *stars (see* Table 2.2*). Notably, the*

Table 2.2 National Distribution of Overall Hospital Ratings

Overall Rating (stars)	N = 4,573 January 2019	N = 4,586 January 2020	N = 4,534 April 2021	N = 5,299 July 2022
5	293 (6.41%)	407 (8.88%)	455(10.04%)	429 (8.1%)
4	1,086 (23.75%)	1,138 (24.82%)	988 (21.8%)	890 (16.8%)
3	1,264 (27.64%)	1,120 (24.42%)	1,018 (22.45%)	890 (16.8%)
2	800 (17.49%)	710 (15.48%)	690 (15.21%)	693 (13.08%)
1	282 (6.17%)	228 (4.97%)	204 (4.5%)	192 (3.6%)
N/A	848 (18.54%)	983 (21.43%)	1,179 (26%)	2,205 (41.6%)

Source: Assembled from various CMS reports: https://www.cms.gov/medicare/quality-initiatives-patient-assessment-instruments/hospitalqualityinits/hospitalcompare

number of hospitals with 5 stars has remained steady or somewhat increased over time demonstrating the value that hospitals place on achieving high ratings. Some hospitals submit more data points than others, although only hospitals that have at least three measures within at least three categories, including one outcome group (mortality, safety, or readmission), are eligible for an overall hospital rating. The average number of data points hospitals submitted in 2019 was 37.

On April 29, 2020, CMS announced that if the COVID-19 outbreak would prevent it from validating data or would create systemic data integrity issues for the 2021 Star Ratings, it would use data based on care delivered in 2018 for the 2021 Star Ratings. The measurement period and data for all other measures, where there was not a health and safety risk from the COVID-19 outbreak in collecting the data, did not change from what was finalized in the April 2018 Budget Act. CMS treated newer contracts (where 2021 would be the first year that they would receive a star rating) as "new" for an additional year since it would not have enough data to assign a rating.

Differentiation and Choice

The star ratings drive systematic improvements in care and safety as hospitals strive to sustain high ratings to leverage competition, lower costs, and improve care quality. Promoting the areas with the higher scores helps hospitals advance their quality-of-care goals. Consumers and patient advocates point to *Hospital Compare* and the star ratings as important resources they rely on to make informed choices. Many hospitals rely on these ratings to project the strengths of their brand and PR messages, promote their reputation, attract patients by attracting physicians, and further differentiate themselves as providing high-quality patient experience. This includes offering nonclinical benefits such as private and family-friendly rooms, a 5-star hotel lobby atmosphere, stunning views, hotel-style room service for meals, massage therapy, and other exceptional amenities. Research shows that patients often value the nonclinical experience as being equal or even more important than the clinical reputation in making hospital choices, creating a halo effect of patient preference.

Now, yet another new style of competition appears to be emerging, in which hospitals compete for patients directly, on the basis of amenities. Though amenities have long been relevant to hospitals' competition, they seem to have increased in importance — perhaps because patients now have more say in selecting hospitals.... Physicians said that when deciding where to refer patients, they placed considerable weight on the patient experience, in addition to considering the hospital's technology, clinical facilities, and staff. Almost one-third of general practitioners even said they would honor a patient's request to be treated at a hospital that provided a superior nonclinical experience, but care that was clinically inferior to that of other nearby hospitals. Patients themselves said that the nonclinical experience is twice as important as the clinical reputation in making hospital choices (Goldman et al., 2010).

...with a sample of 3,000 U.S. hospitals, we find that neither medical quality nor patient survival rates have much impact on patient satisfaction with their hospital. In contrast, patients are very sensitive to the "room and board" aspects of care that are highly visible. Quiet rooms have a larger impact on patient satisfaction than medical quality, and communication with nurses affects satisfaction far more than the hospital-level risk of dying. Hospitality experiences create a halo effect of patient goodwill, while medical excellence and patient safety do not. Moreover, when hospitals face greater competition from other hospitals, patient satisfaction is higher but medical quality is lower. Consumer-driven healthcare creates pressures for hospitals to be more like hotels (Young & Chen, 2020)

Giving a consumer focus to service quality is a fundamental marketing concept and patient experience-based differentiation is an effective strategy to achieve a competitive advantage in healthcare marketing and advertising. The cleanliness or quietness dimensions of hospital facilities, important HCAHPS measures, also have a big impact on patient satisfaction scores, highlighting the role that the hospital environment has on patient experience.

With open access to multiple channels of communication, consumers are becoming major players in the mass consumption of information and in the creation and distribution of messages and reviews with hospitals and healthcare systems reciprocally utilizing social media to allow users to provide selective feedback and ratings. In fact, the percentage of hospital website usage has increased from 22% in 2012 to 32% in 2016 with 41.5% of consumers who visited a hospital website indicating that patient ratings and reviews of doctors are the most important information they sought. This trend continues as patient reviews and feedback are crucial for building brand affinity and driving patient choice.

- 51% of American adults in 2018 shared healthcare experiences online, up 30% from 2017.
- 68% of young millennials (ages 18–24) shared healthcare experiences online, a 95% increase from 2017.
- 95% of patients say online review and rating sites are "somewhat" to "very" reliable.
- 70% of patients say online sites have influenced physician selection.
- 63% of patients use ratings and reviews from hospital or clinic websites or Google to choose a physician.
- 72% of patients (ages 27–64) read online ratings and reviews when considering a new healthcare provider with 65% of patients indicating a preference toward providers that respond publicly to patient reviews (Reputation.com, 2022).
- 80% of consumers trust online reviews as much as personal recommendations.
- 90% of patients use online reviews to evaluate physicians (Healthgrades, 2022).

The extra layer of transparency has added another level of intensity to the competition among hospitals based on intangibles that more directly impact the financial incentives hospitals receive from CMS. This was especially true during the major disruptions caused by the COVID-19 pandemic with most hospitals experiencing a sizeable reduction in operating margins. The *American Hospital Association* (AHA) estimated the financial impact of COVID-19 on U.S. hospitals and healthcare systems during 2020–2021 at $202.6 billion in lost revenue, an average of $50.7 billion per month. Kaufman Hall's index shows that hospitals' median monthly margins have been in the red throughout 2022, starting with negative 3.4% recorded in January 2022 and continuing to persist due to the Omicron surge.

Hospitals may be able to offset these financial losses through improved quality of care and increased outpatient care capabilities but also through stronger patient recommendations. Indeed, top-rated hospitals (those with 4 and 5 stars) with better patient experience, better records in safety, technical quality, reduced length of stay, and lower readmission rates also perform better on the key global HCAHPS measures: "Likelihood to Recommend" and "Overall Rating". These hospitals enjoyed higher net margins, had lower spending in the first 30 days post discharge, and received higher reimbursement per beneficiary during the episode of care than low-quality hospitals (Press Ganey, 2017). Thus, linking financial reward to compliance with quality indicators makes sense. Health systems also benefit from a positive public image, favorable stakeholders' evaluation, better performance credibility, and ultimately increased patient satisfaction and loyalty. When a hospital receives a high grade on any national rating system, it also relies on social media outlets to help tell its story and boost its reputation.

Gaps in Quality Indicators

Leaders' perceptions of quality care do not always match the data, and many hospital leaders tend to overestimate the performance of their organizations. Surveys show that most hospitals have a greater than 10% gap in quality indicators. Payer mix, registered nurse staffing, size, case mix index, accreditation, being a teaching hospital, market competition, urban location, and region are strong predictors of gaps, although the direction of the association with gaps is not uniform across patient outcomes. Gaps of 8%–23% between hospitals' actual and expected, (i.e., best possible) patient outcomes, indicate that hospitals might not be performing at their best capacity given their resources (Unruh & Hofler, 2016).

Part of the problem involves the ability of health systems to game the results by advertising the rating of their highest performing hospitals, even if some of their hospitals are not qualified. Health systems usually report to the CMS under a single CMS certification number, which can mask the performance of a low-performing hospital and make all the systems' hospitals look better than they are. Consider the evidence.

Researchers from the Harvard Medical School examined the extent to which hospitals utilize social media and whether user-generated metrics on Facebook correlate with a *Hospital Compare* metric, specifically 30-day hospital readmission rates. Participants were 315 hospitals performing better than the U.S. national rate on 30-day readmissions and 364 hospitals performing worse than the U.S. national rate. High-performing hospitals were more likely to use Facebook than lower performing hospitals (93.3% vs. 83.5%; $p < 0.01$). The average rating for hospitals with low readmission rates (4.15±0.31) was higher than that for hospitals with higher readmission rates (4.05±0.41, p < 0.01). A 1-star increase in Facebook rating was associated with increased odds of the hospital belonging to the low readmission rate group by a factor of 5.0 (confidence interval [CI]: 2.6–10.3, p < 0.01), when controlling for hospital characteristics and Facebook-related variables (Glover et al., 2015).

Another study examined 1089 hospitals that reported voluntary *Leapfrog Safe Practices Score* (SPS) with more than 50% self-reporting perfect scores for all but 1 measure. No SPS measures were associated with standardized infection ratios (SIRs). One SPS was associated with lower odds of hospital-acquired condition (HAC) penalization (odds ratio, 0.86; 95% CI, 0.76–0.97). Among hospitals not reporting SPS (N = 1,080), 98% and 54% saw grades decline by 1+ letters with first and tenth percentiles of SPS imputed, respectively; 49% and 54% saw grades improve by 1+ letter with median and highest SPS imputed. The researchers concluded that voluntary Leapfrog SPS measures skew toward positive self-report and bear little association with compulsory Medicare outcomes and penalties (Smith et al., 2017). SPS significantly affects Leapfrog's Hospital Safety Score (HSS) grades, particularly when lower SPS is reported. With increasing compulsory reporting, Leapfrog SPS seems limited for comparing hospitals' performance.

LEAPFROG HOSPITAL SAFETY GRADES

Leapfrog provides a standardized framework to evaluate overall patient safety in general acute care hospitals in the United States. A single, publicly available letter grade, representing overall performance in keeping patients safe from preventable harm and medical errors, is assigned to almost 3,000 general acute care hospitals across the United States twice annually. Along with the safety grades, Leapfrog issues a separate report highlighting inpatient patient experiences, analyzing data from CMS' Hospital Consumer Assessment of Healthcare Providers and Systems (HCAHPS) survey.

Public reporting of Safety Grades increases consumer awareness about patient safety in hospitals. It serves as an important resource for consumers to make informed choices and drives systematic improvements in quality of care, safety awareness, and patient communication as hospitals strive to achieve and sustain high grades to leverage competition, lower costs, and improve care quality. The *Safety Grade* acts as a national benchmark to encourage improvement efforts and assist hospital leaders in identifying areas for improvement and enhance public accountability in healthcare by increasing transparency. *Safety Grade* offers a mechanism through which purchasers and payers can set minimum performance thresholds for inclusion in provider networks, recognizing and rewarding performance through value-based purchasing programs. The results for 2022 show that 932 hospitals earned an "A" (33%); 679 hospitals earned a "B" (24%); 1,021 hospitals earned a "C" (36%); 194 hospitals earned a "D" (7%); and 17 hospitals earned an "F" (<1%).

Overall, 20.3% of hospitals earned higher safety scores when compared with 2021. However, 22.4% of hospitals received lower grades than they did last year. Still, 57.2% of hospitals earned the same grade in 2021 and 2022 (https://www.advisory.com/daily-briefing/2022/05/12/leapfrog-safety).

An analysis of the results of two hospitals' performance across Leapfrog's process/structural measures (Table 2.3) reveals that Hospital 1 performed at or almost at the level of the best performing hospital. In contrast, Hospital 2 declined to report on three of the process/structural measures and, for five out of the eight remaining measures, performed close to the average performing hospital. The differences in performance between the two hospitals are even more evident across the outcome measures. For "dangerous object left in patient's body," Hospital 1 performed at the level of the best performing hospital and Hospital 2 performed in between the levels of the average performing hospital and the worst performing hospital. Similarly, for "infection in the urinary tract," "death from treatable serious complications," and "harmful events," Hospital 1 with Grade A performed within the levels of the best performing hospital and the average performing hospital, while Hospital 2 with Grade D performed within the levels of the average performing hospital and the worst performing hospital.

Bilimoria and colleagues (2019) compared U.S. News, CMS star ratings, Leapfrog, and Healthgrades according to impact, improvement, scientific acceptability, transparency, usability, and potential for misclassification. Across each rating system, the researchers identified flaws in data collection with most of the rating systems using administrative data collected for billing instead of clinical purposes, which limits the effectiveness of each rating system. Additionally, variation in measurement methodologies, regression of low-volume hospitals toward the mean, lack of peer review, apples to oranges hospital comparisons, and potential financial conflicts detract from the overall functionality of these ratings. Indeed, hospital ratings should be

Table 2.3   Grade A and Grade D Hospitals

Outcomes Measures (include errors, accidents, and injuries this hospital has publicly reported)	Grade A Hospital 1	Grade D Hospital 2	Best Performing Hospitals	Avg Performing Hospitals	Worst Performing Hospitals
Dangerous object left in patient's body	0	0.177	0	0.02	0.373
Infection in the urinary tract	0.529	1.044	0	0.85	3.337
Death from treatable serious complications	125.89	190.56	95.65	159.68	206.08
Harmful events	0.88	1.71	0.6	1	3.34
Process Measures (include the management structures and procedures a hospital has in place to protect patients from errors, accidents, and injuries)					
Specialty trained doctors care for ICU patients	100	5	100	64.46	5
Effective leadership to prevent errors	110.77	Declined to report	120	117.09	46.15
Staff work together to prevent errors	120	Declined to report	120	116.88	0
Enough qualified nurses	100	Declined to report	100	98.36	0

evaluated with a grain of salt. No matter how objective the methodology for data collection and metrics for evaluation, ratings are inherently subjective.

One thousand six hundred forty hospitals were evaluated by every rating system. Six hundred thirty-eight unique hospitals were identified as high-performing by at least 1 rating system; however, no hospital was ranked as high-performing by all five rating systems. Four hundred fifty-two unique hospitals were identified as low-performing; however, no hospital was ranked as low-performing by all the three rating systems which define low-performing hospitals. Within the study subsample of hospitals evaluated by each system, little agreement between any combination of rating systems (κ < 0.10) regarding top-tier or bottom-tier performance was found. It was more likely for a hospital to be considered high-performing by one system and low-performing by another (10.66%) than for the majority of the five rating systems to consider a hospital high-performing (3.76%) (Shah et al., 2020).

Improving Measures of Patient Experience

Over time the CMS star system generated a considerable amount of controversy. Issues regarding the methodology and potential biases involving certain hospital types and factors, such as demographics served, and high-risk hospitalization were raised. A research note published in *JAMA* concluded that failure to account for hospital variability may limit the utility of the star ratings, particularly when comparing different hospital types, e.g., critical access hospitals, teaching hospitals, and specialty care facilities. Other concerns involved the leverage that multi-hospital settings have in gaming the ratings system for their own benefit, which discourages hospitals from improving in other areas by using a single certification number and by promoting the rating of their high-performing hospital to make the lower performing hospitals look better overall.

Another issue is the statistical method that CMS utilizes which is based on a "Latent Variable Model", making changes in rating difficult to interpret. For example, the readmission measure in the CMS "Overall Rating" accounts for a heavier weight of the total score, placing tertiary care medical centers and hospitals treating patients with frequent readmissions at risk for lower performance on their hospital star rating. Likewise, recalibrating readmission scores for hospital volume may adversely influence the scores for large hospitals and academic medical centers, due to biases related to socioeconomic status, hospital size, and patients that require "heroic care", or high-risk treatment.

In response, CMS devised plans to update the methodology in the future. It is also considering adjusting for socio-demographic risk factors to make it easier to compare hospitals, although it might adversely affect urban hospitals or create disincentives for safety-net hospitals with a high number of low socioeconomic patients to improve readmissions if the ratings for serving higher risk patients are adjusted for them. Allowing users to customize star ratings by weighting measures according to their own preferences has also been floated. However, not all the measures used in the star ratings would be relevant to the consumer's condition or helpful since most consumers lack medical expertise to judge the quality of care being delivered.

Notably, when measures are grouped into user-friendly formats, patients can decipher the meaning of the measures more clearly and understand how the measures relate to their personal care. Research shows that consumers tend to select hospitals with high clinical quality scores even before the scores are publicized. However, the effect of clinical quality on hospital choice is relatively small. On the other hand, satisfaction with prior hospital admission has a large impact on future hospital choice. Arguably, patients tend to be accurate in their assessments of quality despite a lack of medical and clinical training punctuating the value of personal recommendations and word-of-mouth marketing in the healthcare sector. The effectiveness of provider-patient communication is likewise critical for the success of hospitals and willingness of patients to recommend doctors and hospitals.

Communication and Hospital Ratings

The success of provider-patient communication and its relationship to overall ratings of a hospital has been identified as a critical driver for patient satisfaction. In a study of 3,382 U.S. hospitals, responses to HCAHPS surveys were used to correlate those HCAHPS composite measures that most relate to overall hospital ratings. The researchers found a strong correlation between the six composite HCAHPS measures and the overall hospital rating.

Table 2.4 shows the Pearson correlation coefficients for the six composite HCAHPS measures and overall hospital rating. All correlations were positive, relatively strong, and statistically significant ($p < 0.0001$). Among these composite measures, the strength of the partial correlation with overall hospital rating was the largest for care transition followed by nurse communication and doctor communication (Belasen et al., 2021a,b).

Table 2.4 Pearson Correlation Coefficients for HCAHPS Composite Measures and Overall Hospital Rating 2020

	Care transition	Communication about Medicines	Discharge Information	Doctor Communication	Nurse Communication	Staff Responsiveness
Overall hospital rating	0.866	0.738	0.680	0.763	0.856	0.753
Care Transition		0.774	0.742	0.771	0.817	0.747
Communication about medicine			0.660	0.683	0.749	0.783
Discharge information				0.575	0.678	0.647
Doctor communication					0.807	0.679
Nurse communication						0.820

Partial correlations between communication about medicine and nurse communication as well as doctor communication were calculated controlling for the other four composite measures. The researchers found that both doctor and nurse communication are significant but weakly associated with communication about medicine. Interestingly, when controlling for other composite measures, both nurse-patient communication and doctor-patient communication were poorly correlated with communication about medicines. A possible explanation is that patients rarely discuss prescriptions with their care providers, often opting to speak with their pharmacists (Laven & Arnet, 2018). This is particularly true at times of outbreaks such as COVID-19 where community pharmacists, healthcare professionals with a high public availability, are likely to be many patients' first option for care information (Carico et al., 2020).

The three HCAHPS questions associated with care transition are as follows:

- During this hospital stay, staff took my preferences and those of my family or caregiver into account in deciding what my healthcare needs would be when I left.
- When I left the hospital, I had a good understanding of the things I was responsible for in managing my health.
- When I left the hospital, I clearly understood the purpose of taking each of my medications.

These questions relate to communication with physicians, nurses, and other allied health practitioners such as physical therapists and social workers. As one may suspect, given that patients spend more time communicating with their nurses than their doctors, nurse communication has a much stronger relationship than doctor communication with respect to hospital rating. Similarly, the two HCAHPS questions that relate to the composite measure of communication about medicine are as follows:

- Before giving you any new medicine, how often did hospital staff tell you what the medication was for?
- Before giving you any new medication, how often did hospital staff describe possible side effects in a way you could understand?

Best communication practices increase patients' willingness to disclose information along with their motivation to adhere to medical treatment plans. This leads to a nearly 50% reduction in diagnostic tests and referrals, shorter length of stay, and fewer complications, better recovery, and improved emotional health long after discharge. Positive communication (i.e., being attentive and encouraging patients to participate) is associated with better patient outcomes, safer work environments, decreased preventable errors, decreased transfer delays, lower readmission rates, and lower mortality rates, with the combined effect of better patient satisfaction and higher hospital ratings.

However, it is important to note that most of the HCAHPS ratings are unidirectional as patients rate the quality of their experience through responses to close-ended questions, while provider-patient communication is often interactive, encompassing many of the feelings and expectations that patients have had through the delivery of care. Researchers examined the impact of handwritten comments on the HCAHPS two global outcome measures: "overall hospital rating" and "intention to recommend." Using content analysis, they categorized the narratives as positive, negative, neutral, and mixed. Regression analysis showed that negative comments significantly affect the prediction of the two global outcome measures. Coefficients for negative comments were significant for both the overall hospital rating ($p<0.011$) and intent to recommend ($p<0.004$) measures. The coefficients for positive, neutral, and mixed comments were not significant, indicating that these comments did not contribute more information than quantitative ratings did (Huppertz & Smith, 2014).

Ethnicity and International Medical Graduates

Ethnicity and intercultural differences are important considerations in provider-patient interactions particularly since international medical graduates (IMGs) play a vital role in the U.S. healthcare system. These graduates represent 25% of physicians in practice and 24% of residents in specialty programs and often may experience acculturation challenges associated with the transition to practice in the United States. For example, residency programs are periods of intense adjustment, and many programs fail to devote sufficient time and attention to support IMGs as they seek to learn ways of managing communication and cultural differences with not only patients, but with peers as well. Accordingly, IMGs may enter their profession in the United States at some disadvantage with respect to building communication bridges with a range of stakeholders. It is not uncommon for IMGs to pass through residency programs with few, if any, formal opportunities to learn how health philosophies of their native countries may differ from that of the United States and how those differences may be bridged or overcome.

Examining the physician-patient encounter in an interpersonal context, Street (2003) argues that ethnicity influences the encounter in three ways. First, there may be differences in language or dialect which may manifest most vividly with respect to metaphors, idioms, and culture-specific uses of certain terms. Second, certain styles of communication are preferred over others as we move from one culture to the next. Individuals from Western cultures – i.e., those with more individualistic-oriented cultures – may be more prone to expressive and assertive communication styles, while those from more collectivist cultures may exhibit greater communicative restraint and more deference. Third, people from different cultures have different ways of explaining their health or may point to different factors which they believe may account for their health issues. Each level contains the potential to prevent the communication experience from flowing in a meaningful and productive manner. The accuracy of information transmission could be less than optimal, and all the attending benefits of a constructive communication with patients could be compromised.

IMG physician interaction is such that it involves elements of intercultural, interpersonal, and intergroup communication because it involves communication between people of two different cultures who are also members of two distinct groups, but [also] ...because physicians and patients have prescribed roles in medical interaction. However, IMG physicians may attempt to deemphasize the traditional physician-patient power dynamics by accommodating to unique linguistic or behavioral characteristics of the patient. In treating the patient as an individual, and not solely as a member of the patient population or a representative of his/her culture, the interaction becomes one that can be characterized as interpersonal in nature... IMG physicians can take advantage of such expectations to initiate small talk with the patients and to build rapport and long-term relationship. Of course, this strategy could also backfire, but perhaps patients might appreciate differences and use those to develop relationship with the IMG physician. IMG physicians might also use these differences to maintain their cultural identity. Moreover, they might find the maintenance of differences more pragmatic than converging as these differences sometimes provide them a way to start conversations with their patients... Language classes [should also] be made available for international physicians. The focus of the language classes should be upon teaching culturally appropriate language and acculturation with respect to the usage of slang words, idiomatic English, and other colloquial terms prevalent in that part of the United States where the IMG practices (Jain & Krieger, 2011).

Positive Outcomes

When patient satisfaction is high, it triggers multiple benefits. These benefits may include an increase in compliance with treatment and care directives and an enhanced tendency to follow up on instructions from doctors. Other benefits include a decrease in the inclination to initiate medical malpractice lawsuits against healthcare providers. Patients who reported high satisfaction with their overall care experience were 39% less likely to be readmitted than patients who were not as satisfied. Patients' agreement with the doctor about the nature of the treatment and need for follow-up was also found to be strongly associated with their recovery and with better emotional health two months after discharge. Effective patient communication leads to a shorter length of stay and fewer complications, and a reduction of about 50% in diagnostic tests and post-primary care referrals.

Meaningful patient communication can enhance patient satisfaction and compliance as well as contribute to patients' understanding of illness and the risks and benefits of treatment. What's more, optimizing physician-patient communication can lead to better patient health and outcomes for patients and hospitals and even to reduce malpractice suits that are brought not because of complaints about the quality of medical care but as an expression of anger about some aspects of patient communications.

Communication methods (Table 2.5) to help reduce the potential for medical errors and ensure efficient and effective patient-provider interactions are SBAR, STICC, BATHE, and AWARE.

Physicians who understand and who respond appropriately to the emotional needs of their patients are less likely to be sued. When accomplished, patients participate more fully and actively in the exchange and depart with enhanced motivation to carry out care management requirements. Combining knowledge of patients' background and concerns with sensitivity skills and consultative style is empowering and correlates with positive outcomes.

When intentions and outcomes are aligned, they create a powerful medium by which healthcare leaders can evaluate the gaps that exist between patient care measures and thresholds (e.g., HCAHPS) and mitigate organizational or technological factors relevant to improving the patient experience. For example, better design of electronic health records (EHR) and participation in communication and cultural competency training can help physicians integrate EHR meaningful use into the clinical encounter, thus improving the patient's overall

Table 2.5 Patient-Centered Communication Methods

Internal Communication Strategy	For Briefing and Ensuring Comprehension	To Establish Rapport with Patient	Improving Patient Experience
S – Situation – What's going on with the patient? **B** – Background – Full background information gathered **A** – Assessment – Evaluating the status **R** – Recommendation – Course of action to take	**S** – Situation – Explain the situation and the problem **T** – Task – Explain the recommended course of action **I** – Intent – Explain why that action should be taken **C** – Concern – Explain any issues that may arise and what to look out for **C** – Calibrate – Invite the person to say if they do not understand. Ask if there is any reason why an action cannot be taken and for the receiver to express any concerns.	**B** – Background – What is going on in your life? **A** – Affect – How does that affect you? **T** – Troubles – What troubles are you experiencing? **H** – Handling – How are you handling them? **E** – Empathetic statement – e.g., That must be very difficult for you.	**A** – Announce provider's presence **W** – Welcome the patient and smile **A** – Ask if patient needs anything **R** – Review interaction, its importance **E** – Exit the room with kindness

experience. They can also consider the links between communication processes (e.g., responsiveness of hospital staff; pain management; communication about medicines) and outcomes (e.g., increased adherence and compliance; readmission; healthcare delivery costs; hospital overall ratings) and track the patient experience.

Effective patient communication has the potential to help regulate patients' emotions, facilitate meaningful exchange of medical information, and allow for better understanding of patients' needs, perceptions, and expectations. Positive outcomes include increased adherence and compliance, adjustment of expectations, self-regulation, and better pain management. The benefits of treating patients respectfully are likely to be substantial. Respect engenders trust, and having a trusting relationship makes it far more likely that physician and patient can work together as partners.

Effects of the COVID-19 Pandemic

Patient perceptions of quality associated with what had been routine care has been transformed due to the COVID-19 pandemic, which may affect the way future surveys will be filled out. The rapid adoption of telemedicine and a partial shift to the delivery of care via telehealth was necessary due to stay-at-home orders and self-quarantine measures. Many patients were rapidly transitioned to telemedicine solutions, at times involuntarily. Understanding patients' perceptions of their experiences during COVID-19 and how these perceptions affect satisfaction and perceived quality requires renewed attention. When staffing shortages, vital equipment and PPE become a significant problem that impacts patient care, hospitals may be blamed for service disruptions which could skew HCAHPS results and lower hospital ratings, reduced willingness to recommend, and create domino effects for hospitals' reputations. The global pandemic placed especially severe strains on hospitals located in densely populated urban centers.

As discussed in Chapter 3, patients' willingness to recommend hospitals is critical, especially in large urban areas with highly heterogeneous patient populations, since potentially lower ratings could affect hospitals' reimbursement and bottom-line outcomes. Researchers (McFarland et al., 2015) analyzed surveys from 934,800 patients in 3,907 hospitals in more than 3,100 counties and found lower HCAHPS scores are clustered in heterogeneous population-dense areas. Another study examined county-level data, including population density, population diversity, and hospital structural factors, as predictors of patient satisfaction and found that county-level factors accounted for 30% and 16% of the variability in patient satisfaction on the HCAHPS measures of doctor and nurse communication, respectively.

An empirical study of 2816 Medicare-certified acute care hospitals across the United States, using January to December 2019 CMS *Hospital Compare* datasets merged with county-level socio-demographic data (Belasen et al., 2021a,b). Group 1 hospitals comprised about 60% of the hospitals with density corresponding to hospitals with patients having on average more favorable and consistent experiences than hospitals in Group 2.

The findings showed that Group 1 hospitals not only enjoyed higher ratings on average than Group 2 hospitals but had significantly less variability in patient experience and were less sensitive to demographic factors. These hospitals are likely to have established a stronger brand image than their Group 2 peers which experienced more variability in their HCAHPS ratings, indicative of a weaker overall quality image. Unfortunately, Group 2 hospitals are also located in lower income urban areas which were hit disproportionately hard by COVID-19. Frey (2020) reports that the counties hit hardest by COVID-19 during the initial peak were predominantly urban and had a higher percentage of non-white residents (44.1%) than the counties that experienced the least prevalence of COVID-19 cases (32.8%).

Minority groups are disproportionately affected by chronic medical conditions and reduced access to healthcare, which also contributed to worse COVID-19 outcomes, with higher death rates in African American, Native American, and Latinx communities. By April 2020, 97% of disproportionately Black counties (counties with more than the national average of Black residents) reported at least one case of COVID-19, compared to 80% of all other counties. Twenty-two percent of U.S. counties are in this category, and 90% of those are in the South. Similar results were reported by the United Kingdom's Intensive Care National Audit and Research Centre. Ethnic minorities make up 13% of the U.K. population. However, by the end of April 2020, 16.2% of patients in hospitals in England who tested positive were from Black, Asian, and minority ethnic (BAME) communities.

CMS's July 2020 snapshot of COVID-19 reported that by May 16, 2020, over 325,000 Medicare beneficiaries were diagnosed with COVID-19, and nearly 110,000 of those were hospitalized. The snapshot which broke down COVID-19 cases and hospitalizations for Medicare beneficiaries by state, race/ethnicity, dual-eligibility for Medicare and Medicaid, age, gender, and urban/rural areas – confirmed that COVID-19 disproportionately affected vulnerable populations, particularly racial and ethnic minorities. The highest rates of COVID-19 cases involved Black patients, with 1,658 cases per 100,000 beneficiaries followed by Hispanic, American Indian/Alaskan Native, Asian, white, and then patients listed as "other or unknown," further confirming the longstanding healthcare disparities in these populations.

The findings imply that lower rated hospitals with more variability in their HCAHPS responses are more likely to face adverse patient experiences due to COVID-19 than high-quality hospitals. Pandemics like COVID-19 create conditions that intensify the already high demands placed on hospitals and make it even more challenging to deliver quality care. Hospitals serving a large proportion of minority patients may face greater political and regulatory pressures from local, state, and national constituencies to provide better patient experiences for minority patients. Hospitals, especially public hospitals, seeking ways to bolster HCAHPS scores and improve their ratings should respond more equitably to underserved communities and minority groups to reduce healthcare disparities.

Additionally, examining HCAHPS results over longer time intervals may provide additional insights, especially since hospitals may be blamed for service disruptions which could further skew HCAHPS results. Finally, patient perceptions of quality associated with what had been routine care have probably changed due to COVID-19, which may affect the way future surveys will be filled out and utilized. In some instances, high proportions of patients for whom English is not the preferred language may influence quality improvement efforts.

Conclusion – Closing the Gap Experience

In 2019, the Agency for Healthcare Research and Quality (AHRQ) released its Survey on Patient Safety Culture™ (SOPS®) for providers and staff to assess patient safety culture. The purpose of the survey is to raise staff awareness about patient safety, diagnose and assess the status of patient safety culture, and identify strengths and areas for patient safety culture improvement. It can also be used to examine trends in patient safety culture change over time, evaluate the cultural impact of patient safety initiatives and interventions, conduct internal and external comparisons, and reduce potential gaps between actual and desired outcomes.

The survey consists of ten composite measures (Table 2.6) but it also includes two questions that ask respondents to provide an overall rating on patient safety for their work area/unit and to indicate the number of events they reported over the past 12 months. Event reporting was identified as an area for improvement for most hospitals because underreporting of events means potential patient safety problems may not be recognized or identified and therefore may not be addressed. Famolaro et al. (2016) noted that, on average, 45% of respondents within hospitals reported at least one event to have occurred in their hospital. It is likely that this represents underreporting of events, as respondents naturally are reluctant to report their own mistakes. In comparison, on average, 76% of respondents within hospitals gave their work area or unit a grade of "Excellent" (34%) or "Very Good" (42%) on patient safety.

Table 2.6 AHRQ Patient Safety Culture Composites and Definitions

Composite measures	Scale: 1. Strongly disagree 2. Disagree 3. Neither agree nor disagree 4. Agree 5. Strongly agree
1. Teamwork	• In this unit, we work together as an effective team • During busy times, staff in this unit help each other • There is a problem with disrespectful behavior by those working in this unit (negatively worded)
2. Staffing and work pace	• In this unit, we have enough staff to handle the workload • Staff in this unit work longer hours than is best for patient care (negatively worded) • This unit relies too much on temporary, float, or PRN staff (negatively worded) • The work pace in this unit is so rushed that it negatively affects patient safety (negatively worded)
3. Organizational learning and continuous improvement	• This unit regularly reviews work processes to determine if changes are needed to improve patient safety • In this unit, changes to improve patient safety are evaluated to see how well they worked • This unit lets the same patient safety problems keep happening (negatively worded)
4. Response to errors	• In this unit, staff feel like their mistakes are held against them (negatively worded) • When an event is reported in this unit, it feels like the person is being written up, not the problem (negatively worded) • When staff make errors, this unit focuses on learning rather than blaming individuals • In this unit, there is a lack of support for staff involved in patient safety errors (negatively worded)
5. Supervisor, manager, or clinical leader support for patient safety	• My supervisor, manager, or clinical leader seriously considers staff suggestions for improving patient safety • My supervisor, manager, or clinical leader wants us to work faster during busy times, even if it means taking shortcuts (negatively worded) • My supervisor, manager, or clinical leader takes action to address patient safety concerns that are brought to their attention

(Continued)

Table 2.6 *(Continued)* AHRQ Patient Safety Culture Composites and Definitions

6. Communication about error	• We are informed about errors that happen in this unit • When errors happen in this unit, we discuss ways to prevent them from happening again • In this unit, we are informed about changes that are made based on event reports
7. Communication openness	• In this unit, staff speak up if they see something that may negatively affect patient care • When staff in this unit see someone with more authority doing something unsafe for patients, they speak up • When staff in this unit speak up, those with more authority are open to their patient safety concerns • In this unit, staff are afraid to ask questions when something does not seem right (negatively worded)
8. Reporting patient safety events	• When a mistake is caught and corrected before reaching the patient, how often is this reported? • When a mistake reaches the patient and could have harmed the patient, but did not, how often is this reported?
9. Hospital management support for patient safety	• The actions of hospital management show that patient safety is a top priority • Hospital management provides adequate resources to improve patient safety • Hospital management seems interested in patient safety only after an adverse event happens (negatively worded)
10. Handoffs and information exchange	• When transferring patients from one unit to another, important information is often left out (negatively worded) • During shift changes, important patient care information is often left out (negatively worded) • During shift changes, there is adequate time to exchange all key patient care information

Source: Agency for Healthcare Research and Quality, https://www.ahrq.gov/sops/surveys/hospital/index.html

When healthcare settings are engaged in continuous improvement processes, the composite measures in Table 2.5 can be used as quality criteria to help track progress toward achieving desired outcomes. Over time, a trend line (Figure 2.1) can be established, and quality improvement teams can review the results, explore gaps, and brainstorm ideas and action plans for achieving desired outcomes. One example appears in Figure 2.2.

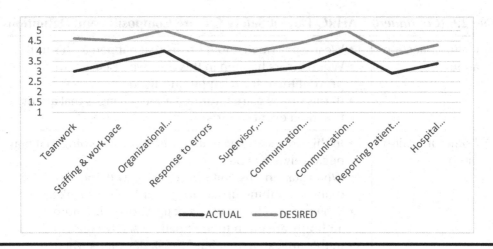

Figure 2.1   Patient safety culture trend line.

Assessments of culture are useful because they help healthcare leaders monitor progress toward desired outcomes. The survey allows respondents to identify important gaps in safety culture – first, as they see the culture of the hospital ("actual"); and second, as they would like to see their culture manifest in the future ("desired"). The gap between the responses (i.e., current vs. desired) provides important clues about prioritizing improvement goals. This involves increasing patient satisfaction through exemplary patient-centered care, effective doctor- and nurse-patient communication, increased hospital staff responsiveness and communication, and improved overall patient safety. In addition, the hospital must systematically measure and evaluate its HCAHPS survey ratings to close the quality perception gap between hospital leaders, patients, and key stakeholders.

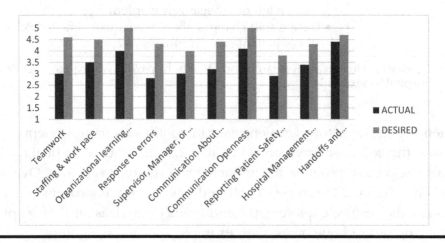

Figure 2.2   Patient safety culture: actual and desired outcomes.

References

Alexander, G. C., Casalino, L. P., & Meltzer, D. O. (2005). Physician strategies to reduce patients' out-of-pocket prescription costs. *Archives of Internal Medicine Journal*, 165(6), 633–636.

Belasen, A. T., & Belasen, A. R. (2018). Doctor-patient communication: A review and a rationale for using an assessment framework. *Journal of Health Organization and Management*, 32, 891–907.

Belasen, A. T., Oppenlander, J., Belasen, A. R., & Hertelendy, A. (2021a). Provider-patient communication and hospital ratings: Perceived gaps and forward thinking about the effects of COVID-19. *International Journal for Quality in Health Care*, 33(1) (https://doi.org/10.1093/intqhc/mzaa140).

Belasen, A. R., Tracey, M., & Belasen, A. T. (2021b). Demographics matter: The potentially disproportionate effect of COVID-19 on hospital ratings, *International Journal for Quality in Health Care. International Journal for Quality in Health Care* (https://doi.org/10.1093/intqhc/mzab036).

Bilimoria, K. Y., Brkemeyer, J. D., Burstin, H., et al. (2019). Rating the raters: An evaluation of publicly reported hospital quality ratings. *New England Journal of Medicine Catalyst*. https://catalyst.nejm.org/evaluation-hospital-quality-rating-systems. Accessed Jan. 14, 2020.

Carico, R. R., Sheppard, J., & Thomas, C. B. (2020). Community pharmacists and communication in the time of COVID-19: Applying the health belief model. *Research in Social and Administrative Pharmacy*, 26 (S1551). doi: 10.1016/j.sapharm.2020.03.017.

Famolaro, T., Yount, N. D., Burns, W., Flashner, E., Liu, H., & Sorra, J. (2016). Hospital Survey on Patient Safety Culture: 2016 User Comparative Database Report, Agency for Healthcare Research and Quality; AHRQ. https://psnet.ahrq.gov/issue/hospital-survey-patient-safety-culture-2016-user-comparative-database-report

Frey, W. H. (2020). Who lives in the places where coronavirus is hitting the hardest? *The Brookings Institution*, 2020; Washington, DC.

Glover, M., Khalilzadeh, O., Choy, G. et al. (2015). Hospital evaluations by social media: A comparative analysis of Facebook ratings among performance outliers. *Journal of General Internal Medicine*, 30, 1440–1446 (https://doi.org/10.1007/s11606-015-3236-3)

Goldman, D. P., Vaiana, M., & Romley, J. A. (2010). The emerging importance of patient amenities in hospital care. *The New England Journal of Medicine*, 363(23), 2185–2187. (https://doi.org/10.1056/NEJMp1009501)

Healthgrades. (2022). Online reviews impact how patients select hospitals & doctors, https://b2b.healthgrades.com/insights/blog/online-reviews-impact-how-patients-select-hospitals-doctors/

Huppertz, J., & Smith, R. (2014). The value of patients' handwritten comments on HCAHPS surveys. *Journal of Healthcare Management*, 59(1), 31–48.

Jain, P., & Krieger, J. L. (2011). Moving beyond the language barrier: The communication strategies used by international medical graduates in intercultural medical encounters. *Patient Education and Counseling*, 84(1), 98–104.

Laven, A., & Arnet, I. (2018). How pharmacists can encourage patient adherence to medicines. *The Pharmaceutical Journal*, 301(7916). doi: 10.1211/PJ.2018. 20205153.

McFarland, D. C., Johnson Shen, M., & Holcombe, R. F. (2017). Predictors of satisfaction with doctor and nurse communication: A national study. *Health Communication*, 32(10), 1217–1224.

McFarland, D. C., Ornstein, K. A., & Holcombe, R. F. (2015). Demographic factors and hospital size predict patient satisfaction variance: Implications for hospital value-based purchasing. *Journal of Hospital Medicine*,10, 503–509. doi:10.1002/jhm.2371.

Press Ganey. (2017). Achieving excellence: the convergence of safety, quality, experience and caregiver engagement. *Strategic Insights Report*. Press Ganey Associates.

Shah, R. F., Manning, D. W., Butler, B. A., & Bilimoria, K. Y. (2020). Do hospital rankings mislead patients? Variability among national rating systems for orthopaedic surgery. *The Journal of the American Academy of Orthopaedic Surgeons*, 28(17), e766–e773. (https://doi.org/10.5435/JAAOS-D-19-00165)

Smith, S. N., Reichert, H. A., Ameling, J. M., & Meddings, J. (2017). Dissecting Leapfrog: How well do leapfrog safe practices scores correlate with hospital compare ratings and penalties, and how much do they matter? *Medical Care*, 55(6), 606–614. (https://doi.org/10.1097/MLR.0000000000000716)

Street, R. L. (2003). Communication in medical encounters: An ecological perspective, in Thompson, T., Dorsey, A., Miller, K. & Parrott, R. (Eds.), *Handbook of Health Communication* (pp. 63–89). Mahwah, NJ: Lawrence Earlbaum.

Unruh, L., & Hofler, R. (2016). Predictors of gaps in patient safety and quality in U.S. hospitals. *Health Services Research*, 51(6), 2258–2281. (https://doi.org/10.1111/1475-6773.12468)

Young, C., & Chen, X. (2020). Patients as consumers in the market for medicine: The halo effect of hospitality. *Social Forces*, 99(2), 504–531. (https://doi.org/10.1093/sf/soaa007)

Chapter 3

The Critical Nature of the Nurse-Patient Relationship

Introduction

Culturally appropriate, technically accurate, and emotionally supportive nurse-patient communication is essential for patients to have consistently positive interactions with the healthcare system. Simply put, nurse-patient communication is integral to the quality of the patient experience. Perhaps more than any other healthcare profession, nurses work in environments across the spectrum of healthcare, yet in each situation effective communication is key. From the intensive care unit to labor and delivery to outpatient clinics to in-home hospice care, nurses are front and center when it comes to listening to, assessing, and educating patients. Navigating these exchanges takes skill, experience, and support from the broader healthcare system. As discussed in Chapter 2, communication, when handled well, contributes to a good chance that the patient will see their experience in a positive light. If handled poorly, the chances of an overall positive patient experience diminish.

Rapid societal changes in technology and demographics continue to make these nurse-patient communications ever more challenging. This chapter will examine some of the evidence supporting the central role of nurse-patient communication (including Hospital Consumer Assessment of Healthcare Providers and Systems, or HCAHPS scores), and it also highlights some of the challenges brought by rapid technological and demographic change. Specifically, changes in technology have forced nurses to learn new skills at an ever-accelerating pace to work effectively with their patients. At the same

DOI: 10.4324/9781003431077-3

time, rapid demographic shifts involving population migration and changes in the racial and ethnic populations served have highlighted the need for education and skill with cultural humility and culturally competent care.

As we move deeper into the 21st century, it will be essential for nurses to prioritize keeping themselves up to date on technological advances as they pertain to healthcare delivery, but it is also essential that they maintain an awareness of and connection to the specific needs of the communities they serve. These skills will need to be hardwired into undergraduate and graduate nursing curricula, but employers will also need to set aside time and resources to allow nurses to continue their education once in the workforce. These are great challenges, and nurses will need the support of the greater healthcare system at both the local and national levels in order to achieve these ambitious goals.

There are several ways in which healthcare organizations and government entities measure performance and track patient outcomes. The HCAHPS survey is one of the more widely used and commonly referenced instruments that illuminates the patient experience at inpatient hospitals and select facilities. Patient experience can also be defined in a number of ways. The Beryl Institute (2023) provides a broad definition as a point of reference, defining the patient experience as "the sum of all interactions, shaped by an organization's culture, that influence patient perceptions across the continuum of care". The presumption is that an improved patient experience is directly linked to better performance and patient outcomes. HCAHPS specifically links nursing-patient interaction to the patient experience and suggests that the latter is closely linked to a positive interaction with the nurses caring for them during their inpatient hospital stay.

The HCAHPS survey results as discussed in Chapter 2 (Table 2.1 HCAHPS Patient-Level Correlations) interestingly, but not surprisingly, suggest that two of the strongest correlations exist between a positive view of nurse-patient communication and the likelihood to rate the hospital favorably (correlation coefficient of 0.64), and a positive view of nurse-patient communication and the likelihood to recommend the hospital to others (correlation coefficient of 0.58). Effective communication with nurses is also closely correlated with more positive responses on the survey items of responsiveness of hospital staff, correlation coefficient of 0.54. These strong correlations between positive and effective nurse-patient communication with hospital rating, willingness to recommend, and responsiveness of staff highlight the need to place value and focus on effective nurse-patient communication.

Further, given that the **willingness to recommend** is deemed critically important to attracting and retaining patients in competitive markets, it follows that the importance of fostering organizational environments where **communication with nurses** can thrive is also critically important. There is also evidence that overall quality of care, health outcomes, and health equity are impacted by effectiveness of communication across all aspects of the healthcare system. This further suggests that understanding effective communication and how it impacts quality of care and health outcomes is worthy of the attention of all healthcare administrators, clinicians, and the academics who prepare the healthcare professionals, staff, and administrators who serve in these roles.

While the correlations between effective nurse-patient communication and the likelihood that a patient will rate a hospital favorably or recommend a hospital to others are very strong, this is not to say that there is no room for improvement. The question then becomes how best to further improve nursing communication with patients, enhancing the patient experience and the likelihood that the patients will both rate the hospital favorably and recommend it to others. There are multiple areas to consider, and these include the following: (1) the culture of the organization; (2) how nursing professionals are valued in terms of their professional growth and development needs; (3) the support nurses receive to provide their patients safe and high-quality care; and (4) attention to an environment that supports and nurtures diversity, equity, and inclusion (DEI).

In addition, there is a growing sentiment that there has been an erosion of what is core to the discipline of nursing: the value of the therapeutic nurse-patient relationship. This erosion has occurred due to several factors directly related to the considerations noted above, including nurses feeling disrespected and underappreciated, nurses encountering bullying in the workplace, nurses reporting unsafe working conditions due to staffing issues, and the aging population of the nursing workforce (Kwame & Petrucka, 2021; American Nurses Association [ANA], 2015). Further, this erosion in valuing and ensuring the conditions for the therapeutic nurse-patient relationship to thrive ultimately compromises optimum patient-centered care, patient-centered communication, and the overall patient experience.

There are some significant drivers changing the way in which nurses communicate with patients and other health professionals and staff as well as with society more generally. It is important for healthcare leaders to be aware of these changes as they are shaping the access, delivery, quality, and safety of care both within the U.S. health system but also globally. The changes are simultaneously shaping the way in which patients are experiencing care across all sectors of the healthcare industry. Given the accelerating rate of change, there has never been a time when a therapeutic, positive nurse-patient relationship has been more critical to the improvement of patient outcomes and the quality of care. Nurses working on the front lines in all types of healthcare organizations, ranging from primary care to home care, hospice, nursing homes, rehabilitation centers, and inpatient hospitals, are consistently holding the hands of patients and families across the continuum of the patient experience ranging from some of their most joyful moments to times of great sadness and tragedy. It is in these crucibles, these intense, vulnerable moments that the nurse-patient relationship is solidified and remembered by patients long after they leave a particular healthcare system.

Some of the notable areas where we have witnessed sweeping changes include the following: (1) technology used for communication with and the assessment of patients; (2) the demographics of the U.S. population; (3) delivery of care focused on understanding the impact of social determinants on health and health disparities; and (4) an increasing awareness of the importance of DEI.

More particularly, the use of electronic medical records in general and patient portals specifically for asking and answering questions is now ubiquitous. Patients have an unprecedented ability to access their own medical records, review data, and ask questions of the nurses and healthcare team. As detailed later in this chapter, U.S. demographics are shifting rapidly, emphasizing the increasing need for delivering care with cultural competence care and cultural humility. Likewise, a greater understanding of the importance of social determinants is continuously reminding healthcare providers to look beyond acute visits or hospitalizations and focus more on the underlying causes of healthcare concerns. Lastly, with a rapidly increasing national focus on DEI, nurses are challenged to bring to the forefront concerns with fairness and evenhandedness as they care for and advocate for their patients.

These changes are forcing a refocus on the importance of the nurse-patient relationship, how healthcare organizations are supporting the patient experience, and the overall communication between health professionals and the patients they care for. As evidence-based practices in these areas continue to evolve, nurses and healthcare providers in general will need to learn new skills without losing proven techniques. Additionally, health systems are learning to navigate these changes with a greater attention to the connections they have with the communities they serve and with an overall more global perspective.

Communication and Connection

Various methods of communication are used by nurses and health professionals to connect with patients, and for good reason. Culturally and situationally appropriate communication is critical to assessing, diagnosing, and providing appropriate intervention in the right setting at the right time. Without effective communication the ability to connect with patients is greatly compromised, leading to concerns for the quality and safety of care. Beginning two decades ago with back to back reports from The National Academy of Medicine (Institute of Medicine, 2000; 2001) and continuing with publications from other professional organizations in the years since, a number of landmark reports have noted that there are several ways ineffective communication exchanges between patients and healthcare professionals compromise a patient's ability to receive optimal care and achieve optimal health outcomes. The root cause of these ineffective exchanges often stems from a patient's perception of whether they are being listened to, respected, and valued. Equally important is the level of trust the patient has in the healthcare professionals and the healthcare system they interact with. Naturally this is easier in situations where continuity is possible, more challenging when the nurse and patient are previously unknown to each other.

Listening as an aspect of the communication process is important in two related ways. First, listening is important from the perspective that the patient feels they are being heard with a belief that the other is interested in understanding them. If a patient does not feel listened to, the relationship between patient and nurse erodes. A patient can certainly develop feelings of distrust and feelings that they are not valued, respected, or cared about. These feelings of distrust and not feeling valued can be additive and lead to circumstances where important information being delivered by the nurse is ignored by the patient. It can also result in a patient withholding information or not fully disclosing information because they do not feel as though they are going to be listened to.

Second, and by extension, this breakdown in any given nurse-patient interaction can have serious implications for a patient in both their overall satisfaction and experience but also in the ability of a nurse to adequately assess a patient. For example, a woman seeking healthcare in the early stages of a pregnancy who does not make a connection and feel trusted, valued, and respected may withhold information about drug and alcohol use, smoking, and domestic partner violence – which, if not addressed, can have devastating health outcomes for the woman and the baby. It can also lead to the patient deciding not to pursue additional follow-up care for the remainder of the pregnancy. A physical exam of a patient is without question a valuable tool used by health professionals to assess the status of a patient, but the verbal exchange that takes place between the patient and health professional can reveal important and key aspects about a patient that are needed to properly diagnosis and recommend treatment. In short, the history, the patient's story, is often the key. The ability of a nurse and other health professionals to make a connection with a patient where the patient feels they can be open and honest can make all the difference to the appropriate plan of care, treatment, and long-term health outcomes.

In the inpatient setting, this appropriate plan of care continues straight through to discharge, and it is often skilled delivery of these discharge instructions that can make all the difference in whether a patient once discharged experiences a readmission. Preventable readmissions are not only problematic and at times devasting for a patient, but they are also enormously expensive for healthcare systems. Whether the readmission occurs within the same 24–48 hours or within a week, in either of these scenarios the mere fact of the readmission should force us to ask why. Was ineffective nurse-patient communication a part of the cause? If not, then what factors contributed to the readmission?

While there are several medical complications that can occur after a patient returns to their home from an inpatient hospital stay, there are also a number of areas where gaps in communication could be a causative factor in why a patient needs to be readmitted. Discharge instructions may be contradictory or confusing, medication reconciliation may be rushed or superficially performed, and plans for outpatient follow-up may be unclear. Medications and home health equipment may not be appropriately ordered, family members may not be appropriately updated on a patient's status, and external healthcare providers may not be appropriately updated on a patient's condition.

A patient's successful transition from the hospital to home is one of many examples of how several, often sequential, communications are needed between the patient and the team of health professionals caring for the patient. Newer technologies, such as patient portals, email, and videoconferencing, can be used to help facilitate these communications, but ultimately attention to detail and a nurse tailoring the appropriate type and level of communication to meet the needs of a particular patient and their family is crucial.

Who Are Nurses Communicating to – Changing U.S. Demographics

An important finding in the HCAHPS results is that lower scores tend to cluster in areas where the population is more heterogenous and dense. This is not surprising, as more heterogenous-dense communities are populated with more diverse populations. The increased diversity of the patient population can make effective nurse-patient communication more challenging, particularly if the nurses and other healthcare professionals do not mirror the population receiving care. Data demonstrate that patient experiences across the country are not the same, and that communities with more diverse populations frequently have more evidence of healthcare inequalities. Researchers find that persons living in these communities more commonly express feeling excluded or ignored, a consequence of the largely inherent cultural and structural barriers that exist across the U.S. healthcare system (Belasen et al., 2021). It is also in these environments where barriers to effective communication and an optimal patient experience are potentially the most challenged, and it follows that it is in these environments that strategies to improve communication must be a priority.

To promote effective communication, training in intercultural competence has long held an important role in the discipline of nursing and professional nursing practice. The American Nurses Association (ANA) Standards and Scopes of Practice notes that a key role of nurses is that, "Nurses design and direct culturally congruent practice and services for diverse consumers to improve access, promote positive outcomes, and reduce disparities" (2015, p. 31).

Intercultural care and communication are threaded throughout both nursing education curriculum standards and standards of professional practice. The ANA Standards and Scopes of Practice further defines culturally congruent practice as the "application of evidence-based nursing that is in agreement with the preferred cultural value, beliefs, worldview, and practices of the healthcare consumer and other stakeholders" (2015, p. 31) and parallels the connections, documented in the literature, between cultural understanding and sensitivity in the delivery of optimal patient care health outcomes. The more closely patients feel understood the more likely they are to engage with the health professionals from whom they seek care.

With an increasingly culturally diverse population in the U.S., it is becoming more and more evident that the need to fully explore how nurses can shape the experiences of patients with a keen attention to cultural differences is critically important. Being able to communicate and thus connect with patients in a culturally attuned manner can impact a conversation with a patient that further impacts the experience the patient has with the healthcare system and can potentially influence overall long-term health outcomes. The geographic distribution and increasing diversity of the U.S. population requires an understanding of how U.S. demographics are changing, and how these changing demographics directly affect health disparities and inequalities, necessitating the development of a complex communication skill set to address determinants of health. Understanding the interplay of these dynamics needs to be situated with attention to geographic and cultural differences evolving across the U.S. health systems.

Significant changes occurred in the racial and ethnic makeup of the U.S. population between 2010 and 2020. The 2020 U.S. Census data provides a snapshot of the current geographic population distribution by state. In 2020, the last year the U.S. Census was taken, the U.S. population measured just over 333 million residents (US Census Bureau, 2021). Importantly, this number does not include the total number of persons living in the United States., which would also include unhoused persons and unauthorized immigrants. Estimates of the true U.S. population, which would include these two groups, would add upward of an additional 10.5 million people (Lopez, Passel, & Cohn, 2021).

Longstanding trends showing increased population growth in the South and West (as defined by the U.S. Census Bureau) accelerated between 2010 and 2020, with increases of 10.2% and 9.2%, respectively. This is in comparison to the Midwest, which showed an overall population growth rate of only 3.1%. At the state-specific level, the Western states of Utah (18.4%), Idaho (17.3%), and North Dakota (15.8%) have seen the most significant shifts in overall population growth (2021). Texas, with a growth rate of 15.9%, has seen the largest growth rate in the South. In comparison, Midwestern states such as Wisconsin (3.6%), Pennsylvania (2.4%), and Ohio (2.3%) are reported as having lower overall growth rates, and West Virginia has seen the largest decline in population growth rate with a negative 3.2% (US Census Bureau, 2021).

The overall population changes and shifts are only one aspect of the changing U.S. demographics. There have also been racial and ethnic changes. The U.S. Census Bureau report by Jones et al. (2021) also noted that during the same period between 2010 and 2020, the Hispanic or Latino population grew by 23% and accounted for more than half of the total U.S. population growth. By 2020, Latinos accounted for 18.7% of the total U.S. population. While the Latino-identifying population reported the overall highest growth numbers, all population groups grew except for whites. This includes groups classified as Black or African American, American Indian, Alaska Native, Asian, Native Hawaiian and Other Pacific Islander group, along with the multiracial population classification.

Changes in the design of the U.S. Census collection also help to explain a large growth in the multiracial population identification, a 276% increase. Attention to these demographic shifts is important, as it helps to explain some of the noted regional health outcome disparities. The COVID-19 pandemic illuminated many of these growing disparities (Belasen et al., 2023).

As discussed in Chapter 2, COVID-19 was in many ways a wakeup call, shedding light more brightly on the gross disparities and social inequities that exist in our health system. Stark disparities in both the death rates and the hospitalization rates in the Hispanic and Black populations, as compared to whites, brought a renewed awareness of where communication barriers may exist related to language, culture, and other determinants of health impacting health outcomes. Research conducted by the Missouri Foundation, in concert with the George Washington University Milken Institute for Public Health, revealed some of the gross disparities that exist among diverse population groups (Mead et al., 2023). Blacks and Latinos across the country were "more likely" to not only experience higher infection rates, but also compounding "hardships" related to increased rates of job loss, housing insecurity, and overall economic struggles.

Additionally, in a Pew Research Report, growth of the Hispanic (Latino) population in the United States is noted as an important consideration not only because of potential language and cultural barriers but because the population is "less likely than other Americans to have health insurance and to receive preventative medical care", and "were more likely to be hospitalized during COVID" (Funk & Lopez, 2022). The population shifts noted in the latest U.S. Census mirror the changes and growth of the Latino population in the United States, with the greatest increases seen in the South and West.

The pre-pandemic Commonwealth Fund 2020 Scorecard on State Health Systems underscores the point that the United States is a varied picture of access to care, quality of care, health outcomes, and health disparities (Radley et al., 2020). In similar findings from the Pew Research report, The Commonwealth Fund 2020 Scorecard reflects the growing evidence that Black people die from treatable and early medical conditions at twice the rate of white people. The report tracks 49 indicators as a measure of health system performance in each state.

Key indicators which contributed to disparities between people of color and whites include rising out-of-pocket costs, access to primary care, and a still largely uninsured population in several states such as Texas, Missouri, and West Virginia. Texas, the second largest growth state, ranked 42nd and falls in the bottom quartiles for access and affordability, prevention and treatment, avoidable cost, and 30-day readmissions. Some of the states ranking lowest on income disparity measures were Mississippi, Oklahoma, Missouri. In other words, these states have some of the largest income or wealth disparities as compared to other states.

Overall, the report indicated that the U.S. health system does not provide equal care to people of color or to those with low-to-moderate incomes leading to an overarching conclusion of the report that there is considerable geographic variation by state in the quality of healthcare delivered. For example, The National Institutes of Health (2023) reports that the United States has among the highest rates of maternal mortality in industrialized countries, with nearly 700 women dying of pregnancy-related complications annually. This includes deaths that occur up to one year postpartum. Like other poor health outcomes tracked by the Commonwealth Report, these mortality rates vary from state to state and are disproportionately higher for Black and Indigenous women.

Health disparities are evident across the United States but there are few places where the disparity in health outcomes is more evident than the mortality rates of Black women in the peripartum period, where nationally Black women are nearly three times more likely to die from pregnancy-related complications than white women: The National Center for Health Statistics reports that in 2020, the maternal mortality rate for Black women was 55.3 death per 100,000 live births. The rate for white women was 19.1 deaths per 100,000 live births (Hoyert, 2020; Green, 2023). It is a continuing tale of a country that has failed to address some of the key determinants of health that have plagued both the healthcare system and left disadvantaged populations underserved and the needs of racial groups ignored for many decades.

To illustrate the historical perspective, the famous Norman Rockwell painting "Doctor and Doll" or W. Eugene Smith's landmark 1950s photo titled the "Midwife- Nurse Maude Callen, attending a Women in Labor" visually remind us of the complex art of the patient-health professional relationship and a bygone era where almost every aspect of a conversation between the patient and a health professional was not documented in a database. However, what is striking, and in some ways most significant to consider when reflecting on the landmark photo of Maude Callen, is what is captured beyond the nurse-patient relationship and shared with society. The photo at the time was considered a first glimpse into the work of a healthcare professional, a Black nurse-midwife, in the rural south in the 1950s, who cared for "thousands of desperately poor patients". It was featured as part of a photo essay in Time Magazine, and at the time it was noted to be what some consider the first glimpse of poor rural southern life that the readers of Time Magazine had ever seen (Cosgrove, 2013). The published image generated thousands of dollars in donations to help Maude Callen care for her patients.

While this image and others taken by W. Eugene Smith captured a period in U.S. history almost 75 years ago, to this day even with the advances in medical sciences, technology, and over $4 trillion spent on healthcare in the United States, much is unchanged when examining the health outcomes for some of the most vulnerable patient populations. Today we continue to see tragically high maternal child death rates across the country with rates highest among rural poor Black women, the very same population Maude Callen is captured caring for in the 1950s. Stories are being told about Black women coming in to seek care, but are they being listened to? Or is there an effective exchange of communication between provider and patient taking place to assess the full story and examine the determinants of health, both current and past, which are contributing to the welfare of the patient during her pregnancy? There is no place where there may be a greater breakdown in communication, and consequently no place with a greater need to address a failing communication system in healthcare, than that between health professionals and Black pregnant women.

In early 2023, *The New York Times* reported on a story that reflects other similar stories that have brought growing attention to the morbidity and mortality rates of pregnant Black women and their babies. This story was about a 34-year-old pregnant Black woman who arrived in an emergency room seeking care because she did not feel well and complained of swollen feet. She was diagnosed with a probable bladder infection and then sent home with antibiotics. She returned two days later, but by then the time to accurately diagnose and save the new mother had passed. The swollen feet became more uncomfortable, causing this woman to seek care in an emergency room. In the emergency room, the swollen feet were correctly identified as a symptom of a much more serious condition, toxemia (poisoning) from pre-eclampsia. Tragically, the diagnosis came too late for this woman, and she died two later from complications of pre-eclampsia.

There were certainly several variables present during her initial interaction and communication with the healthcare system, and we have no way of knowing all of the details, but we do know there is pattern of stories just like this one and that regardless of socioeconomic status there is a "maternal mortality health crisis among Black women" – they are dying at higher rates than affluent white women (Green, 2023). How does a health system get to a place where patients are fully listened to, pain is not minimized, symptoms are not trivialized, and reports of mistreatment are rare to nonexistent? One of the potential answers involves building a healthcare system where the makeup of the healthcare workforce more closely reflects the population it cares for, and mastering communication practice grounded in cultural humility and competent care.

Nursing Workforce Demographics

The changes in the diversity and geographic distribution of the population have taken place at a rate where the current nursing workforce is not reflective of the population they care for, which may have implications related to communication and cultural barriers and raises concerns as it relates to providing quality care and building trust. There is a growing body of literature highlighting research linking communication, health disparities, health outcomes, and the quality of care to the lack of diversity in the U.S. healthcare workforce. Over the last two decades the demographic shift in the United States has led to an increasingly diverse general population, while the diversity of the healthcare workforce has changed much more slowly.

The lack of diversity in the U.S. nursing workforce has been and continues to be a significant issue, so much so that it is a key focus of the Academy of Sciences Future of Nursing 2020–2030: Charting a Path to Achieve Health Equity report. It describes the effects of the failure to make progress on diversity growth in the nursing profession on the quality of healthcare in the United States. As hospitals and other healthcare organizations seek to strategize ways to improve communication, quality of care, and patient outcomes, continued engagement and attention to the diversity of the workforce and the patient populations served need to be a priority.

In looking for opportunities to improve health outcomes across populations, there has never been a more critical time to focus on increasing the representation of diverse populations in the nursing workforce and finding more ways to reduce barriers in communicating across population groups. However, diversifying the nursing workforce in addition to reducing the nursing workforce shortage presents a number of challenges. Increasing diversity in the healthcare workforce is not only a responsibility of the healthcare systems that hire nurses, but as Buerhaus (2008) noted, to expand the future supply of nurses, policy makers must support efforts to remove barriers to entry into the workforce. For the most part, the literature on these barriers to entry in the nursing profession focuses on the post-secondary nursing programs, focusing on such matters as capacity restraints, faculty shortages, and availability of educational sites (Buerhaus, 2008). Other cited barriers to entry to practice for certain ethnic groups include the lack of diversity of nursing faculty, perceived discrimination by faculty, and financial burdens (Villarruel, Canales, & Torres, 2001).

So, what does the nursing workforce currently look like? In 2008, in the absence of knowledge of the 2019 pandemic, healthcare economist Peter Buerhaus predicted a deficit in the supply of RNs relative to the expected demand that would begin around 2015. Consistent with Buerhaus, The National Center for Health Workforce Analysis (2022) predicts a shortage of "78,160 full-time equivalent (FTE) RNs in 2025 and a shortage of 63,720 FTE RNs in 2030." Additionally, the nursing workforce demographics have consistently not been representative of the diverse U.S. population. In 2005 Hispanics made up 14% of the entire U.S. workforce, but only 4% of the approximately 2.5 million RNs in the nursing workforce (Zangaro, Streeter, Tiandong, 2018). In 2018, roughly a decade later, the 2017 National Nursing Workforce reported that 5.3% of the RN population were Hispanic while at that time Hispanics made up 18% of the entire U.S. population and 16.8% of the U.S. Labor workforce (National Council on the State Boards of Nursing [NCSBN], 2018; Smiley et al., 2018).

According to The National Council on the State Boards of Nursing (2020) and The 2020 National Nursing Workforce Survey, in 2020 nearly 81% of registered nurses were white/Caucasian, males accounted for 9.4% of the nursing workforce, Blacks represented 6.7% (a mere 0.7% increase from 2013), 7.2% reported their ethnicity as Asian and 5.6% reported their ethnicity as Hispanic. In looking at the demographics in the 2020 United

States Census, the nursing workforce falls far short of being reflective of the U.S. population and has seen very little change in the past decade.

The data suggest that over the last decade very little progress has been made toward increasing the number of Hispanic/Latino and Black/African American women in the nursing workforce. This lack of progress should raise alarms given mounting awareness of the importance of culturally competent communications, and an understanding that communication and more importantly healthcare outcomes may be improved when the healthcare workforce better mirrors the population it serves. As part of an overall strategy to ensure a more diverse nursing workforce to provide more patient-centered communication and culturally competent care, the American Association of Colleges of Nursing (AACN) has made progress in aligning nursing curriculum to focus even more attention on culturally sensitive care, social injustices, and inequalities that exist in the U.S. health system.

Role of Nursing Education in Communication

The American Association of Colleges of Nursing (AACN), an academic governing body whose purpose it is to outline the "educational framework for the preparation of nurses at four-year colleges and universities", published a 2021 iteration of The Essentials: Core Competencies for Professional Nursing Education document highlighting a framework that calls attention to several educational areas but specifically to the areas of informatics and healthcare technology and population health, and person-centered care. Other areas include quality and safety, interprofessional partnerships, professionalism, scholarship, and leadership. The AACN importantly calls attention to the idea of what makes a nurse "work ready"? What do they need to learn to be able to communicate and work in this complex healthcare environment where policy, social structures, economics, and politics are impacting the delivery of care more than at any previous time in history.

In addressing this "work ready" concept, the AACN notes that not only is DEI a concept critical to embed and integrate throughout the curriculum, but that it also, "requires intentionality, an institutional structure of social justice, and individually concerted efforts" (2021, p.5). It is this complex interplay of so many changes occurring that is shaping the way in which nurses communicate with patients, communities, and society at large. As previously noted, the communication between a nurse and patient can make a difference in patient behavior, readmissions to hospitals, and ultimately long-term health outcomes.

The discipline of nursing has always been grounded in theoretical frameworks centered on the "well-being pattern of human behavior", the "relationships with others", "health", "caring", and the way in which humans interact with their environment (American Association of Colleges of Nursing [AACN], 2021, p. 2). Moving forward into the 21st century where the environment is changing so dramatically, it follows that nursing as a discipline needs to examine the impact these changes will have on healthcare delivery and outcomes.

Specifically, it is important to study and understand how relationships are changing, how human behavior is changing, and how humans are interacting with their environment, especially given the advances in technology, changes in U.S. demographics, and the need for more diverse, equitable, and inclusive approaches in all aspects of society. The AACN notes that for nurses to fully develop as professionals and approach the practice of nursing, the foundational educational core of nursing needs to be in the liberal arts and sciences (2021). It is in this way that nurses will be able to fully embody "the richness of perspective and knowledge" and the "capacity to engage in socially valued work and civic leadership in society" (2021, p.3).

The AACN recognizes the continued need to reinforce educational preparation in communication for the future nursing workforce and has dedicated accreditation language for baccalaureate nursing programs to incorporate into their programs. This focus on communication is grounded in frameworks that guide the discipline of nursing and the growing evidence on the importance of communication to patient quality and safety both within the discipline and across disciplines.

However, the nursing workforce in many healthcare environments is diverse in terms of its educational background, preparation, and scope of practice; it ranges from nurses holding a bachelor's degree from an AACN-accredited university to licensed vocational nurses, registered nurses holding an Associate Degree or registered nurses holding a Diploma Certificate, as well as to advanced practice nurses (nurse practitioners and midwives) (National Academies of Sciences, Engineering, and Medicine, 2021). The educational preparation of nurses has changed significantly over the past several decades, with the AACN only "recognizing the degree of Bachelor's in Nursing as the minimum educational requirement for professional nursing practice", but it is important that the focus of nursing education across all levels involves teaching culturally competent communication and importantly ways nurses can the reduce of barriers contributing to inequalities in health outcomes across the healthcare system.

Nursing Communication and Technology

Over the last decade, changes in the U.S. demographics are not the only significant change impacting healthcare. There has also been a dramatic shift in the way health professionals interact and communicate with patients. In parallel to the rapid changes in the U.S. demographics, there has also been equally rapid changes in the advances in technology. The 21st-century technological era has not only propelled advances in several areas in the medical sciences and bioengineering sciences, but over the course of the era, the advances in technology have changed the way health professionals communicate with patients. While the first World Wide Web was launched in 1993, and subsequently jump-started the accelerated use of the internet by the public at large, it was Thomas Friedman who aptly asks, in his book *Thank you for Being Late an Optimist's Guide to Thriving in the age of Acceleration*, "What the Hell happened in 2007?" In this very year alone a number of online communication platforms surfaced. The social media platforms of Twitter, Facebook, and YouTube were launched, and IBM pushed the barriers in capturing data analytics technology in its Watson System- a computer that became "the first cognitive computer, combining machine learning, and artificial intelligence" (Friedman, 2016, p. 22).

Today we see the evolution of this very first artificial intelligence technology in the development of carebots or care robots. Despite raising a number of ethical concerns in the way in which personal data are being collected, incidences involving potential deception, and privacy infringements, carebots are marketed as AI-generated companions (Robots) to provide physical and mental healthcare to vulnerable populations (Yew, 2021). It is with this technology that there may be even greater changes in patient communication on the horizon, in that a healthcare professional is absent in the conversation. New questions consider how AI can be best used, and concerns exist about how it could be misused.

Regardless of the direction surrounding the emerging use of AI in healthcare communication, in the 21st-century era of healthcare delivery it is a rarity for a health professional to engage with a patient without the use of a computer in some capacity. A computer can be found in almost every patient care area. Patient information is used not only within a single health system, but it is often shared across many systems. Unimaginable to many, the launch of the World Wide Web in 1993 propelled the current day use of the internet as one of the primary sources used by patients to learn about their healthcare diagnosis and needs, and it has led to patients bringing questions to their health professionals in a way never seen before. It has changed the dynamic of the conversations between patients and health professionals in all types of healthcare settings.

Through the use of technology and easy access to information, patients have come to expect to communicate in a different way, a way that acknowledges the information they are finding. Patients not only want to share their physical symptoms but also want to be heard and discuss the information they have learned through their internet searches. Through patient portal systems patients no longer must wait for a follow-up visit or even a phone call in some instances to access the results of medical tests. Personal patient medical portals also allow patients to access and review their own data and charts, and in some cases, they may do so before they have had a chance to speak with their healthcare provider. Use of portal messaging with healthcare providers enables a two-way online communication platform outside of direct face-to-face interaction.

The use of telemedicine, or virtual patient visits, has enabled patients to remain in their own homes during what would have been in the past a face-to-face visit in an office setting. The expansion of the internet has provided on-demand healthcare information and opportunities for increased communication between healthcare providers and millions of patients who otherwise would not have access. The expansion and use of technology has happened so fast that it is almost difficult to imagine a conversation with a patient without technology by the bedside.

To follow the example of the patient portal, nurses have for years grown adept at in-person and at times phone conversations with patients. There is both learned skill and an art to this type of communication. Likewise, there are very real and distinct skills necessary for effective portal communication with a patient. For example, the nurse needs significant judgement and experience to know when to continue an exchange on what is essentially HIPAA-compliant email, versus deciding that a phone call or in-person patient visit is in order. If the email exchange is to continue, the nurse must be confident with the language and responses they are giving, knowing that the "patient cases" become a permanent part of the medical record. It takes a combination of knowledge of the medical situation at issue, the cultural and educational situation of the patient on the other end of the computer, and level of technological comfort with the electronic medical record in use to deliver this type of care effectively and efficiently. Done well, the patient experience is enhanced. If done poorly, the interaction may lead to a patient complaint.

Friedman notes that in the age of acceleration and in all things technological, one of the hardest things for the human mind to grasp is the power of exponential growth in anything – "what happens when something keeps doubling or tripling or quadrupling over many years and just how big the numbers get" (2016, p. 38). While Friedman was referring to Gordon Moore's 1965 Law on the computational speed of microchips, it provides a framework for trying to understand how difficult it can be to keep pace with the current pace of change in communication and language systems occurring in our health systems and the global society. While the pace of change leading into the 21st century has been fast and is often embedded in great complexity with no end in sight, nursing professionals are poised to adapt and strengthen the impactful nature of effective communication and the patient experience across healthcare systems, but this type of success cannot be achieved by working in silos.

Taking a strategy out of the playbook of global corporate organizations that are trying to keep pace with the rate of change, Clancy and Warren (2017) provide a thoughtful strategy for the future of effective nurse-patient communication in the age of acceleration and that is the development of academic and practice partnerships, particularly between nursing schools and health systems. This is like corporate companies that have partnered with higher education entities to help train and reskill their workforce. They note that there are just too many aspects of learning and changes occurring to go it alone. Beyond the obvious competence in the uses of electronic health record data systems, there is as Clancy and Warren note, the "standardized language, information system design, analysis of nursing workflow, telehealth, consumer informatics, patient engagement, clinical decision-making support, robotics, mobile technology, information literacy, data science and a whole host of other areas" (2017, p. 186). For nurses to be prepared for communicating with patients in a technology-laden environment, partnership with nursing schools and health systems can provide the exposure and digital literacy to work with "state of the art information systems". Partnerships also enable collaborations in education, training, and research needs for both students and working professional nurses.

Conclusion

As society moves forward there is no question that human adaptability will continue to be challenged, social contracts will be examined, and scarce resources will remain the center of competition and strategy for many organizations. However, as nursing professionals adapt, the patient experience needs to be reflective of patient safety, quality of care, and effective communication. Using HCAHPS and similar data sets to measure the performance of a healthcare system will remain a useful tool to assess progress and to focus healthcare leaders on areas needing improvement.

The current environment requires a skill set attuned to the advances in medical science and technology but also aware of the growing diversity in the population. Advances in medical science and technology are constantly stretching the interventions that patients receive across all disease processes. While we marvel at the advances in medical care and life-saving treatments, there is also a staggering and growing body of literature identifying the disparities in the U.S. health system across differing populations. It has become clear that a lack of attention to these inequities is contributing to poor patient outcomes and trust in the healthcare system.

Fostering a culture in healthcare that is inclusive and culturally sensitive, where all patients feel valued, respected, and listened to needs to be central to the mission of healthcare organizations. Operating in silos and taking a one size fits all approach when providing patient care with the hope of achieving optimal patient outcomes, high-quality care, and a positive patient experience will leave healthcare organizations falling short on every measure.

In order for patients to have positive experiences with the healthcare system, high-quality nurse-patient communication will remain a priority. Current data, as highlighted in the HCAHPS data, supports this approach. Nurses can and should be trained to master existing healthcare technologies, and they should be given opportunities and support to develop new skills once they enter the profession. Likewise, as highlighted in this chapter, rapidly changing demographics in the United States and a deeper societal understanding of longstanding health inequities emphasize the need for nurses to both develop initial skills in delivering culturally competent care, but also to continuously refine and enhance these skills as they move further into their careers. Successfully accomplishing these distinct but very much complementary goals will greatly enhance the likelihood of positive patient experiences in the years and decades to come.

References

American Association of Colleges of Nursing (AACN). (2021, April 6). *The Essentials: Core Competencies for Professional Nursing Education.* American Association of the Colleges of Nursing. Washington, D.C.

American Nurses Association (ANA). (2015). *Nursing Scope and Standards of Practice.* American Nurses Association. Silver Springs, MD.

Belasen, A. R., Belasen, A. T., & Bass, M. (2023). Tracking the uneven outcomes of COVID-19 on racial and ethnic groups: Implications for health policy. *Journal of Racial and Ethnic Health Disparities.* (https://doi.org/10.1007/s40615-023-01692-5)

Belasen, A. R., Tracey, M. R., & Belasen, A. T. (2021). Demographics matter: The potentially disproportioned effect of COVID-19 on hospital ratings. *International Journal for Quality in Health Care*, 33(1), 1–7. DOI:10/1093/intqhc/mzab036

Buerhaus, P. (2008). Current and future state of the US nursing workforce. *Journal of the American Medical Association*, 300 (20), 2422–2424. DOI: 10.1001/jama.2008.729

Center for Medicare and Medicaid Services. (n.d.) *Hospital Consumer Assessment of Healthcare Provider Systems.* https://www.hcahpsonline.org

Clancy, T. R., & Warren, J. J. (2017). Informatics. In G. Sherwood & J. Barnsteiner (Eds.), *Quality and Safety in Nursing: A Competency Approach to Improving Outcomes* (2nd ed., pp. 173–195). Wiley Blackwell.

Cosgrove, B. (2013). W. Eugene Smith's Landmark Photo Essay, "Nurse Midwife". *Times Magazine.* https://time.com/26789/w-eugene-smith-life-magazine-1951-photo-essay-nurse-midwife/feed/

Friedman, T. L. (2016). *Thank You for Being Late: An Optimist's Guide to Thriving in the Age of Accelerations.* Picador. New York, NY.

Funk, C., & Lopez, M. H. (2022, June 14). *Hispanic Americans' Experience with Health Care. Chapter 2. Hispanic Americans' Trust in and Engagement with Science.* Pew Research Center. https://www.pewresearch.org/science/2022/06/14/hispanic-americans-experiences-with-health-care/

Green, E. (2023, Jan.18). 'I do not want to Die': Fighting Maternal Mortality Among Black Women. *The New York Times.* https://www.nytimes.com/2023/01/18/us/doula-black-women.html

Hoyert, D. L. (2020). *Maternal Mortality Rates in the United States, 2020.* Centers for Disease Control and Prevention National Center for Health Statistics. U.S. Departments of Health and human Services https://www.cdc.gov/nchs/data/hestat/maternal-mortality/2020/maternal-mortality-rates-2020.htm

Institute of Medicine. (2000). *To Err Is Human: Building a Safer Health System.* National Academies Press. Washington, D.C. DOI: 10.17226/9728

Institute of Medicine. (2001). *Crossing the Quality Chasm: A New Health System for the 21st Century.* National Academy Press. Washington, D.C.

Jones, N., Marks, R., Ramirez, R., & Rios-Vargas, M. (2021, August 21). *Improved Race and Ethnicity Measures Reveal U.S. Population is Much More Racial.* U.S. Census Bureau. U.S. Government. https://www.census.gov/library/stories/2021/08/improved-race-ethnicity-measures-reveal-united-states-population-much-more-multiracial.html

Kwame, A., & Petrucka, P. M. (2021, Sept. 3). A literature-based study of patient-centered care and communication in nurse-patient interactions: Barriers, facilitators, and the way forward. *BMC Nursing,* 20 (1). (https://doi.org/10.1186/s12912-021-00684-2)

Lopez, M.H., Passel, J.S., & Cohn, D. (2021, April 13). Key facts about changing U.S. unauthorized immigrant population. *Pew Research Center.* Washington, D.C. https://www.pewresearch.org/short-reads/2021/04/13/key-facts-about-the-changing-u-s-unauthorized-immigrant-population/

Mead, H., Banos, J., Trott, J., & Regenstein, M. (2023, January). *Experiences of Back and Latino Residents During the COVID-19 Response in Missouri. Milken Institute School of Public Health* (pp. 1–25). The George Washington University & The Missouri Health Foundation. Washington, D.C.

National Academies of Sciences, Engineering, and Medicine. (2021). *The Future of Nursing 2020–2030: Charting a Path to Achieve Health Equity.* The National Academies Press. Washington, D.C. (https://doi.org/10.17226/25982)

National Center for Health Workforce Analysis. (2022, November). *Nurse Workforce Projections 2020–2035.* Health Resources & Services Administration. Washington, D.C.

National Council of State Boards of Nursing. (2018). The 2017 National Nursing Workforce Survey. *Journal of Nursing Regulation,* 9(3), S4–S5.

National Council of State Boards of Nursing. (2020). *National Nursing Workforce Study.* National Council of State Boards of Nursing. Chicago, IL. https://www.ncsbn.org/research/recent-research/workforce.page

National Institutes of Health. (2023). *Maternal Morbidity & Mortality Web Portal.* NIH Office of Research on Women's Health. https://orwh.od.nih.gov/mmm-portal/what-mmm

Radley, D., Collins, S. R., & Baumgarter, J. C. (2020). *2020 Scorecard on State Health System Performance.* The Commonwealth Fund. https://www.commonwealthfund.org/publications/scorecard/2020/sep/2020-scorecard-state-health-system-performance

Smiley, R. A., Lauer, P., Bienemy, C., Berg, J. G., Shireman, E., Reneau, K. A., & Alexander, M. (2018). The 2017 national nursing workforce survey. *Journal of Nursing Regulation: Supplement,* 9(3), S1–S85.

The Beryl Institute. (2023). *Defining Patient and Human Experience.*https://theberylinstitute.org/defining-patient-experience/

United States Census Bureau. (2021, April 26). *Historical Population Change Data (1910-2020).* United States Government. https://www.census.gov/data/tables/time-series/dec/popchange-data-text.html

Villarruel, A.M., Canales, M., & Torres, S. (2001, Sept.), Bridges and Barriers: educational mobility of Hispanic nurses. *Journal of Nursing Education,* 40(6), 245–251. DOI: 10.3928/0148-4834-20010901-04

Yew, G. C. K. (2021). Trust in and ethical design of carebots: The case for ethics of care. *International Journal of Social Robotics,* 13(4), 629–645. DOI: 10.1007/s12369-020-00653-w

Zangaro, G. A., Streeter, R., & Tiandong, L. (2018). Trends in racial and ethnic demographics of the nursing workforce: 2000 to 2015. *Nurisng Outlook,* 66(4), 365–371. https://doi.org/10.1016/j.outlook.2018.05.001

Chapter 4

Board Leadership and Stakeholder Engagement

Introduction

The development and expansion of systems in the U.S. healthcare and life sciences industry has occurred on a relatively unrelenting basis in the past 30 years. In the period of 2010–2021 alone, there were 2,733 ownership change transactions in the healthcare industry (Singh, 2022), involving a staggering $2.4 trillion in assets (Mikulic, 2023). In recent years, the number of transactions has trended slightly downward, while the value per transaction has increased, suggesting that mergers and acquisitions (M&A) of hospital-based systems, as opposed to takeovers of individual hospitals, are occurring more frequently.

Indeed, the healthcare delivery system has undergone an inexorable transformation over the past three to four decades. The purpose of this chapter is to (1) identify the forces underlying that broad corporate consolidation; (2) examine how such consolidation shifted the priority focus of hospital systems' board of directors away from member hospital interests and to overall corporate interests; and (3) recommend a governance structure with a more balanced distribution of authority lines between parent and local boards to strengthen sensitivity to community health needs and member hospitals' organizational cultures.

The Expansion of Hospital Systems

Peering through a macro lens, and with the benefit of hindsight, we understand that the consolidation phenomenon came about as a result of a

 DOI: 10.4324/9781003431077-4

coalescence of economic, clinical, technological, and other drivers. Today, the vast majority of the approximately 6,100 hospitals in the United States are part of an affiliation. Some systems are more complex and vertically integrated, housing multiple hospitals as well as medical practices, outpatient facilities, and even medical equipment companies and insurance companies. Others are horizontally configured, meaning that the system comprises providers that perform similar functions and offer similar services, for example, a collection of a few hospitals under a common corporate umbrella.

But despite the complexity or simplicity of the corporate structure, there is one thing that all systems have in common, and that is a collective interest in scaling services across a continuum of care. This is not to suggest that the resources that the parties bring to the relationship are of equal value or that relationship formation occurs exclusively among peers. For example, takeovers typically occur when a stronger player exercises decision-making leverage over a target that has little choice in the matter.

Strategic interests guide decision-making with respect to affiliating. This is the case even when some hands are positioned in a clearly superior manner. For example, a relatively modest-sized community hospital may simply not be able to survive without the economic, referral, and staffing benefits offered by membership in a system. But even under such conditions, that hospital may have some leeway in selecting which system to join and under what terms.

Certainly, there are examples of hospitals joining a system and largely retaining their distinctiveness, identity, and institutional culture, not to mention their market base, operational protocols, and programmatic emphasis. But even when this occurs, there is some need to fit into the whole, to adapt to some degree. That is, individual identities may adapt to and embrace the "brand" of a broader organizational identity through assimilation, when members of the acquired health facility willingly adopt the cultural values of the acquiring, larger health system.

The goals of the individual provider entities are framed to some degree by corporate or system goals. An organization that had done things completely on its own, with executives and boards operating with relative autonomy, becomes accountable to the larger corporate entity which now encompasses it. The degree of oversight varies from hospital system to hospital system. Nevertheless, as extended in Chapter 5, decisions at the individual hospital level – the "local" level – are now made in a more complex, layered governance and strategic environment. Even if the hospital enjoys considerable latitude in doing so, such latitude is rarely, if ever, unconditional.

Thus, we may view an organization's post-affiliation strategic decision-making on a continuum with endpoints consisting of complete autonomy and complete assimilation. The autonomy endpoint would be reserved for those institutions in the larger system that maintained the decision-making structure and processes that existed prior to the affiliation. The complete assimilation endpoint would mark those situations in which the organization essentially cedes its executive function to the system or to the dominant entity in the system.

It is posited that those endpoints are essentially ideal, that while some executive functions may fall close to one endpoint or the other, it would be rare to see cases of pure autonomy retention or pure executive acquiescence. Retaining executive privileges is a function of key factors, including the nature of the affiliation agreement, the power and resource balance or imbalance between the affiliating organizations, and the size of the hospital system. Fundamentally, however, the location on the continuum at which its decision-making prerogatives lie has much to do with the board of directors and its role in formulating institutional strategy and in representing the communities served by the organization.

It is important to consider that until recently, the majority of mergers and acquisitions in healthcare had been approved by regulatory and other government agencies with authorization responsibility, like the *Federal Trade Commission*. The principal arguments employed by those proposing ownership consolidations have tended to be threefold: first, that coordination of care can occur more effectively when the provider entities exist under one corporate umbrella; second, that the economy of scale that would accrue from the affiliation would mean that costs can be more effectively managed (Noether & May, 2017); and third, that the resources of a larger provider network would translate into an enhanced ability to serve communities through greater investment capabilities.

Concerns About Pricing: A Turning Point?

Recently, some pushback on merger proposals has occurred. For example, in 2022, the Biden administration blocked four merger petitions, citing a concern that prices would likely rise in a diminished competitive environment (Meyer, 2022). By extension, they claimed, the potential for such an adverse impact on pricing merits more rigorous scrutiny than had been exercised in previous years. Moreover, while prices have risen as competition diminishes, improvements in quality have not been comparable (Abelson, 2018). The impact on access is equally noteworthy: larger health systems with increased bargaining power with insurers have been able to negotiate higher prices for medical services, often leading to reduced access for the most vulnerable populations and marginalized groups due to hospital closures or strained resources in consolidated markets as was also evident during the COVID-19 pandemic (Belasen et al., 2023).

The evidence related to pricing spikes has been mounting. The Medicare Payment Advisory Commission examined relevant studies and in a report to Congress stated that the "preponderance of evidence suggests that hospital consolidation leads to higher prices" (MedPAC, 2020). Among the considerable body of research referenced in the report is the determination that "Prices at monopoly hospitals are 12 percent higher than those in markets with four or more rivals" (Cooper et al., 2018).

Similar results were reported by Dafny et al. (2018) who found that mergers of two hospitals in the same state led to price increases of 7%–9%. The phenomenon is not limited to in-state acquisitions. As Lewis and Pflum (2017) found: "Prices at hospitals acquired by out-of-market systems increase by about 17% more than unacquired, stand-alone hospitals and confirm that out-of-market mergers result in a relaxation of competition, the prices of nearby competitors to acquired hospitals increase by around 8%."

Moreover, market-dominant hospitals may extend their competitive strength by employing mechanisms such as hospital referral regions (Kocher et al., 2021). This enables them to control pricing even beyond their "catchment" area, that is, outside of the primary population of a hospital, thereby tamping down competition beyond the communities directly served by those organizations. And by offering comprehensive services through the network of providers, third-party payers are at a disadvantage with respect to pricing negotiations.

In short, there is simply no one else with whom they can negotiate, well, at least in terms of another system that offers a full range of healthcare services. Absent competition, third-party payers have little leverage but to negotiate less favorable terms with the dominant system in a given market.

Despite the recent pushback, the tide is unlikely to turn with respect to hospital system expansion – after all, this model of hospital systems replacing the individual hospital as an independent entity has become an ingrained feature in the U.S. healthcare landscape. And the economic clout of those hospital systems, especially the larger ones, has provided them with much influence in policy development.

At the same time, the trend of accelerated pricing increases is unlikely to be sustainable. When healthcare inflation regularly and considerably exceeds the consumer price index (CPI), corrective forces tend to be triggered. Thus, in the 1980s, when healthcare inflation rates were two and three times the CPI, Medicare stepped in with the diagnostic related grouping prospective payment plan (Böcking & Trojanus, 2008) and managed care took root to gain some control over needless tests and procedures.

How did hospitals respond to a narrower flow of reimbursement? In seeking to achieve economies of scale, hospitals started to merge, ushering in what would become a sweeping and largely unabated trend of hospital system formation. The irony is that the very action intended to manage cost control efforts by the federal government and third-party payers has, today, intensified the very problem it was intended to correct.

At some point, however, much like what occurred in the 1980s, it is expected that price increases will again get the attention of policy makers and third-party payers. What may also get their attention is the fact that quality has remained stagnant, undermining a key element of the rationale in merger proposals. If corporate boards act preemptively, that is, if they anticipate that some action may be taken – and if they view the recent elevated level of scrutiny over merger petitions as an omen – they may be prompted to revisit how they develop and manage their priorities. If so, this will be welcome news, not only because those are vital considerations for the economic character of the healthcare industry but also for the health and well-being of those receiving care. But beyond that, a review of priorities may be essential for another matter, and that is how effectively boards understand and represent the interests, economics, and socio-cultural characteristics of the communities served by their organizations. This would have far-reaching implications for access, community health, and population health.

Centralization of Board Authority

Traditionally, hospital boards, much like nonprofit boards more generally, have had at least two broad spheres of responsibility: fiduciary and community representation. These two areas are highly interrelated. Directors of nonprofit organizations such as 501(c)3 corporations are statutorily obligated to act in ways that protect and advance the interests of their organizations. In so doing they must abide by three fiduciary duties: loyalty, care, and obedience.

The duty of *loyalty* means that all actions must be taken in the interest of the organization's stakeholders, not for oneself. The duty of *care* specifies that they must exercise reasonableness, diligence, prudence, and soundness of judgment in carrying out responsibilities in the interest of shareholders. The duty of care pertains to the actions taken and decisions made, not the results. The fiduciary duty of *obedience* means that board members are required to comply with laws and policies relevant to the organization as well as abide by the organization's rules of governance, for example, its bylaws (Center for Healthcare Governance, n.d.).

Taken as a whole, the fiduciary duties cover much ground. The shareholders in a publicly traded hospital system surely constitute a stakeholder group, with an understandable focus on overall corporate performance. Thus, the core question is what is the relative priority of those shareholders in relation to the residents of communities served by the individual providers in a hospital system?

CLEVELAND CLINIC STATEMENT ON FIDUCIARY DUTY OF LOYALTY

Directors and trustees are subject to a comprehensive conflict of interest policy that requires disclosure of interests that may pose a conflict. Each transaction or interest is reviewed by the Law Department and the Conflict of Interest and Managing Innovations Committee for potential conflict of interest issues. The Director or Trustee does not participate in the negotiation or approval of such transactions or review of such interests. Directors and trustees are also subject to the Cleveland Clinic Code of Conduct (Cleveland Clinic, n.d.).

Has the healthcare system in the United States evolved in such a manner that one set of stakeholders is more likely to be prioritized over the other? Or has it arrived at a place in which the priorities are well-balanced, and even if there is some give-and-take, is there room in the system for the interests of multiple stakeholder groups to be addressed adequately and with reasonable equity?

The answer is not simple. Indeed, the increasing concentration of hospital systems has had many benefits for communities and their residents, including the capacity to offer continuity of care across a vertical array of facilities. This makes it easier and more convenient to enter the hospital system at any entry point and to cycle through its ambulatory and acute entities with relative one-stop shopping ease. Such potential seamlessness would undoubtedly be more challenging to achieve in an environment in which such infrastructure linkages were not present. In their compilation of interviews of hospital CEOs, Noether and May (2017), emphasize the crucial nature of expanding scale to keep up with industry trends, explaining that such growth justifies the building of IT infrastructure and other data management systems while allowing for the distribution of risk.

The phrase "bear risk" is worth examining and very important. Risk and investment are two sides of the same coin. To achieve the complex infrastructure for capital improvement and expansion, considerable investment is required. As an example, HCA Healthcare, which is among the largest hospital systems in the United States, reports capital expenditures of $34 billion in the period of 2010–2022, highlighting its ability to deliver shareholder value, which for the same period includes $3.2 billion in special dividends, $2.5 billion in quarterly dividends, and $29.2 billion in share repurposes (HCA Healthcare, 2023).

Attracting capital is infeasible in a return-on-investment (ROI) vacuum. Most typically, it would be within the purview of the corporate board to establish system-wide goals, including those relating to capital improvement. HCA Healthcare doesn't shy away from proclaiming its business orientation, referencing its impact boldly on its website: "HCA Healthcare's founders envisioned a company that would deliver healthcare differently: one that would revolutionize the healthcare landscape by applying business principles of scale to hospitals, without ever losing sight of the patient's needs. Today, more than 50 years later, that original vision thrives… Our scale enables us to deliver everything from first-class cutting-edge clinical research to individualized patient health solutions" (HCA Healthcare, n.d.).

Scaling Up Could Result in Missing What's on the Ground

In scaling up with an eye toward maximizing the gains in a market domination scenario, the community in which the individual member hospital resides can fall through the cracks. This does not mean inevitable or outright neglect. Nor does it mean that the individual patient will not be afforded a high level of quality care. It also does not mean that corporations will fail to be forthcoming with respect to capital upgrades, marketing support, training for employees, and facility upkeep for the individual hospitals in that corporation.

But if the local hospital board is in a largely subservient position relative to the corporate board, and if the corporate board is disproportionately focused on market share and ROI, then the local board may be less able to give full attention to community health needs. It is that plain and simple. And while all communities have health needs, some communities' needs are more pronounced.

Taking this notion of potential competing priorities between the corporate level and the community level, we may envision that the relationship between these two governing bodies to be central in finding a balanced approach to ensure that all priorities are addressed.

In examining the community priorities, we may start with the notion that community needs vary considerably. But one thing is certain: the general health of residents in Black, Brown, and poor communities is not the same as it is for residents living in white and middle-class communities (Belasen et al., 2021, 2023).

- Among adults with any mental illness, Black (39%), Hispanic (36%), and Asian (25%) adults were less likely than white (52%) adults to receive mental health services (as of 2021).
- At birth, AIAN and Black people had a shorter life expectancy (65.2 and 70.8 years, respectively) compared to white people (76.4) as of 2021.
- Black infants were more than two times as likely to die as white infants (10.4 vs. 4.4 per 1,000). Black and AIAN women also had the highest rates of pregnancy-related mortality.
- Black (13%) and Hispanic (11%) children were over twice as likely to be food insecure than white children (4%) as of 2021 (Hill et al., 2023).

As noted above, research has demonstrated that quality has not been shown to improve as healthcare systems enlarge. Whether access has improved is made complicated by the notion that in communities in which health literacy is weak, engagement with the system occurs at low levels even if health services are free or if highly subsidized care is available. The Centers for Disease Control and Prevention (n.d.) cites studies which underscore the inverse relationship between health literacy and seeking care, or "activation."

A study by Nijman et al. (2014), which is referenced in the CDC report, demonstrates the point by noting that comprehension of forms asking about medical condition is a factor in whether the person will actually pursue engagement with a provider; the greater the confidence in ability to understand what information is requested, the greater the likelihood that the individual will seek care. The trends related to pricing and quality, in conjunction with our growing understanding of health disparities may prove difficult to ignore in an emerging environment in which public reporting requirements are increasing and in which policy shifts favoring outcomes rather than a number of tests and procedures are increasingly at the center of reimbursement models.

As this takes root, we would expect that healthcare organizations will seek to prepare themselves for the challenges these policy shifts will present. Progressive hospital systems also provide ancillary services and will not simply seek to adapt. Rather, they would anticipate the trends, identify them in their early stages, and proactively plan for them. They could even seek to influence what may prove to be a rapidly evolving set of policy considerations.

A progressive tack is unlikely to occur absent a reconfigured approach to the hospital boards. As hospital systems enlarge, managing competition is inevitably and quite understandably a priority of considerable magnitude. The risk in the present board environment is that community needs may get dwarfed. Under the present model of progressively dominant corporate boards, pricing may not get under control without regulatory or legal guardrails in place. But even more, quality, as discussed in Chapter 7, and community health needs may fail to have a proper voice in strategic direction.

Thus, in this chapter we propose that in the coming years, a more balanced governance configuration should be considered, one which allows for hospital system-wide priorities to be developed and pursued but also allows for the interests of communities represented by the member hospitals to have a real voice in strategy development. Predictably, care quality will be enhanced. This is because the more that health literacy levels are elevated, the more that community health needs are understood, the greater the ability of providers to meet those needs. If this occurs, it follows that quality would have a better chance of being positively affected.

A Balanced Configuration Between Corporate and Local Boards

Achieving a well-balanced configuration requires diligence, effective board leadership, and a sound understanding of trends affecting the healthcare industry. For boards to make progress toward the goal of a balanced configuration, the following six recommendations are offered:

> First, hospital systems are encouraged to develop a Population Health Advisory Board that would organize its purview in relation to a three-part framework: (1) define a population's health characteristics and conditions, including the environmental factors that contribute to those conditions; (2) align those health conditions as well as the risk factors with members of the provider community most suitable to the management of those health conditions and most capable of mitigating risk; and (3) monitor, track, and assess utilization, quality, and costs associated with such efforts.
>
> (Murphy et al., 2011)

Ideally, the advisory board would be co-chaired by an epidemiologist and medical sociologist with membership comprised of (1) experts in the field of community medicine, primary care, and health disparities, (2) board members from selected local hospitals in the system, and (3) selected community representatives from member hospitals.

As an advisory board, the entity would not have formal authority to implement policy but would have responsibility for at least the following:

■ Provide educational activities for the corporate board, local boards, senior management, clinical directors, and relevant others on population health, trends of relevance to the system and individual member hospitals, and public health initiatives that have bearing on epidemiological phenomena
■ Advise the corporate board on how public health concepts intertwine with system-wide strategic initiatives
■ Assess the system's strengths and weaknesses relative to population health and offer recommendations for improving its population health capability

Second, hospital system boards are encouraged to allocate 20% of their board seats to board members from their individual hospitals. Typically, the larger the hospital system, the greater the need for board members to bring high levels of expertise in such areas as finance, economics, legal affairs, clinical, marketing, and regulatory matters. The more that board membership is dominated by those with a macro-orientation in those areas, the greater the potential for local matters to be overlooked. This would be especially relevant when a disadvantaged socio-economic profile of a member hospital's service area adversely affects the residents' health prospects.

Allotting just one or two seats to members of the local hospital boards would not guarantee a sufficient voice. To achieve a productive and healthy local presence, it would be reasonable to have at least one-fifth of the corporate board membership held by board members of local hospitals. Such an 80:20 ratio would not prevent the board from providing concerted attention to broad, system-wide issues. But it would also allow for a community perspective to be included in agenda setting, deliberations on policy initiatives, and strategic planning.

It should be noted that board composition in general is not without controversy. For example, it has not been uncommon for nurse participation to lag physician participation (Sundean et al., 2017). And while it is important to ensure adequate representation from these and other key constituencies, it should not come at the expense of community representation. Thus, it may be prudent to select a member hospital representative with a nursing background. A nursing executive would be a fine choice, but perhaps even more pertinent would be a nurse with a community health background. Such a selection could satisfy multiple areas of need.

It would be most beneficial for those board seats to rotate every 18 months to 2 years. One-year rotations would not allow time for individual board members to become sufficiently oriented and make an impact. Three-year assignments may prohibit an adequate number of hospitals in the system from participating. The length of the assignment would be at least partially dependent on the size of the hospital system. As the hospital system expands, a somewhat shorter rotation period may prove necessary to ensure a broad range of representations from local hospitals.

Third, presentations from the management teams of local hospitals should be made on a regular basis at corporate board meetings. In fact, to cultivate awareness of the importance of getting to know each individual hospital, such presentations should occur at every scheduled board meeting. While it would be understandable that financial and reimbursement data, service offerings, capital and strategic initiatives, and prospects for the future would constitute regular agenda topics, a portion of every presentation should focus on the community or communities served by the hospital. This would help board members get to know the culture, demographics, and health needs of the community, to view and understand the residents as people, not just numbers in some aggregation. Presenters would be encouraged to highlight a few patients, those whose stories express something meaningful about the community.

It is recommended that the presentations not be delivered exclusively by the member hospital chief executive. Others ought to participate in the presentation, with the goal of bringing to life what working at the hospital involves and feels like, as well as the patient's perspective of the experience in that hospital. The HR executive, for example, could provide insights into the organizational culture, that is, identify what makes staff proud to work there and what might be undertaken to continuously improve the employee experience at the facility. The nursing executive could describe for the board the clinical programs and how those benefit the community. And of course, a community education specialist could offer insights into the activities pursued by the hospital to remove barriers to care and promote health literacy.

Fourth, at least one board meeting per year should be held on the site of one of the member hospitals. This would reinforce the notion that the corporation is a compilation of its members, not merely one large entity. Consider that even communities that are quite close geographically may be separated by virtual light-years when it comes to the health of their residents (Belasen et al., 2023). Evidence reveals the extent to which life expectancy in cities varies by neighborhood: "Chicago had the largest gap in life expectancy across neighborhoods at 30.1 years. Washington, DC had a life expectancy gap of 27.5 years, followed by New York City at 27.4 years, and New Orleans and Buffalo, both with gaps of 25.8 years" (NYU Langone Health, 2019).

By way of explanation, each of the cities had considerably higher racial and ethnic segregation scores, more than double the average for a 500-city compilation. The experience of New York City is revealing. Residents of East Harlem, a largely Black and relatively poor community, have a lifespan average of 71.2 years, while those living just a few blocks away, on the Upper East Side, a predominantly white upper middle-class community, have a lifespan average of 89.9 years (NYU Langone Health, 2019).

The most glaring of such gaps was found in the Chicago suburbs of Streeterville and Englewood, just 9 miles from one another. The average life expectancy in Streeterville, a relatively affluent white suburb, is 90. Englewood, a poor African American community, has a life expectancy of 60 – a gap of 30 years (Eisenberg, 2021). There is quite a difference seeing such data buried in a report to the board and seeing firsthand the actual environment in which care occurs, to walk through the community where the residents live, and to have a sensory experience of what social disparities look like. Such direct and upfront experience is important to energize board members.

Like in managing by walking around (MBWA), executives who learn about their organizations not just by reading reports but through direct communication with employees and other stakeholders, the same would hold for board members. In healthcare this would be especially important since, as discussed in Chapter 5, most hospital boards still tend to recruit members with business experience. In fact, less than 15% of board members overseeing U.S. top hospitals have a professional background in healthcare (Emerson, 2023).

Fifth, in keeping with the fiduciary responsibility of obedience, board members at both the corporate and local levels are obliged to become familiar with policy and trends that relate to population health. Three aspects of population health are notable in this regard. First, over the past hundred years, and even in the face of political headwinds, health policy has evolved, progressing (albeit with glacier-like pacing) toward the goal of whole population coverage. Starting with the Social Security Act in 1935, and continuing with Medicare and Medicaid in 1965, and up through the Affordable Care Act of 2010, many groups, including workers, the elderly, and those who are poor, have become entitled to receive coverage.

Notwithstanding, access remains unevenly distributed. For many groups, even those eligible for care, health services can seem out of reach. Low health literacy rates may stifle an ability or willingness to engage with the provider community. Lack of trust in the system may also contribute to a decision to avoid seeking care; for example, Funk (2022) found that with respect to Black people, "a majority (56%) say they've had at least one of several negative experiences, including having to speak up to get the proper care and being treated with less respect than other patients." Other barriers, including transportation difficulties, taking time off from work, and higher copays for prescription drugs are all more prevalent in marginalized communities. Accordingly, the great challenge for the healthcare system is to remove those barriers and aspire to align access with eligibility, all the while broadening the latter.

The second aspect relates to moving healthcare resources more directly into the communities in which the target populations reside. In the traditional model of healthcare, providers waited until patients walked through their doors to get care. In the emerging model, shifting resources outside the hospital's walls is an important means of facilitating access.

Community health focuses largely on primary care and education with an emphasis on wellness, injury and illness prevention, nutrition, weight management, pregnancy, and mental/behavioral health. Nontraditional venues include schools, the workplace, houses of worship, libraries, pharmacies, community, and recreation centers, as well as outpatient clinics and medical offices.

In a throwback to what had been the earliest and most traditional of settings, community health can even mean providing health services directly in homes. The Montefiore Health System in the Bronx provides an excellent example. Residents in the largely Black and poor communities in the system's main hospital's vicinity experienced higher rates of life-threatening diabetes, cardiac issues, and co-morbidities at considerably younger ages than residents of white, middle-class suburban communities just 10 miles away. The community health plan established by Montefiore was organized on the premise that bringing assessment resources directly into residents' homes was essential given the limited health literacy in the community and the lack of confidence that residents had with health system engagement.

As such, they began by knocking on doors and using venues such as local houses of worship, barbershops and salons, and civic centers at which they would arrange for appointments to develop health profiles. In so doing, community health teams would examine such issues as food insecurities, transportation needs, economic stability, health histories, substance abuse, and social connections. The community health team was also focused on building trust with residents so that necessary medical interventions would seem less daunting. In a five-year period, the incidence of death from manageable diseases experienced an appreciable decline (Eisenberg, 2021).

The third aspect related to population health involves the shift from reimbursement based on the number of tests and procedures (fee for service) to the quality of the outcome, what the industry refers to as value-based pricing (VBP). Since VBP places emphasis on the effectiveness of the medical intervention, the healthcare industry has been examining more fully the quality of the work of those who contribute to the caregiving process. This involves not only the physician and hospital staff but also the rehabilitation facility that cared for the patient, the home health service program, and all others who collectively comprise the care chain.

While VBP is not new, it is expected to develop quite rapidly. Much like hospitals adapted to the constrained revenue flow from the shift to prospective payment decades ago, they will surely adapt to VBP. Two trends will undoubtedly occur with respect to VBP. One is that the metrics employed to determine value will become increasingly sophisticated. Thus, today, if a hospital experiences a significant volume of what are deemed to be preventable readmissions, it may experience a financial penalty from Medicare.

As such, today's metrics are based principally on aggregate data. But as the tools for measuring value become more advanced, and as the body of data against which an individual outcome can be compared becomes more robust, VBP will undoubtedly expand. The second trend is that public reporting is on the rise. Hospital outcome data will be published and available in a way that will allow consumers to make choices based on providers' result profiles. Such data will factor into marketing efforts and presumably become more foundational to a hospital's reputation.

Hospitals that are on the leading edge of these trends will have an advantage in an increasingly VBP environment. And boards will have the special obligation to lead. As Lynn (2014) states, "To accomplish this goal, hospital and health plan boards must reshape governance structures, acquire new competencies, and forge new alliances outside the hospital walls. Improving population health requires much more than a vague mission statement. The task demands dynamic, informed board leadership."

Moreover, the synergy between the corporate board, which can establish system-wide goals relative to VBP, and local boards, which are closer to the networks of care that serve communities, should prove vital in ensuring that quality of care is first and foremost a priority in community health initiatives. The partnership between the corporate board and the local board will be more critical than ever as VBP and community health occupy an increasing presence in national healthcare priorities.

Sixth, transparency in reporting of clinical data is fundamental to institutional credibility and community representation (Belasen & Eisenberg, 2023). Transparency constitutes a vital control for motives that may otherwise compete with the best interests of the organization from penetrating the decision-making apparatus. Without transparency, political, economic, and/or other interests have a greater opportunity to influence policy development and institutional strategy. If an insular decision-making culture takes root at the system-wide board level, opportunities for effective engagement with local boards will be constrained.

A closed decision-making system, by definition, lacks mechanisms for transparency and, in some situations, may lead to conformity or groupthink, in which group members insulate themselves from messages which challenge their beliefs in their unassailable correctness (Janis, 1972). Boards can understandably get lulled into groupthink tendencies. Consider that board members are often selected because they have amassed considerable accomplishments, have proven track records in leadership and problem-solving, and understand strategy and organizational planning. These are important traits for those serving aboard. The problem occurs when a cultural climate emerges in which these traits offer unchecked justification for blurring the boundaries between management and the board or for a board to operate in an insular fashion. Potential consequences flow, including the failure to analyze alternative options, the failure to adequately assess risk, avoidance of contingency plan development, and inattentiveness to the decision's impact on the full range of stakeholders.

Genuine transparency can occur only in the context of an open system. Transparency means that decision-making occurs openly and that communication regarding decision-making and the various processes that lead to decisions takes place between the board and the various stakeholder and constituency groups that the board is entrusted to represent. Again, transparency is the single most critical mechanism to control for board encroachment on management prerogatives as well as for motives that compete with the best interests of the organizations and those it serves to be prevent from influencing decision-making.

Achieving transparency requires deft board leadership skills. Leaders who promote transparency typically avoid communicating their positions until others have had an opportunity to do so; arrange for experts to provide advice and council on matters prior to board deliberation; ensure that space in deliberations is provided to devil's advocacy; promote discussion of solutions not only to problems but also to the definition of the problem itself; consult with stakeholders on their definition of the problem, potential solutions, and how different solution scenarios would affect them; and respect the primacy of the relationship with management by ensuring proper and ongoing consultation (Belasen & Eisenberg, 2023).

The greater the transparency, the greater that a board's commitment to the full range of its fiduciary responsibilities will be honored in a balanced manner. Transparency is an essential precondition for accountability which, in turn, fosters a more ethically responsible decision-making climate. And most pertinently to this discussion, it fosters more productive, meaningful, and constructive channels between the corporate board and its local affiliates.

Communication Is Key

Over the extended 40-year period in which the health services industry transformed from one of thousands of independent entities into vertically and horizontally aligned corporate structures, the voice of the individual entity can be obscured. This is not unique to healthcare. It is a naturally occurring phenomenon in any market-driven industry, and healthcare certainly has a sufficiently market-driven orientation to render it susceptible to large interests dwarfing smaller ones. That is why it is not surprising that quality has, at best, remained stagnant, while merger and acquisition activity gained steam. After all, in such a growth scenario, senior management must exercise a certain entrepreneurship, embracing a transformational decision-making culture, while middle management has the transactional duties of ensuring task completion, day-to-day regulatory compliance, and operational continuity. In this era, senior management orients toward change; middle management orients toward stability.

Ultimately, it is the board that sets the tone for how the organization defines priorities related to growth, stability, and quality. Can the organization effectively integrate those potentially discrepant drives? If they fail to do so, tensions invariably arise and the organization will be less capable of adjusting to industry trends, at least on a sustained basis. Certainly, boards have the major responsibility of selecting a chief executive, an obligation central to how those drives are managed. However, that is not where a board's responsibility for setting the tone for organizational culture ends. Fundamentally, a major responsibility is communication. We use this term throughout our lives with the idea that it is about creating meaning. Although the term communication is bandied about in everyday conversation, so much so that it can be seen as trite, in the context of restoring the role and influence of a local hospital board, it can be remarkably profound.

Faithfulness to fiduciary obligation does not require boards to disregard a potential chief executive's entrepreneurial capabilities. After all, seeking to retain and even strengthen a competitive position in the marketplace is a vital consideration for the organization. It is part of the fiduciary network of commitments. But if that competitive strength becomes too dominant a drive, as it appears to be in many corners of the industry considering the evidence that quality has not improved, other priorities may be getting short shrift.

If the corporate board enables the communication mechanisms necessary to achieve balance between its prerogatives and those of the member hospital boards, it is likely that they will, together, discover ways of improving quality while enhancing sensitivity to community health needs. These, of course, go together. The more that community needs are identified, the greater that the barriers to obtaining care can be recognized, enabling efforts to be undertaken to dismantle or neutralize them. As that occurs, community residents will be more apt to connect with their local providers. As they do, and to the extent that the hospital can facilitate means for the community members to engage responsibly and effectively, the greater likelihood of a quality healthcare experience.

The probability of this occurring is increased if central boards focus less exclusively on growth, profit, and short-term gains. By no means ignore them – that would be irresponsible, not to mention a violation of fiduciary obligation. But it does mean that their focus should broaden, that they continuously strive to understand the needs of communities in their hospital systems and encourage member hospitals to pursue programs that serve those needs. Communication engagement between both levels of boards is essential to make this work. And by instituting the mechanisms of advisory boards focused on population health, corporate board seat allocation to local board members, regular local board presentations at corporate board meetings, holding meetings at member provider facilities, ensuring awareness of policies relevant to community health, and promoting decision-making transparency, the board will have gone the distance toward building a communication environment worthy of their missions.

References

Abelson, R. (2018). When hospitals merge to save money, patients often pay more. *The New York Times*. https://www.nytimes.com/2018/11/14/health/hospitalmergers-health-care-spending.html

Belasen, A. R., Belasen, A. T., & Bass, M. (2023). Tracking the uneven outcomes of COVID-19 on racial and ethnic groups: Implications for health policy. *Journal of Racial and Ethnic Health Disparities*. https://doi:10.1007/s40615-023-01692-5. Advance online publication. https://doi.org/10.1007/s40615-023-01692-5

Belasen, A., & Eisenberg, B. (2023). Building trust for better crisis communication: Lessons for leadership development. In Pfeffermann, N. & Schaller, M. (Eds.), *New Leadership Communication - Inspire Your Horizon*, Springer 2023.

Belasen, A. R., Tracey, M., & Belasen, A. T. (2021). Demographics matter: The potentially disproportionate effect of COVID-19 on hospital ratings, *International Journal for Quality in Health Care*. *International Journal for Quality in Health Care* (https://doi.org/10.1093/intqhc/mzab036).

Böcking, W., & Trojanus, D. (2008). Diagnosis related groups (DRGs). In: Kirch, W. (eds) *Encyclopedia of Public Health*. Springer, Dordrecht. (https://doi.org/10.1007/978-1-4020-5614-7_79)

Center for Healthcare Governance. (n.d.). Best practice guideline: board legal fiduciary duties. *American Hospital Association*. https://trustees.aha.org/sites/default/files/trustees/board-legal-fiduciary-duties.pdf

Centers for Disease Control and Prevention. (n.d.). *Patient engagement*. https://www.cdc.gov/healthliteracy/researchevaluate/patient-engage.html#comprehension-use

Cleveland Clinic. (n.d.). Financial information and annual reports. *Cleveland Clinic*. https://my.clevelandclinic.org/about/overview/financial-information

Cooper, Z., Craig, S., Gaynor, M., & Van Reenen, J. (2018). The price ain't right? hospital prices and health spending on the privately insured. *National Bureau of Economic Research*. https://www.nber.org/system/files/working_papers/w21815/w21815.pdf

Dafny, L., Ho, K., & Lee, R. (2018). The price effects of cross-market hospital mergers. *National Bureau of Economic Research*. https://www.nber.org/system/files/working_papers/w22106/w22106.pdf

Eisenberg, B. (2021). The pandemic and the health care system: where do we go from here? *All About Mentoring*. SUNY Empire State University, 55, Autumn. 4-10. https://www.sunyempire.edu/media/ocgr/publications-presentations/all-about-mentoring/AAM-55_FullIssue_AccessibleVersionKLaB.pdf

Emerson, J. (2023). Most board members at the nation's top hospitals have no healthcare background: Study. *Beckers Hospital Review*. https://www.beckershospitalreview.com/hospital-management-administration/most-board-members-at-the-nations-top-hospitals-have-no-healthcare-background-study.html

Funk, C. (2022). *Black Americans' Views About Health Disparities, Experiences With Health Care*. Pew Research Center. https://www.pewresearch.org/science/2022/04/07/black-americans-views-about-health-disparities-experiences-with-health-care/

HCA Healthcare, Investor Update Q4 2022. (2023). https://s23.q4cdn.com/949900249/files/doc_presentations/2023/Mar/07/final-q4-investor-update-2022.pdf

HCA Healthcare, Investor Relations. (n.d.) https://investor.hcahealthcare.com/overview/.

Hill, L., Ndugga, N., & Artiga, S. (2023). Key data on health and health care by race and ethnicity. *KFF*. https://www.kff.org/racial-equity-and-health-policy/report/key-data-on-health-and-health-care-by-race-and-ethnicity/

Janis, I. (1972). *Victims of Groupthink: A Psychological Study of Foreign-Policy Decisions and Fiascoes*. Houghton Mifflin., Boston, MA.

Kocher, R., Shah, S., & Navathe, A. (2021). Overcoming the market dominance of hospitals. *Journal of the American Medical Association*, 325(10), 929–930.

Lewis, M., & Pflum, K. (2017). Hospital systems and bargaining power: Evidence from out-of-market acquisitions. *The RAND Journal of Economics*, 3(48), 579–610. (https://onlinelibrary.wiley.com/doi/10.1111/1756-2171.12186)

Lynn, G. (2014). *Empowering Board Members to Improve Population Health Through Value-Based Care*. Center for Healthcare Governance. https://trustees.aha.org/sites/default/files/trustees/14-empowering-board-members.pdf

MedPAC (2020). March 2020 report to the Congress: Medicare payment policy. *Medicare Payment Advisory Commission.* https://www.medpac.gov/wp-content/uploads/import_data/scrape_files/docs/default-source/reports/mar20_entirereport_sec.pdf

Meyer, H. (2022). Biden's FTC has blocked 4 hospital mergers and is poised to thwart more consolidation attempts. *KFF Health News.* https://kffhealthnews.org/news/article/biden-ftc-block-hospital-mergers-antitrust/

Mikulic, M. (2023). Transaction value of mergers and acquisitions in the U.S. healthcare and life sciences industry from 2009 to 2021. *Statistica.* https://www.statista.com/statistics/331801/total-value-of-merger-and-acquisitions-in-us-healthcare-and-life-sciences/

Murphy, S. M., Castro, H. K., & Sylvia, M. (2011). Predictive modeling in practice: Improving the participant identification process for care management programs using condition-specific cut points. *Population Health Management,* 14(4), 205–210.

Nijman, J., Hendriks, M., Brabers, de Jong, J., & Rademakers, J. (2014). Patient activation and health literacy as predictors of health information use in a general sample of Dutch health care consumers. *Health Communication,* 19(8), 955–969.

Noether, M., & May, S. (2017). Hospital merger benefits: views from hospital leaders and econometric analysis. *Charles River Associates in connection with American Hospital Association.* https://www.aha.org/system/files/2018-04/Hospital-Merger-Full-Report-FINAL-1.pdf

NYU Langone Health. (2019). Large life expectancy gaps in US cities linked to racial & ethnic segregation by neighborhood. *NYU Langone Health NewsHub.* https://nyulangone.org/news/large-life-expectancy-gaps-us-cities-linked-racial-ethnic-segregation-neighborhood

Singh, A. (2022). 2021 M&A in review: a new phase in healthcare partnerships. *KaufmanHall Featured Insights.* https://www.kaufmanhall.com/insights/research-report/2021-ma-review-new-phase-healthcare-partnerships

Sundean, L., Polifroni, E., Libal, K., & McGrath, J. (2017). Nurses on health care governing boards: An integrative review. *Nursing Outlook.* 65(4), 361–371. https://www.sciencedirect.com/science/article/abs/pii/S0029655417300453

Chapter 5

Communicating Quality – Hospital Leadership and Performance Outcomes

Introduction: Quality of Care Matters

Provider-patient communication is not only important for its impact on patient outcomes but also because of its role in influencing patient ratings and willingness to recommend the hospital. When patient satisfaction is high, it triggers multiple benefits. These benefits may include an increase in compliance with treatment and care directives and an enhanced tendency to follow up on instructions from physicians. Other benefits include a decrease in the inclination to initiate medical malpractice lawsuits against healthcare providers. Patients reporting that their physicians listened to them carefully are also 32% less likely to be readmitted.

Positive communication, in which providers are attentive to patients' needs and engage them in consultation, is associated with a 50% reduction in diagnostic tests and referrals, shorter length of stay, fewer complications, better recovery and improved emotional health long after discharge, and lower mortality rates. Understanding the context of patient safety and social environment through effective partnership and patient engagement is empowering and correlates with positive hospital outcomes. Thus, a critical factor in the effectiveness of healthcare delivery is sustaining patient centeredness through meaningful provider-patient communication. The benefits of treating patients respectfully are likely to be substantial. Respect

DOI: 10.4324/9781003431077-5

engenders trust, and having a trusting relationship makes it far more likely that physicians, PAs, NPs, and patients can work together as partners.

An important measure of provider-patient communication and patient satisfaction is the Hospital Consumer Assessment of Healthcare Providers and Systems (HCAHPS). Under the Hospital Value-Based Purchasing (VBP) Program, Medicare makes incentive payments to hospitals based on how well they perform on each measure of the HCAHPS survey and/ or how much they improve their performance on each measure compared to their performance during a baseline period. The goal of HCAHPS is to promote consumer choice, public accountability, and greater transparency in healthcare. Daily more than 30,000 patients receive HCAHPS surveys about their recent hospital experience, and more than 8,400 patients complete it. In July 2016, the U.S. Centers for Medicare and Medicaid Services (CMS) began displaying HCAHPS Star Ratings on the Hospital Compare website as part of the initiative to add 5-star quality ratings of hospitals.

The basic sampling procedure for HCAHPS involves drawing a monthly random sample of eligible discharges, except for smaller hospitals that survey all HCAHPS-eligible discharges. Responses about patient experiences at a given hospital are collected throughout each month of the 12-month reporting period and are aggregated quarterly for each hospital. The survey response rate and the number of completed surveys are reported on the *Hospital Compare* website. CMS linearly transforms responses to numerical values and adjusts for differences in patient mix and survey mode across the last four quarters to produce a score between 0 and 100 for ten domains of patient experience, which are publicly reported for each participating hospital. The domains are communication with nurses and doctors, hospital staff responsiveness, communication about medicine, cleanliness and quietness of hospital environment, discharge information, care transition, hospital rating, and recommendation of hospital.

CMS objectively evaluates six outcomes of care: mortality, patient safety, readmission rates, effectiveness of care, timeliness of care, and efficient use of medical imaging. Together with the HCAHPS patient experience measures, CMS provides an overall summary of healthcare quality via the star ratings. These ratings drive systematic improvements in care and safety as hospitals strive to sustain high ratings and further differentiate their services based on patient satisfaction. Consumers and patient advocates point to *Hospital Compare* and its star ratings as important resources to help patients make informed choices. Studies have shown that hospitals in the top HCAHPS quartile with better patient experience also had better records in safety, technical quality, length of stay, and readmission rates. Hospitals try hard to sustain high ratings to leverage competition to lower costs and improve care quality. CMS can revoke the license of a plan rated below 3 stars for three years in a row and notify its members that they are in a low-performing plan.

CEO RELEASES PLAN FOR STAR RATING TURNAROUND

Medicare Advantage Star Ratings declined this year, as predicted prior to their release on October 6, but Centene said this week that the results were slightly worse than expected.

Only four plans received a low 2-star rating, compared to none last year in the 1–5 star rankings. All were Wellcare plans by Centene Corp., according to the star ratings list released by the Centers for Medicare and Medicaid Services.

"While the final results were slightly worse than our internal expectations, the vast majority of the revenue headwind was known to us months in advance, as we share transparently with the investor community," Centene CEO Sarah London said on October 25, during the company's third-quarter earnings call.

London outlined "aggressive action" underway to turn around results, including hiring an experienced chief quality officer, assigning strong operational leaders to manage key operations and administration programs, investing in new technology to enhance access to clinical data around gaps in care, and integrating the company's platforms into a single workflow.

In addition, a newly installed management team this year added quality improvement as a key compensation metric for every Centene employee. The goal is to achieve 60% of members in 4-star plans, London said. The decrease in ratings impacts the 2024 revenue year, London explained during the call.

The bottom line is that star ratings are important to plan, not only as a way to attract new members when the results are good but also as revenue. Plans that do well get a 5% quality bonus payment. The money is used by insurers to increase extra benefit offerings, which attracts more enrollees (Morse, 2022).

We begin this chapter by describing the role of hospital executive leadership in influencing hospital best practices, pandemic leadership and quality care, hospital resource utilization, and patient outcomes. Evidence from recent studies is used to show how and why physician-led hospitals have higher quality ratings as compared with other hospitals. The balanced scorecard (BSC) with key performance indicators (KPI) and metrics for improving hospital performance and patient experience concludes this chapter.

Hospital CEOs

Hospital CEOs today have a critical role in the promotion and development of advanced technology, patient care, employee relations, community involvement, financial strategies at times of crisis, wellness programs, and hospital innovation. They often hold deeper skills and exposure to a breadth of strategic and operational issues, including quality measures and patient satisfaction, both of which factor into value-based care.

The Bureau of Labor and Statistics (BLS) defines a chief executive officer (CEO) as the professional who determines and formulates policies and provides the overall direction of companies or private and public sector organizations within guidelines set up by a board of directors or similar governing board. Most hospital CEOs come from a healthcare administration background with about eight to ten years of experience in administrative, management, and healthcare positions such as chief operating officers (COOs) of hospitals. They have experience in strategic management and executive leadership and most hold Master of Hospital Administration (MHA) or Healthcare MBA degrees that help them to build proficiency in areas such as business administration, ethics, human relations, law, and financial management.

More than a decade ago, the *American Hospital Association* noted that hospitals should evolve from traditional "hospitals" to "health systems," partnering with community organizations and patients to advance the wellness and health needs of communities. It is recognized that efforts have been made in the past to reconfigure new systems, especially due to merger and acquisition (M&A) activities across the healthcare field (see Chapter 4). However, this recommendation is different as it emphasizes that without effective linkage to the community, this evolution will not be as successful. Some hospitals consolidated long-term and post-acute services and moved discharge planning and case management under common leadership. The evolution toward the creation of local and regional non-equity alliances (as compared with joint ventures) to facilitate better coordination as well as enhance the level of care is imminent.

With a continued increase in M&A in the healthcare industry, the number of standalone hospitals is diminishing quickly even in the critical access group. In virtually every state and across state lines the rate of hospital transactions and partnerships is accelerating. Each facility, though, will continue to need an "officer in charge" to run the local operations. In New York, the Department of Health (DOH) continues to require a "local board" for each hospital. But generally, it is subservient to a parent board which has certain reserve powers over the local boards. The hospital CEO often reports to a local board and a parent (i.e., integrated system) CEO. You can imagine the complexity of matrix demands coming out of that structure.

The "true CEOs" are far fewer in number when considering the pyramid. Even the titles are changing – President, Senior Vice President (SVP), Chief Administrative Officer (CAO) – those are all out there. And the forecast calls for an increase in the pace of M&A. In Albany, NY, St Peter's Hospital was initially part of Eastern Mercy Health System (17 hospitals), then part of Catholic Health East (33 hospitals), and it was then acquired by Trinity Health System in Michigan (to date with 88 hospitals).

Roles and Responsibilities

As health systems are becoming more centralized due to the expansion of corporate offices, local CEOs within mega-systems, like Tenet Healthcare, Trinity Health, HCA Healthcare, or Ascension Health, have begun to experience less autonomy working with boards that have become more advisory in nature. Increasingly, the role of the local CEO is drifting away from strategic or visionary to operational with the local culture resembling a more corporatized health system.

As discussed in Chapter 4, understanding the differences between corporate and advisory boards and developing the ability to manage those dynamics present learning opportunities for aspiring healthcare leaders. The extent that CEOs report to a governing board vs. an advisory board often reflects the type of hospital structure and its affiliation with a system. Nonetheless governance has become more complex and tiered as hospitals figure out ways to affiliate to achieve economies of scale and survive in an environment that requires doing more with less.

Hospital CEOs and physician executives and leaders are challenged to clarify priorities and strategies, improve the overall efficiency and productivity of the organization, inspire employees to transform their ways of thinking about patient care and the culture of the organization, and employ evidence-based best practices to improve patient quality and safety.

Successful CEOs focus their efforts on innovating the operating model, reducing costs of care by increasing operating efficiencies and economies of scale, adding core competencies, using analytics to improve the patient experience, and developing leadership capacity. To achieve these goals, CEOs are expected to execute in key healthcare areas and assume important responsibilities and roles.

Hospital CEOs serve as moral leaders who articulate the hospital's mission and vision to the community. These seasoned executives have a strong strategy orientation to champion the planning process and set the tone for its development and implementation. They determine priorities, formulate policies, and provide overall direction of the hospital within guidelines set up by the board of directors. They offer leadership guidance to the hospital's executive management team (i.e., chief nursing officer, chief medical officer, chief operating officer, chief financial officer) to ensure sustained success and future growth opportunities, engage the board of directors who provide input and oversight of quality and safety, and coordinate key stakeholders to establish a shared vision.

The governing board's traditional responsibility is to select and retain an effective CEO. The CEO is the link between the day-to-day *operations* of the organization and the board. With the support of senior executives, physician leaders, and staff managers, CEOs plan, direct, and integrate strategic development initiatives with operational activities at the highest level of management. Typical responsibilities of chief executive officers include the following:

- Delivering high-quality patient care
- Modeling the way in both work ethics and personal values
- Shaping positive culture
- Setting standards for operational excellence
- Hiring, rewarding, and promoting executive talent
- Monitoring productivity and satisfaction of the hospital team
- Allocating resources for the implementation of clinical procedures and policies
- Reinforcing consequential compliance with laws, regulations, and hospital policies
- Sustaining relationships with partner organizations, community, and referring physicians
- Planning, deploying, and delivering financial performance based on strategic objectives
- Improving operational efficiency and focusing on cost reduction

- Keeping performance metrics in line with quality goals
- Investing in health IT
- Implementing EHRs across the continuum of care
- Employing rapid cycle improvement and lean methodologies
- Increasing overall hospital ratings and patient satisfaction (HCAHPS)

As the yearly turnover rate of hospital CEOs continues to linger at 16–17% over the last decade (ACHE, 2021), governing boards and senior leaders need to remain vigilant, especially during the challenges posed by the COVID-19 pandemic, in promoting leadership development as a strategic imperative. Building a leadership team with those already working within the organization improves existing capabilities of managers as well as nurtures new leaders. From recruitment to onboarding, it costs less to develop and retain a cadre of leaders in-house than to hire and train new executives. Surprisingly, however, senior executives in healthcare organizations often de-emphasize the need to cultivate the next cadre of talent champions by increasing their span of control over operational levels, dodging middle managers and aspiring physician leaders (Belasen & Belasen, 2016).

Pandemic Leadership

With the persistence of COVID-19, many hospital executives and CEOs have adopted an entrepreneurial orientation pursuing innovative strategies and practices and actively engaging patients, care teams, staff members and communities in contributing to and implementing innovation. Resilience is key. Hospital leaders must be advocates who build resiliency and flexibility into their management structures and work on behalf of their workforce and patients with higher levels of accountability and transparency (Belasen, 2022).

Fortune/Deloitte (2021) surveyed 110 CEOs across more than 15 industries for its summer 2021 CEO survey. Nearly two years into the pandemic, most CEOs expressed confidence that their organizations will continue to cope with the disruptions associated with the enduring uncertainty of COVID-19. While 60% expected strong or very strong growth of demand for healthcare services, over 75% of these CEOs highlighted the need to attract and retain health professionals as well as invest in designing post-pandemic workplaces. This is important considering a poll that showed 32% of registered nurses (RNs) in the United States indicated they may leave their current direct-patient-care role primarily due to burnout (McKinsey & Company, 2022).

Another survey by Ernst & Young (2022) found that a majority (58%) of CEOs see technology and increasing digital customer interaction as buffers against rising costs from supply chain disruption and an ongoing staffing shortage but also as an important opportunity for growth in the next five years. Most (70%) CEOs also plan to actively pursue mergers and acquisitions to reduce the costs of health delivery.

Pandemic leadership is not an enviable position to be in. One small decision can change the outcome for the better or worse. A wrong move could erode the trust of employees, patients, and stakeholders and trigger unnecessary tensions that may exacerbate the existing conditions. The true test of executive leadership does not occur when everything is running smoothly; it occurs during unexpected situations when it is crucial to act quickly and communicate "the why" effectively.

It is also important for leaders to maintain a sense of continuity, to be relevant and consistent in the dissemination of information, to remain calm, and to be visible, truthful, trustworthy, and responsive. Accurate and timely communication is vital during major disruptions. Effective hospital leaders acknowledge transitions, communicate with compassion, show understanding, and are empathetic. They use mixed strategies of messaging, at times using persuasion to promote cooperation and, in some circumstances, resorting to authority to achieve the desired results and continuity. Messaging that appeals to the collective values and history plays a key role in enhancing public trust and stakeholders' acceptance (Belasen & Belasen, 2019).

However, future-proofing the leadership pipeline in healthcare settings with talents and skills for leading diverse teams and individuals during major disruptions is critical for the success of hospital operations. Effective leaders find ways to balance risk-taking and accountability through a mix of centralized control to achieve operating efficiency with local adaptation for effective delivery of patient care. They promote employee engagement and interfunctional collaboration across the continuum of care by leveraging diversity and clinician inputs into important decision-making, particularly in times of major disruption.

A recent Gallup (2021) survey showed that managers account for 70% of the variance in employee engagement. In the healthcare industry, a disengaged workforce may impact the patient's experience and could lead to an increase in infections, medication errors, and even higher rates of mortality.

Successful hospital leaders learn to embrace relational, teamwork, and emotional intelligence (EI) skills and capabilities to improve interprofessional collaboration across diverse care teams. Further, they rely on rapid decision-making and digital-first strategies (e.g., online patient portals) for responding to patients and stakeholders. Increasing morale, reducing burnout in physicians and nurses, improving care team communications, and using motivational strategies to engage employees and providers are critical for providing high-quality patient care.

Physician Leadership

Aspiring physician leaders are well positioned to deal with financial challenges and personnel shortages, as well as to tackle behavioral health/addiction issues and meet regulatory mandates and patient safety and quality standards, the top challenges for hospitals. Hospital administrators, no matter how well-intentioned, do not go through the same interactions and direct patient care experiences as physicians, a reality that can lead non-physician CEOs toward a different set of values and metrics of success.

While non-physician executives do not have the hands-on experience of working on the hospital floor and making difficult, life-altering decisions in a high-stress work environment, they think physicians do not have a full grasp of overcoming challenges with strategy and scope of running a complex hospital network or integrated system. The perceptual gap between physicians and administrators can create a cultural disconnect and may lead to unnecessary tension, feelings of disempowerment, burnout, and frustration that could affect physician engagement or even the quality of patient experience.

Non-physician CEOs do not have clinical knowledge associated with in-depth medicine, experiential understanding of hospital life, or even peer-to-peer credibility among fellow physicians. Moreover, the credibility that comes with medical experience, compared to non-medical professionals, can be leveraged vis-a-vis external stakeholders (e.g., future clinicians, patients, pharma executives, and donors), broadening the physician executive's social capital amongst their peers and within their communities.

A high degree of credibility, trust of other physicians, and effective interpersonal communication skills were found to be among the most important skills reported by physician CEOs themselves. It comes as no surprise that the global executive search firm Witt Kieffer has seen a 20% increase in the demand to include physicians with experience in improving managed care and population health as candidates in their CEO searches, a trend due in part to the shift of healthcare from volume to value-based care.

The increasing demand for physician leaders has also been recently met by the growing number of physicians who are interested in assuming senior-level and C-suite leadership positions. In recent years, physicians have also begun to attend business schools after completing their clinical training through full- or part-time MD/MBA programs to gain systems thinking and strategic planning skills. Others attend leadership programs or take specialized courses in business to improve critical financial, operational, and management skills and learn to accept risks and support new business ventures to qualify for C-suite positions or boardroom roles.

Other motivations for physicians to join C-Suite or boardrooms include the high CEO turnover rates (16%–17%) and the willingness to step in, but also due to burnout, which ranges from 30% to 65% across medical specialties. Many are looking for an off-ramp from day-to-day patient care with the highest rates among physicians in the front line of care, including emergency medicine and general internal medicine (Corder, 2018). Another incentive might be compensation. From 2005 to 2015, mean compensation for major nonprofit medical center CEOs increased 93%, from $1.6 million to $3.1 million. During that period, the wage gap between CEOs and clinicians rose from 3:1 to 5:1 for orthopedic surgeons, from 7:1 to 12:1 for pediatricians and from 23:1 to 44:1 for RNs (Du et al., 2018).

We cannot escape the conclusion that recruiting physicians to lead hospitals, especially during catastrophic times, has many potential advantages. Moreover, an effective hospital succession plan is essential for building the leadership development pipeline and the orderly transitions of clinical leadership positions. Physician development helps sustain the culture of safety and ensures continuity in care services as well as acting as an incentive for aspiring physicians to pursue a leadership role and improve their engagement and performance.

Physician involvement with other health professionals in prioritizing hospital quality improvement is critical when it comes to improving patient safety and quality outcomes. Hospital settings with physicians who were provided with patient satisfaction education saw an average increase of 7.1% on the HCAHPS ratings of patients who strongly agreed to recommend the hospital to friends and family members (Belasen & Belasen, 2018). Furthermore, physicians who received leadership or management training were found to perform well in executive leadership roles, including driving system-wide care delivery transformation, employee engagement, and physician alignment.

Surprisingly, however, most hospital boards still tend to recruit members whose expertise centers around business experience and community leadership rather than healthcare backgrounds. Remarkably, the practice of recruiting non-physicians to hospital boards negates the rationale that in the value-based care model, physicians add great expertise to the board in determining what adds value to healthcare delivery.

Consider the evidence – notably, 13 of the 21 hospitals on the 2019 U.S. News & World Report's Best Hospitals list were physician-led, and all the top-rated 6 hospitals were physician-led. Overall quality scores in physician-run hospitals were also 25% higher than those run by non-physicians. Moreover, while in 2019 only 5% of hospitals in the United States were led by CEOs with medical degrees, 11.3% of the 5-star hospitals on Hospital Compare during 2019 were physician-led. And the trend continues. In 2022, overall, 13 hospitals led by physicians (10%) received a HCAHPS recommended rating of 5, while 80 hospitals (5%) led by non-physicians received a rating of 5.

Washington, DC – June 23, 2022 – Healthgrades released the hospitals that received its 2022 Outstanding Patient Experience Award on June 21, and 55 of the 399 recognized hospitals were physician-led hospitals. Nationally, physician-led hospitals make up less than 5% of the nation's total number of hospitals.

In Texas, over half (13) of the 24 total recipients of the award are physician-led hospitals, even though physician-led hospitals make up less than 15% of the hospitals in Texas.

In Pennsylvania, 21% of the hospitals named to this distinguished Healthgrades list were physician-led hospitals although they only represent 1.5% of all hospitals in the commonwealth. *Every physician-led hospital in PA* made the list.

In Arizona, two of the three hospitals awarded are physician-led hospitals.

Of the 109 hospitals in Arkansas, the one recipient of the award is a physician-led hospital.

Half of the hospitals selected in Oklahoma are physician-led hospitals.

"It's not surprising that physician-led hospitals outperformed this important patient experience award," said Frederic Liss, MD, the president of Physician-Led Healthcare for America (PHA). "Our hospitals place an emphasis on the patient-physician relationship and are driven by value-based care models and transparency. Physician-led hospitals consistently outperform their competitors on patient satisfaction, quality of care and cost ratings."

The annual award is based on an analysis of 3,173 hospitals that submitted at least 75 patient experience surveys to the Centers for Medicare and Medicaid Services between July 2020 and March 2021. The scoring methodology applies to ten patient experience measures, including physician and nurse communication, medication and post-discharge care instructions, hospital cleanliness, and whether a patient would recommend the hospital to family or friends. Healthgrades excluded hospitals that were in the bottom 20%for overall quality (PHA, 2022).

The advantages that physicians have over other executives in leading complex health systems seem to extend to hospital resource utilization. Tasi et al. (2019) found that physician-led hospitals achieve higher quality ratings across all specialties and inpatient days per hospital bed than non-physician-led hospitals, with no differences in staffed beds, inpatient days, total revenue, or profit margins. Of the top 115 hospitals, almost 30% were physician-led. Physician-led hospitals had a higher average number of inpatient days per hospital bed than did non-physician-led hospitals. Did they also do a better job of managing the challenges brought by COVID-19 in terms of capacity utilization as compared to hospitals led by non-physicians? The next sections describe a study that was aimed at finding an answer to this question.

Hospital Utilization

Hospital resource utilization is driven by complex dynamics between input, output, and the number of available beds and capacity management methods are used to balance beds, staff, and hospital resources with patient flow. Efficient patient flow helps increase revenue streams and more importantly keeps patients safe and satisfied. Understanding variation in hospital utilization and spending across organizations, rather than across geographic areas, is important because care is delivered by health networks and hospitals and interventions and cost savings increasingly focus on organizations. In normal times, hospitals maximize bed occupancy while *maintaining* the *overflow* rate at a reasonable level, which often has a negative effect on patient outcomes. Patient mix (e.g., medical vs. surgical, observation vs. full admission patients) and payor mix (e.g., private vs. Medicaid-Medicare) – all make an enormous difference.

During disruptions, however, determining the optimal number of hospital beds becomes highly complex and requires models and techniques which are sensitive to interaction effects among variables such as demographic and socioeconomic factors, average length of stay, admission rates, and bed occupancy rates.

Most hospitals moved in the direction of centralizing operations during COVID-19 by adjusting their capacity planning. Lack of bed capacity, shortage in supplies, and high occupancy rates further increase the complexity of capacity planning. ICU overflow during the COVID-19 pandemic – the proportion of supplementary beds specifically created for COVID-19 ICU care to the previously existing total number of ICU beds – appeared to have a positive impact on mortality rate among critically ill patients. To prevent overflow, hospitals employed interventions such as suspension of non-essential medical, surgical, and dental procedures and expansion of capacity for COVID-19 patients depending on the patient load and intensive care units' (ICU) bed availability. Other means included installation of field hospitals, use of private hospitals, and deployment of former or newly qualified medical staff. Declarations of emergency from state governments allowed temporary expansions of scope for various non-physician providers and recently retired nurses and providers to quickly reenter the workforce.

Healthcare providers who participate as an accountable care organization (ACO) in the voluntary Medicare Shared Savings Program (MSSP) have financial incentives to reduce spending for Medicare patients while being rewarded for efficiency and quality. Because ACOs are designed to reduce resource utilization, the bonus—or share of estimated savings received by an ACO—is one factor that significantly influences ACO profitability. Large networks of ACOs with a range of services often provide care for patients not covered by their ACO contracts and subsequently may lose substantial fee-for-service profits unless they reduce utilization to ACO-covered patients.

Physician-led ACOs with a smaller range of services often have stronger incentives to limit utilization and create more savings by reducing unnecessary hospitalizations, outpatient hospital procedures, and imaging studies for patients in general, without targeting specific patients. McWilliams et al. (2018), for example, conducted a difference-in-differences analysis to compare changes in Medicare spending for patients in ACOs before and after entry into the MSSP (2012–2014) with concurrent changes in spending for local patients served by providers not participating in the MSSP (control group). By 2015, the mean differential change in per-patient Medicare spending was −$474 (−4.9% of the pre-entry mean, $p < 0.001$) for physician-group ACOs that entered in 2012, −$342 (−3.5% of the pre-entry mean, $p < 0.001$) for those that entered in 2013, and −$156 (−1.6% of the pre-entry mean, $p = 0.009$) for those that entered in 2014. The corresponding differential changes for hospital-integrated ACOs were −$169 ($p = 0.005$), −$18 ($p = 0.78$), and $88 ($p = 0.14$), significantly smaller savings than for physician-group ACOs ($p < 0.001$). Spending reductions in physician-group ACOs constituted a net savings to Medicare of $256.4 million in 2015, whereas spending reductions in hospital-integrated ACOs were offset by bonus payments.

However, during the pandemic, operating at or near capacity with COVID-19 patients limited the financial gains that could have been garnered from elective surgeries or required treatments that are reimbursed at higher rates than the capped COVID-19 reimbursements. In the long run, hospitals may be able to offset these financial losses through increased volume by virtue of the stronger patient recommendations stemming from their quality of care. Indeed, the pandemic created an enormous demand shock for healthcare with a big impact on hospitals' utilization.

The Physician CEO Advantage

Belasen et al. (2023) report on multiple studies with a relationship between expert leadership and hospital performance with evidence suggesting that physician-led hospitals have better clinical outcomes, have improved financial performance, and enjoy higher average quality ratings. Similar studies reported higher quality ratings and lower morbidity rates in hospitals with physician board members or with physicians in multiple levels of management.

Other confirming evidence was also found for the relationship between physicians' board participation and overall hospital performance. Higher rated hospital boards had superior performance by hospital management staff and used clinical quality metrics more effectively on target setting and operations (Tsai et al., 2015).

Research has found that leaders with graduate-level degrees are more likely to exhibit transformational leadership behaviors such as role modeling that provides a strong motivation to achieve well-defined goals. Likewise, leaders with graduate degrees that are grounded in theory, research, and utilization of findings based on empirical research are, like leaders with terminal degrees (e.g., Doctor of Medicine [MD], Doctor of Philosophy [PhD], Doctor of Science [DSc], Doctor of Science in Nursing [DSN], Doctor of Public Health [DrPH], and others), more likely to use evidence-based practices. Notably, physician executives are more likely to use evidence-based decision-making with an increasing emphasis on quality metrics and patient outcomes, driving higher patient ratings (Galstian et al., 2018).

As the COVID-19 pandemic continued to disrupt hospitals' performance, hospitals began to see a shift in utilization of essential services due to lockdown policies and suspension of elective surgeries, stay-at-home orders, and demand for telemedicine. While the studies referenced above showed that hospital quality ratings are positively associated with the patient experience of care and may predict patients' future acute care utilization, the COVID-19 pandemic provided a unique lens through which patient ratings of their quality of care and hospital resource utilization can be examined as a function of the CEO's professional background.

A recent study (Belasen et al., 2023) investigated the impact of CEO characteristics on hospital resource utilization during the time leading up to and including the peak of the COVID-19 Delta variant wave in 2021. Finding out how CEO characteristics and HCAHPS quality measures influence hospital utilization allowed researchers to infer whether a CEO's impact on operating efficiency is through the overall perceived quality of the patient experience. Hospital capacity utilization, measured by the percentage of days that the hospital is operating at full capacity, was used to capture hospitals' operating efficiency. A decline in utilization for non-COVID-19 medical care, particularly early in the pandemic, was expected due to the suspension of non-essential medical, surgical, and dental procedures.

These researchers included physician CEOs and CEO tenure as the independent variables. Tenure is a continuous variable calculated as the number of years in the current CEO position. Since hospitals with higher bed capacity are less likely to reach full capacity, controlling for population, they included a number of beds per 1,000 population as an additional control variable and added state-fixed-effects since the pandemic peaked in different states on variable dates due to swings in daily COVID cases and the lifting of social-distancing restrictions. Finally, they used the HCAHPS global measures (hospital overall rating; willingness to recommend) as explanatory variables.

Findings suggested that physician CEOs have positive impact on hospital utilization, while CEO tenure did not have any effect during the pandemic. More specifically, physician-led hospitals had 44% more days at capacity during 2021 when hospitals needed to run more efficiently, due to the sharp rise in cases and increase in daily patient demand. The coefficient for hospital rating was not significant, but the coefficient for hospital recommendation was significant and positive, suggesting that a 0.01 higher hospital recommendation score increased hospital utilization by 1.5%. The results suggested that physician CEOs improved operating efficiency through the utilization of hospital beds during the pandemic. Some of this efficiency was captured in the HCAHPS global measures and some were not.

To find out whether physician-led hospitals with higher ratings on the HCAHPS communication composite measures achieved more favorable hospital efficiency than non-physician-led hospitals, they focused on the interaction variables between physician CEOs and HCAHPS communication scores. Results suggested that, during the COVID-19 pandemic, physician-led hospitals with higher patient satisfaction saw an improvement in operating efficiency. Notably, a 0.01 increase in any of the patient experience of care scores ("Communication with Nurses," "Communication with Doctors," "Responsiveness of Hospital Staff," "Communication about Medicines," "Discharge Information and Care

Transition") for physician-led hospitals was associated with 0.52%–0.79% increase in hospital utilization (% of days at capacity).

These findings added support to the physician leadership advantage argument during times of crisis. During the fight against the COVID-19 pandemic, with limited resources and a rise in demand for inpatient beds, physician-led hospitals continued to provide a high-quality care and improved their hospitals' operating efficiency as compared with those led by non-physician leaders. The less significant correlation between physician CEO and non-physician CEO tenure suggested that physician CEOs have some inherent qualities that are different from those of their non-physician counterparts, and these qualities are hardwired and developed with clinical expertise and deep experience over time. Among top-tier hospitals, physician-led hospitals are more likely to achieve higher ratings through patient-centric care approaches. While this may lead to better patient outcomes, higher hospital recommendation rates may also potentially trigger higher patient flow and place a greater demand on inpatient beds, translating into fuller hospitals over a longer duration than non-physician-led hospitals.

Dual CEO

The wave of mergers and acquisitions in healthcare, which increased substantially after the pandemic, has brought back the question of whether two CEOs are better than one. Critics argue that accountability at the top of the pyramid must be undivided, a single point of accountability that exists in the solitary model. Similarly, some argue that the dual CEO makes it much more challenging to coordinate activities or collaborate across functional lines.

When Netflix co-founder Reed Hastings developed plans for his succession, however, he assigned his former COO as co-CEO and later elevated the current COO to the co-CEO position. Reed became the Executive Chairman. In his blog, he explained – "Ted and Greg have developed great trust and respect for each other through their collective successes and failures. In addition, they can always be relied upon to put Netflix's interests first. These qualities – combined with their complementary skill sets, deep knowledge of entertainment and technology, and proven track record at Netflix – create a unique opportunity to deliver faster growth and greater success long term with them as co-CEOs" (Hastings, 2023). And the focus on long term makes sense. While co-CEO structures tend to evolve during transitional periods (e.g., M&A), the CEO tenure is not significantly different than the average tenure of solo CEOs (about 5 years), lasting on average 4.5 years.

We recently took a careful look at the performance of 87 public companies whose leaders were identified as co-CEOs. We found that those firms tended to produce more value for shareholders than their peers did. While co-CEOs were in charge, they generated an average annual shareholder return of 9.5% – significantly better than the average of 6.9% for each company's relevant index. This impressive result didn't hinge on a few highfliers: Nearly 60% of the companies led by co-CEOs outperformed. And co-CEO tenure was not short-lived but more or less the same as sole-CEO tenure – about five years, on average.

We're not suggesting that all organizations should rush to adopt a co-CEO arrangement. With so little public company data available to us (under 100 companies in 25 years is not a lot), we have to use caution. For firms in stable industries facing only moderate disruption, having a single CEO may still be the better option. But today the job of running a company has become so complex and multifaceted, and the scope of responsibilities is so great, that the co-CEO model deserves a fresh and close look....

Given the pace of change and disruption we're likely to experience in the years ahead, we can expect more and more companies to try installing co-CEOs – and we hope the guidance we have provided here will help them succeed. Agile organizations are particularly good at managing ambiguity and blurred boundaries, so they may find that the co-CEO model is especially easy for them to implement and sustain. The approach will never be for everybody, but if your company is moving away from command-and-control leadership, as more and more organizations are, putting two leaders at the top may make a lot of sense (Feigen et al., 2022).

To succeed, the co-CEO model requires symmetry in communication, clarity in roles and responsibilities, and mutual understanding of how power is shared, especially in a mega-system. Consider Advocate Aurora Health and Atrium Health which completed their merger in December 2022. The new health system, Advocate Health, is expected to generate revenue of more than $27 billion and operate 67 hospitals and more than 1,000 sites of care in six states. It is nationally recognized for its expertise in cardiology, neurosciences, oncology, pediatrics, and rehabilitation, as well as organ transplants, burn treatments, and specialized musculoskeletal programs. Advocate Health is expected to treat nearly 6 million patients each year. Their co-CEOs Eugene A. Woods and Jim Skogsbergh were recognized among Modern Healthcare's *100 Most Influential People in Healthcare* of 2022.

This prestigious recognition acknowledges and honors individuals who are deemed by their peers and the senior editors of Modern Healthcare to be the most influential figures in healthcare in terms of leadership and impact. They include health system leaders, high-level government administrators, elected officials, academics, and national thought leaders. Thomas C. Nelson, Chairman of Advocate Health board of directors, reflected – "In a year that has brought new challenges and underscored the need for transformation, we could not be prouder of Gene and Jim being selected for the most influential list. Their vision, strategic acumen and operational skill will guide our unified organization as we push past traditional geographic and care delivery boundaries to reshape health care at a national level" (Advocate Health, 2022).

WHY ARE HEALTH SYSTEMS TURNING TO DUAL CEOs?

Dual-CEO models can work as a "bridge to completing a deal" between health systems that might otherwise be skeptical of a merger, and it can be a potentially successful short-term solution.... Hackensack Meridian Health had dual CEOs for about two years after it was created via a merger, that arrangement wound down when co-CEO John Lloyd retired in December 2018.

Robert Garrett, the system's current CEO, who previously served as co-CEO with Lloyd, said there was no power struggle between him and Lloyd, nor was there any ambiguity, as a succession plan had been created early in the merger.

Under Hackensack Meridian's model, the hospitals, physicians, and academic and research divisions reported to Garrett, while the ambulatory, population health, and post-acute departments reported to Lloyd. Meanwhile, departments like finance, human resources, and strategic planning reported to both.

Garrett and Lloyd would meet each Monday morning for overlapping areas, and according to Garrett, they agreed about 95% of the time. On the occasions when they disagreed, they were able to resolve their differences internally... "It really didn't slow the decision-making process," Garrett said. "Looking at what we accomplished in the past two years, we were able to move quickly and complete some major initiatives. We had a good communication structure and didn't get caught up in bureaucracy" (Advisory Board, 2023).

The dual leadership model resembles the dyad leadership framework covered in Chapter 8. Dyad leadership, which pairs physicians with responsibility over the clinical vision for the organization and administrators with responsibility for operationalizing the vision has emerged as an important practice for guiding and managing health settings with over 75% of healthcare leaders indicating that they use dyad leadership in their organizations. In tandem, the partners in the dyad share roles and responsibilities for strategic planning, capital and operational budgeting, and shaping the cultural fabric of the organization. MedAxiom's president, for example, is a practicing cardiologist and works with a team of administrative leaders at each level of the organization. Similarly, the ACC, MedAxiom's parent company, also utilizes the dyad model at its helm (Cardiology Magazine, 2020).

At Lee Health Heart & Vascular Institute, roles and responsibilities are always agreed upon at the start of any dyad relationship. In general, physician leaders are responsible for ensuring quality, evidence-based care; minimizing variations and gaps in care; fostering teamwork; maximizing clinical team productivity; and overseeing clinician-driven resource use and staffing. Administrative partners handle financial and supply chain management, market-share analysis, and capital planning and deployment. Responsibility for maintaining compliance and professionalism tends to go to clinician leaders, while performance reporting usually falls to administrative leaders.

"We've been successful in using the dyad model to create a collaborative culture that's built on and furthers our progress in achieving shared goals, and at the same time keeps the quality of patient care central in all discussions and initiatives," explains Richard A. Chazal, MD, medical director at Lee Health Heart & Vascular Institute in Fort Myers, Fla. "But we couldn't have done that without creating a strong foundation in the beginning" (Ross, 2020).

The Balanced Scorecard and KPIs

The BSC plays an important role in aligning the different functions and departments with the mission, strategic objectives, and performance metrics of health systems. A typical BSC is shown in Table 5.1. It links four broad key performance indicators (KPIs): financial, patient care, operations, and

Table 5.1   Key Performance Indicators for Hospitals

KPIs	Metrics
Financial Performance	
Revenue	Growth in net revenues, volume growth by key service line, number/sources of funds raised, number of contracts received, percentage of contracts relative to competition; revenues from new contracts, patient census, market share, referrals and use, donors' contribution, funds raised for facility improvements, payer mix, number of outpatient visits, research grants, financial growth rate and strategic expansion budgeting.
Productivity	Profit, operating margin, depreciation, amortization, and expense as a percentage of net revenue, total assets by net revenue, cost per case, cost per discharge, supply expense and pharmacy expense, personnel cost, reduced cash, efficiency ratios such as overtime use, unit expenditures, length of stay, and operating room supply expense per surgical case.
Patient Satisfaction	
Patient acquisition	Patient complaint, patient referral rate, percentage of patient recommending the hospital, patient waiting time, access, accurate diagnosis rate, incidents (include falls, medication errors), hospital-acquired conditions, discharge timeliness, preventable readmissions, hospital cleanliness.
Quality of care	Length of stay, case cancelations, waiting time, discharge, readmission rate, mortality rate, number of patient falls, claim processing accuracy, patient complaints, % ER patient triaged within 15 minutes of arrival, billing and collection ratios, staff to patient ratio
Safety	Infection rate, coding error rate (clinic and hospital), medication errors per dose, occupational injuries, restraint usage.
Operations	
Productivity	Cost per capita, cost per diagnosis, cost per produce; staffing utilization, percentage of occupied beds, hours per unit of activity, resource utilization.
Employee satisfaction	Employee satisfaction, physician satisfaction, nurses' retention rate, employee turnover rate, absenteeism rate

(Continued)

Table 5.1 *(Continued)*   **Key Performance Indicators for Hospitals**

KPIs	Metrics
Stakeholder communications	Number of HMO contracts, number complaints, information sharing among stakeholders (e.g., response rate), number of PCP referrals, increased donations
Development	
Human capital	Staff development, dollars spent on training and development, continuing education credits per FTE, publications, tuition reimbursement spent per year.
Technology	EHR implementation, informatics training, work design, interoperability training
Continuous improvement	New service lines offered, new research projects, number of partners participating in joint projects
Development	Leadership development, cultural survey, communication assessment, employee engagement, number of interprofessional collaborations
Innovation	Product innovation, staff training, number of physicians using EHR

innovation (Kaplan & Norton, 1992). The scorecard facilitates a single dashboard view that provides insight into how well the hospital progresses toward achieving its goals. It expands the scope of hospital CEOs beyond backward-looking financial metrics about how goals have been achieved in the past, to assessment of future performance: clinical outcomes, patient satisfaction, financial performance, and staff development. Duke Children's Hospital, an inpatient academic hospital, with 138 beds was the first health organization to implement BSC in 2000, and quite likely the use of BSC helped the hospital convert 11 million dollars of losses into 4 million dollars of profits.

When designed properly and updated in a timely manner, the BSC can present a broader view of the hospital's performance and serve as a guide for strategic decision-making and improve the quality of medical services. The framework is anchored in the axiom that measurable goals get operationalized, but since not all goals can be measured, choosing the right-quality indicators is critical. Hospital leaders may review possible tradeoffs across several goals and measures and take proactive steps to balance regulation with innovation, and patient experience and quality care with financial investment and performance management.

The BSC is also a useful tool for bridging gaps and overcoming cultural misalignment across merged hospitals and healthcare facilities, realigning them with the new strategy for delivering higher value for patients, physicians, payers, and communities.

It is important to note that health systems use adaptations of the BSC to map their unique mission, goals, strategies, and measures. For example, Peel Memorial Hospital in Ontario, Canada, uses six categories: management leadership, human resources, patient care and process management, patient and community focus, quality tools and information utilization, and performance results. Humber River Hospital includes four categories: stakeholders, learning and growth, financial and accountability, and internal processes (infection prevention, mortality rates, surgical safety checklist compliance). Duke Children Hospital (mentioned above) uses patient outcomes as its top priority and research and education since it is a teaching hospital in addition to internal processes and financial outcomes. Mount Sinai hospital includes the patient experience, quality and safety, access and efficiency, organizational financial health, innovation, and new knowledge. Hospital leaders who promote the use of BSCs also improve their hospital operating efficiency, financial results, and patient satisfaction. Other benefits include the following:

- Better alignment between physicians and administrators to create new value
- Improved operating costs and functionality by streamlining operations, reducing waste, and eliminating unnecessary errors and redundancies
- Movement toward value-based care
- Effective interprofessional cooperation
- Increased focus on risk management and patient safety
- Alignment of key areas – clinical, financial, operational, technological, and cultural
- Improved revenue cycle best practices
- Rationalizing the system through external affiliations, partnerships, and consolidation of service lines to achieve greater synergies
- EHR implementation for dissemination and sharing information
- Analytics to measure financial and quality performance on a continuous basis
- Engaging local leaders across the clinical integration network (CIN) with a strong focus on cost-efficiencies and coordinated care
- Hiring care professionals and tech specialists to staff quality teams
- Ensuring development of effective post-discharge plans to improve outcomes and reduce costly readmissions

Conclusion

In recent years and especially during the COVID-19 pandemic, physician-led hospitals, as compared with those run by non-physicians, experienced greater improvement in patient outcomes, enjoyed higher financial performance, and had 25% higher overall quality scores. Evidence also showed a positive relationship between participation of physicians in hospital senior leadership teams and boardrooms and improved performance targets. Outcomes included higher quality ratings, lower morbidity rates, better performance by hospital management staff, and more effective utilization of clinical quality metrics on target settings and operations. Notably, physician executives are more likely to approach important decisions based on the clinical delivery model with greater focus on evidence-based decision-making, quality metrics, and patient satisfaction, thus driving better patient outcomes.

As the COVID-19 pandemic continued to disrupt hospitals' performance, it also provided a unique lens through which acute care hospital utilization and patient satisfaction could be examined as a function of the leader's professional background and education. For example, while the COVID-19 pandemic generated greater demand for inpatient beds, physician-led hospitals improved their hospitals' capacity utilization as compared with those led by non-physician leaders.

Exploring the relationship between physician leadership and hospital ratings and identifying best practices could inform hospitals wishing to improve quality-of-care delivery. It could also trigger a more focused approach to leadership training and development and improve hospital succession planning, the subject of Chapter 10. Further, it could also inform hospital CEO recruitment strategies and selection processes and potentially close the gap created by high CEO turnover rates in U.S. hospitals.

References

Advisory Board. (2023). Are 2 CEOs better than one? Why some health systems are embracing the dual-CEO model, https://www.advisory.com/daily-briefing/2019/03/20/co-ceos

Advocate Health (2022). https://www.advocatehealth.com/news/advocate-health-ceos-eugene-a-woods-and-jim-skogsbergh-recognized-among-modern-healthcares-100-most-influential

Belasen, A. (2022). *Resilience in Healthcare Leadership: Practical Strategies and Self-Assessment Tools*. New York, NY: Routledge. (https://doi.org/10.1093/intqhc/mzab036)

Belasen, A. R., & Belasen, A. T. (2018). Doctor-patient communication: A review and a rationale for using an assessment framework. *Journal of Health Organization and Management*, 32(7), 891–907.

Belasen, A. T., & Belasen, A. R. (2016). Value in the middle: Cultivating middle managers in healthcare organizations. *Journal of Management Development*, 35(9), 1149–1162.

Belasen, A. T., & Belasen, A. R. (2019). The strategic value of integrated corporate communication: Functions, social media, stakeholders. *International Journal of Strategic Communication*, 13, 4. (https://doi.org/10.1080/1553118X.2019.1661842)

Belasen, A., Belasen, A., & Feng, Z. (2023). The physician CEO advantage and Hospital performance during the COVID-19 pandemic: Capacity utilization and patient satisfaction, *Journal of Health Organization and Management*, 37(3), 313–326. (https://doi.org/10.1108/JHOM-04-2022-0126)

Cardiology Magazine (2020). Business of medicine: Dyad leadership model, walking the talk, *American College of Cardiology*, https://www.acc.org/Latest-in Cardiology/Articles/2020/06/01/12/42/Business-of-Medicine-Dyad-Leadership-Model-Walking-the-Talk

Corder, J. C. (2018). We need to reflame the fire before it burns out. *Missouri Medicine*, 115(2), 108–111.

Du, J. Y., Rascoe, A. S., & Marcus, R. E. (2018). The growing executive-physician wage gap in major us nonprofit hospitals and burden of nonclinical workers on the US healthcare system. *Clinical Orthopaedics and Related Research*, 476(10), 1910–1919 doi: 10.1097/CORR.0000000000000394

Ernst & Young (2022). *The CEO imperative: How the health care industry is growing via M&A*. https://www.ey.com/en_gl/ceo/the-ceo-imperative-how-the-health-care-industry-is-growing-via-m-a

Feigen, M. A., Jenkin, M., & Warendn, A. (2022). Is it time to consider co-CEOs? *Harvard Business Review*, 100(4), 50–54.

Fortune/Deloitte (2021). *CEO Survey*, https://www2.deloitte.com/content/dam/Deloitte/us/Documents/about-deloitte/us-fortune-deloitte-CEO-survey-summer-2021-highlights-new.pdf

Gallup (2021). *How Influential Is a Good Manager?* https://www.gallup.com/cliftonstrengths/en/350423/influential-good-manager.aspx

Galstian, C., Hearld, L., O'Connor, S., & Borkowski, N. (2018). The relationship of hospital CEO characteristics to patient experience scores. *Journal of Healthcare Management*, 63(1), 50–61 doi: 10.1097/JHM-D-16-00020

Hastings, R. (2023). https://about.netflix.com/en/news/ted-sarandos-greg-peters-co-ceos-netflix

Kaplan, R. S., & Norton, D. P. (1992). The balanced scorecard: Measures that drive performance. *Harvard Business Review*, 70(1), 71–79.

McKinsey & Company. (2022). *Surveyed nurses consider leaving direct patient care at elevated rates*, https://www.mckinsey.com/industries/healthcare/our-insights/surveyed-nurses-consider-leaving-direct-patient-care-at-elevated-rates?cid=other-eml-alt-mip-mck&hdpid=7243ea41-7631-4c68-9faab07f629b87c3&hctky=12202925&hlkid=1d27768204c14d7588b486237179a04a

McWilliams, M., Hatfield, L. A., Landon, B. E., Hamed, P., & Chernew, M. E. (2018). Medicare spending after 3 years of the medicare shared savings program. *The New England Journal of Medicine*, 379, 1139–1149.

Morse, S. (2022). *Centene CEO Releases Plan for Star Rating Turnaround in Q3 Report*, Healthcare Finance, https://www.healthcarefinancenews.com/news/centene-ceo-releases-plan-star-rating-turnaround-q3-report

PHA. (2022). *Physician-led hospitals outperform Healthgrades' 2022 outstanding patient experience awards*, June 23, https://physiciansled.com/physician-led-hospitals-outperform-healthgrades-2022-outstanding-patient-experience-awards/

Ross, J. R. (2020). 90 days a dyad (or triad): Strategies for success & errors to avoid in the crucial early days of partnership, *Cardiovascular Business*, https://cardiovascularbusiness.com/topics/patient-care/90-days-dyad-or-triad-strategies-success-errors-avoid-crucial-early-days

Tasi, M., Keswani, A., & Bozic, K. (2019). Does physician leadership affect hospital quality, operational efficiency, and financial performance? *Health Care Management Review*, 44(3), 256–262.

Tsai, T. C., Jha, A. K., Gawande, A. A., Huckman, R. S., Bloom, N., & Sadun, R. (2015). Hospital board and management practices are strongly related to Hospital performance on clinical quality metrics. *Health Affairs*, 34(8), 1304–1311.

Chapter 6

Nursing Leadership and the Patient Experience

Introduction

The COVID-19 pandemic was a direct strike on the infrastructure of healthcare systems across the world. It pushed healthcare systems and those who worked in them to unimaginable limits and into previously unthinkable decision-making dilemmas. As such, the pandemic highlighted the importance of strong, effective leadership in healthcare. Again and again, healthcare leaders were forced to make real-time decisions with imperfect information. People across the world were looking for understanding, direction, and guidance, and in some instances, they were making very personal decisions based less on a clear understanding of data and more on a sense of whom they felt they could trust. The pandemic left people feeling vulnerable and fearful as each twist and turn led to more unanswered questions and the need to make decisions with unknown implications. Often the direction that needed to be taken was unclear or ambiguous. The COVID-19 pandemic was and continues to be an unprecedented time for our healthcare systems and society in general. And throughout, nurse leaders were front and center, guiding policy and making decisions surrounding the allocation of scarce human and material resources, all with direct and immediate impact on the patient experience.

As discussed in Chapter 5, the pandemic challenged every aspect of how we communicate and interact with each other. It has also been an inflexion point in thinking about how our healthcare systems are managed and the

DOI: 10.4324/9781003431077-6

type of leadership needed in times of crisis. Nearly two decades ago, the "crisis in healthcare" centered around the release of a seminal report by the Institute of Medicine (IOM), *To Err Is Human: Building a Safer Health System*, that as discussed in Chapter 2 documented the number of medical errors occurring across the U.S. systems, many of which led to the death and injury of patients.

Since that report was issued, there have been additional crises in the healthcare sector. The growing technology age has introduced different systems challenges for the healthcare industry, including massive security breaches of personal patient information and the need for implementation of electronic health record systems. There have also been human capital challenges such as the shrinking of the nursing workforce and a growing shortage of primary care health professionals, especially in regions of the United States with some of the most vulnerable populations. Finally, but certainly not least, have been the challenges of providing access to affordable health insurance to a large number of uninsured Americans. These challenges have impacted individual people, the communities they live in, and healthcare systems in many ways. But a common thread has been the need for healthcare leaders to assess the situation, provide clear guidance, when possible, acknowledge uncertainty when necessary, and ultimately provide empathy and compassion as required.

While the aforementioned *To Err Is Human* report was one of the first widely publicized reports of its kind, opening nationwide discussion about systems issues and patient safety, there have been several key reports during the last decade addressing healthcare leadership, nursing leadership, and either patient outcomes or the patient experience. Several of these research reports, conducted at the request of the U.S. Department of Health and Human Services Agency for Healthcare Research and Quality, have been published by the IOM (National Academies of Science, Engineering, and Medicine [NASEM]). In addition to the IOM, many agencies, associations, and organizations, particularly nursing organizations, have also contributed to the advancement of the discussion on medical errors, adverse events, systems issues, and healthcare leadership. The following is a small sampling of the contributing entities: the Robert Wood Johnson Foundation, the American Nurses Association (ANA), the Joint Commission, the American Association of Colleges of Nursing, the National Committee for Quality Assurance, the National Quality Forum, and the Nursing Alliance for Quality Care. One of the overarching outcomes of the IOM *To Err Is Human* report was a discussion of systems failures: how they happen, who is involved, and what type of leadership can move healthcare organizations in a direction where fewer errors and adverse events happen.

The publication of these reports set in motion conversations among nursing leaders throughout healthcare organizations, in academic settings, in policy settings, and in related community health settings about how nursing leadership and nursing professionals can contribute to and influence patient outcomes and the overall patient experience. While many of these reports have been widely discussed, analyzed, and applied in practice across many healthcare organizations, this chapter will provide a brief reflection on the findings and recommendations found in these reports. It will provide an overview of how nursing leadership has evolved and should continue to evolve as a result of these reports with a focus on patient outcomes.

To do this, the chapter will address three overarching and pressing issues currently facing nursing leadership. The first is how nursing leadership can advance progress toward health equity as outlined in *The National Academies Future of Nursing Report 2020–2030*. The second involves the impact that the COVID-19 pandemic has had on the performance of nursing leaders through a historic disruption to our health system and society. The third is what this chapter will refer to as the *three Bs* – blaming, burnout, and bullying. The aim is for nursing leaders to understand how and why nursing needs to move beyond the *three Bs* as it is not only critical for the well-being of all nurses but also for the well-being of the patients they care for.

Leadership and the Transformational Role of Nursing

Scholarly articles and books on leadership often begin with the question *What Is Leadership?* This is for good reason, as leadership is complex and dynamic. Scholars and practitioners in the field will often have slightly different variations as to what leadership means to them, especially when considering what good leadership or bad leadership looks like. This makes sense, as leadership as a concept is both complex and fluid. It has moral and ethical dimensions, and leadership frameworks are embedded in a number of disciplines such as psychology, sociology, anthropology, and political science. Consideration of leadership theory, practice, and style can take on different importance and dimensions given the consideration of circumstances, organizational culture, and mission, leading to the question of what type of leadership is required in any given organization and in any given circumstance.

It is important to keep in mind that leadership as a concept has also evolved as society has evolved and is reflective of ideological shifts. New and emerging leadership styles have moved away from being more transactional in nature to awareness of the importance of gender-based studies, adaptability, and authenticity (Northouse, 2018). This holds true in healthcare organizations which are characterized by high levels of diversity Additionally, leadership styles and approaches that emphasize trust and collaboration have emerged in which multi-directional engagement with employees enables broader participation in organizational change. Accordingly, staff are invited to have a problem-solving role and thus influence outcomes to support sustainable organizations and, in the case of healthcare, optimal patient outcomes. It has become increasingly clear that nursing leadership is integral to both the patient experience and achieving health equity.

Transformational leadership style as a framework has dominated healthcare leadership scholarship during the past two decades as the importance of shared responsibility has been emphasized to curb patient errors and improve patient safety and quality (Institute of Medicine [IOM], 2001). This is for good reason: transformational leadership is visionary in that it brings about change and in doing so puts an emphasis on being concerned with "emotions, values, ethics, standards, and long-term goals" with a whole-person approach aimed at nurturing intrinsic motivation through engagement (Northouse, 2018). As discussed in Chapters 7 and 8, moving toward an organizational culture that supports shared responsibility and removes structural barriers to bring about change through engagement has not been easy. Major internal transformational organizational change cannot occur without the active participation of many and employees need to be empowered to contribute and they need to be valued for their contributions.

However, some experts have suggested that nurses have traditionally been "over-managed" and "led inadequately," preventing organizations from benefiting from full participation and engagement of nurses in organizational change across healthcare systems (Doody & Doody, 2012). Considering that nurses make up the largest number of employees in healthcare and devote the greatest number of hours to direct patient care, it can be problematic for healthcare organization to achieve optimal patient outcomes if nurses are not fully engaged and valued participants in working toward improving patient satisfaction, the patient experience, patient outcomes, and health equity.

During the last couple of decades healthcare experts and nursing leaders have focused on cultivating a transformational leadership mindset across all healthcare organizations. In the aforementioned report by the IOM, it was purported that creating a work environment that is "conducive to patient safety will require throughout many healthcare organizations a mindset with a vision to help improve patient care and evolve nursing professionals as full participants and contributors to healthcare reform in the U.S." (IOM, 2004). A strategic aim using the principles of transformational leadership provides a conceptual framework for this transition that is based on the importance of relationships, using collaborative practices to achieve a shared vision and empowering others to meet their full potential (Marquis & Huston, 2017). Building and maintaining relationships sits at the core of the framework in that it engages both leaders and their employees in a process of mutual goal setting and movement toward those goals "that represent the values and motivations, the wants and needs, the aspirations and expectations of both leaders and followers" (Burns, 1978, p. 19).

Specifically, change was deemed needed to promote evidence-based practices that could decrease medical errors and adverse events. Borrowing from other industries with potential for high-risk errors, the IOM outlined five key practices that were used in these other high-risk industries but were not routinely used within healthcare to reduce errors. The IOM's report, *To Err Is Human: Building a Safer Health System* (2001), defined errors as "failures of planned actions to be completed as intended, or the use of wrong plans to achieve what is intended," while adverse events were defined as "injuries caused by medical intervention, as opposed to the health condition of a patient" and when "an adverse event is the result if an error, it is considered a preventable event." The report estimated (which they note is most probably an underestimate) that each year between 44,000 and 98,000 hospitalized patients die from medical errors. The five practices highlighted to reduce medical errors, adverse events, and preventable adverse events were as follows:

1. Balancing the tension between production efficiency and safety,
2. Creating and sustaining trust throughout the organization,
3. Actively managing the process of change,
4. Involving workers in decision-making pertaining to work design and workflow, and
5. Using knowledge management practices to establish the organization as a learning organization.

The nursing profession has long been concerned and active in the quality and safety of patient care. There are numerous historical accounts of safety and quality initiatives set in motion by nurses, with one of the most historically and earliest referenced being the work of Florence Nightingale in the mid-19th century. A discussion of the role of nursing in patient safety, quality, and outcomes would be incomplete without mentioning her. Nightingale's influence on nursing practice, the environment in which patients were being cared for, and the sanitation conditions in healthcare settings revolutionized the way in which patients were cared for, but her actions also set in motion the framework for modern nursing practice. In addition to being known for establishing the first secular nursing school in London in 1860, Florence Nightingale is cited throughout nursing literature as the first nurse, or health professional of any kind, to measure patient outcomes related to the conditions in which patients were being cared for.

There have been many nursing professionals and nursing scholars who have followed in advancing health outcomes, patient safety, and quality, such as Linda Norman, a nationally and internationally recognized nursing scholar and the former Dean of the Vanderbilt University School of Nursing who is credited with being among the first nursing leaders to work with other health professionals as part of the Dartmouth Summer Symposia (DSS).

In 1995, the DSS is a collective gathering of healthcare professionals committed to identifying ways that healthcare leaders can improve healthcare by addressing factors contributing to the quality of care from an interdisciplinary perspective (Cronenwett & Barnsteiner, 2017). The DSS stated publicly the goal of promoting this interdisciplinary approach to identify and share best practices and in the process positively impact the quality of healthcare delivery. The DSS is also credited with the early recognition of the damaging effect of the fragmented U.S. healthcare systems, and for advancing the framework outlined in the early IOM reports promoting the recommendation that the education of all health professionals should be grounded in *patient-centered care*, and that they should perform as members of an *interdisciplinary team* using *evidence-based practices, quality improvement approaches*, and *informatics* (Cronenwett & Barnsteiner, 2017, p. 45). As discussed in Chapter 8, interdisciplinary became a central focus of improving the U.S. healthcare system for the next two decades.

Immediately following the release of the IOM's early 2000s reports, there were other initiatives undertaken to examine the connection between patient outcomes and nursing practice. For example, in 2005 the Robert

Wood Johnson Foundation funded an initiative commonly referred to as QSEN, or Quality and Safety Education for Nurses. At its ideological core, QSEN was created with patient quality and safety in mind. Its purpose was to develop competencies needed by nurses to provide high-quality and safe care to patients. QSEN is now a repository of what is called "knowledge, skills, and attitudes" (KSA) to guide teaching strategies based on evidence-based practices to ensure the delivery by the nurse of high-quality and safe patient care (QSEN, 2022).

Occurring in parallel was the development of the National Database of Nursing Quality Indicators (NDNQI). In particular, this database found three nursing workforce characteristics to be significantly related to patient outcomes (Dunton et al., 2007). These workforce characteristics are total nursing hours per patient day, percentage of hours supplied by RNs, and years of experience in nursing. Despite the documented importance of these nursing workforce characteristics, the Hospital Compare website does not provide patients with access to this information, the very data found to be most impactful to patient outcomes. The Hospital Compare website gives consumers of healthcare access to readmission data, timely and effective care, and patient safety, but it does not include data on the nursing workforce characteristics that have been found to most impact the patient outcomes. In other words, the publicly reportable data, readmission data, and timely response data are not tied to the number of mandatory hours worked by the nursing staff or any of the other staff in direct patient care. This raises questions concerning transparency and the way in which hospitals in particular are managing nurse staffing in a way that is centrally focused on patient outcomes.

For many decades nursing practice has benefited, and as a result patients have benefited, from the efforts of those who have worked to define the nursing discipline; centering the discipline in conceptual frameworks which have driven evidence-based practice strategies and illuminating nursing quality indicators. National databases tracking nursing quality indicators against patient outcomes and the patient experience are now replete for consumption. Even prior to the startling IOM reports released in the early 2000s capturing the rates of medical errors, in 1989 the ANA had already established the NDNQI in collaboration with the University of Kansas Medical Center School of Nursing. By the mid-1990s the ANA was launching patient safety and quality initiatives, isolating indicators impacting patient outcomes, and engaging in conversations around the restructuring and design of healthcare (Dunton et al., 2007).

The ANA, being fully aware of research suggesting a linkage between nurse staffing hours and patient outcomes, wanted to be more informed of the linkages through not only a formal and nationwide tracking of data and but also data that could specifically measure nursing-sensitive *structure*, *process*, and *outcome* indicators at the unit level: the "specific site where the care occurs and better comparison among like units" (Dunton et al., 2007).

Nursing process and outcome measures were identified as items such as patient falls and pressure ulcers, now deemed *serious reportable events* or *never events* as defined under the National Quality Forum's Care Management Events 4E. and 4F., respectively. Other nurse-sensitive indicators such as nursing hours per patient day, voluntary nurse turnover, and nurse vacancy rates fell under the *structure* measures category. Restraint use, central line catheter and catheter-related urinary tract infection, nosocomial infection, and ventilator-associated pneumonias fell under the *outcome* measure category.

The growing number of resources available to track patient outcomes challenges health leaders to better understand how nurse-sensitive indicators are being measured and to be attuned to how nursing leadership can impact the *structure, process,* and *outcomes* of these nurse-sensitive indicators. It is in this way that nursing leaders can advocate for nurses, but also set goals aligned with the collective vision of an organization and make decisions that are thoughtful but also grounded in analytical thinking.

Given that the HCAHPS measure patient satisfaction and that healthcare reimbursement is tied to or contingent on quality indicators such as patient satisfaction (Belasen et al., 2021), nursing leaders need to be focused on the intersection between nursing practice and patient satisfaction. Nursing leaders need to assess the quality of interactions with patients and the overall environment that supports or does not support these interactions. Without attention to the way in which the discipline of nursing is being practiced with regard to patient interactions, there will be very little ability to move the needle in terms of improving patient satisfaction and quality of care. The typical workday for a nurse on an inpatient unit, or in other types of healthcare facilities, is often task heavy, and the accomplishment of these tasks is valued more directly than an attempt to measure the overall quality of care and the quality of interactions with patients (Penque & Kearney, 2015).

Drawing from nursing theorist, Penque and Kearney (2015) so eloquently point out in their study on the effects of *nursing presence* on patient satisfaction, the mere act of nursing being with and being there for patients "illuminates the heart of nursing practice." They further note that *nursing presence* entails the act of communicating and connecting with patients. However, communicating and connecting takes time and needs to be both purposeful and intentional. Active listening is essential. However, in work settings that are filled with tasks and in many instances are chaotic, the ability of nursing to perform purposeful, intentional, active listening can get lost. Unfortunately, this may come at the risk of falling patient satisfaction scores that are tied to reimbursement in pay-for performance models.

Nursing Leadership and Advancing Health Equity

While earlier reports on patient outcomes, quality, and safety had focused on medical errors, adverse events, and the transformational leadership needed to reverse these trends, current reports are now rightly focused on how healthcare leaders can reverse the gross and growing disparities in healthcare. As discussed in Chapter 3, a more recent focus on disparities and population health has created newer challenges for nursing leaders and nursing professionals as a whole. It has become clear the essential role they must play in designing a healthcare system to reduce disparities and discriminations found throughout the healthcare system.

Given the scope of needed changes in healthcare to address health disparities and inequities, it is not surprising that *The National Academies Future of Nursing 2020–2030* report re-emphasizes not just the need for transformation, but a need for "sweeping transformation," first introduced in the 2001 IOM *Crossing the Quality Chasm: A New Healthcare System for the 21st Century*. The 2001 report captured the essence and importance of transformational leadership and its importance in achieving health equity was further restated and re-emphasized in the more recent The National Academy of Sciences Future of Nursing 2020–2030 report funded by the Robert Wood Johnson Foundation, in stating that the responsibility of nursing leadership needs to focus on, "Creating and articulating the organization's vision and goals, listening, to the needs and aspirations of those working on the front line, providing direction, creating incentives for change, aligning and integrating improvement efforts, and creating a supportive environment that encourages and enables success" (NASEM, 2021, p. 137).

However, The Future of Nursing 2020–2030 report does not stop there. It further suggests that healthcare leadership has failed to advance health equity and that "a new generation of nurse leaders is now needed"

(NASEM, 2021, p. 275). This new generation of nursing leaders needs to lead with an understanding of the importance of the social determinants of health (SDOH) and diversity and the way in which SDOH impact health equity, especially for the most underserved individuals. Only in this way can new models of care be achieved to bring about improved patient experiences and outcomes. This will require a broad intersection of knowledge and skills.

There are two fundamental ways in which nursing leaders will be able to gain the necessary knowledge and skill set to lead with an intentional focus on improving health equity and the patient experience. One of those is through embedding leadership education throughout nursing curriculum at the undergraduate and graduate level that addresses what it means in a leadership role to connect an awareness of SDOH with patient outcomes. The second is through the principle of lifelong learning, fostered through ongoing evidence-based training and development opportunities that are embedded in the culture of all healthcare organizations. As noted in the Future of Nursing Report 2020–2030, Shapiro et al. (2006) eloquently suggests that "Nurses as a professional group manifest many characteristics of strong leadership- including courage, humility, caring, compassion, intelligence, empathy, awareness, and accountability" (NASEM, 2021, p. 277).

The Three Bs

The three Bs in this chapter are not to be confused with the three Bs of med-surg nursing, introduced in a blog by Wolters Kluwer (2014), referring to "broad, busy, and brimming" to describe the work experience of med-surg nurses. Rather, the three Bs here refer to *blame, burnout,* and *bullying.* These three phenomena have long been issues plaguing the nursing workforce and they require the special attention and focus of nursing leaders. They can have detrimental effects on patient care and the patient experience (Yellowless & Rea, 2022). *Blame* is situated in a type of organizational behavior that treats bad outcomes as a product of an individual or select groups of individual mistakes as opposed to or without regard to any contributing systems issues (Bolman & Deal, 2017). *Burnout,* according to the American Psychological Association (APA) (2023), is the feeling of "physical, emotional, or mental exhaustion, accompanied by decreased motivation, lowered performance, and negative attitudes towards oneself and others."

For the purpose of discussing burnout in the context of this chapter, the APA's definition will be used. And the third B, *bullying*, is defined by the U.S. Department of Health and Human Services (n.d.) as actions, such as "making threats, spreading rumors, attacking someone physically or verbally, and excluding someone from a group on purpose."

Blaming

One of the most significant outcomes of the earlier IOM reports is the concept of moving away from an individual blame culture to a culture where healthcare leadership focuses on a systems approach dedicated to root cause analysis as opposed to solely an individual approach. Systems have far-reaching effects on how individuals perform in any given work environment, and thus it is critical to look at errors through a systems lens. Bolman and Deal (2017) outline what they describe as common fallacies that people often ascribe to explaining problems or failures within an organization. The first is the act of blaming people and that failure is the result of blunders. The IOM (2004) defined these blunders in terms of active failures and notes that they often occur on the front lines. In the healthcare settings, these active failures are occurring during direct patient care.

> Active failures occur at the level of the front-line worker (e.g., airplane pilots; control room operators; healthcare workers, such as nurses, physicians, and pharmacist; and other operators of technology interfacing with people). Such failures are sometimes called the "sharp end" of an error. The types of errors committed by front-line workers involve phenomena such as lapses in memory, misreading or misinterpreting written data, incorrect performance of routine activity as a result of distraction or interruption, or simply human variation in fine motor skills.
>
> *IOM (2004)*

Broadening the definition of individual failure encompasses human behavior problems related to, for example, egotism, bad attitudes, abrasive personalities, neurotic tendencies, stupidity, and incompetence (Bolman & Deal, 2017). Humans by nature are often uncomfortable with ambiguity and often attach meaning to things they cannot explain regardless of whether it is correct. As such, blame is a tool employed to satisfy the psychological predisposition to resolve ambiguity by reducing uncertainty and mystery. When there can be no obvious assignment of blame of an individual, the second common fallacy is the act of placing blame on the larger bureaucracy, and this occurs when blame is placed on items such as a policy, procedures, and abundance of red tape, or unclear goals and strategic plans.

In this case it is easier to place blame in the collective hands of others as opposed to addressing the problems and devising ways to keep the failures from occurring. The third common fallacy lies in the act of assigning problems or failures to leaders or executives thirsting for power. It is an approach where those in executive or leadership roles advance their own self-interest over that of the organization. The authors conclude that each of these fallacies has a "kernel of truth" but oversimplify the explanation of problems and causes of failure.

Instead, to be effective, leaders need to understand four key characteristics. One is that *organizations are complex*, second that *organizations are surprising*, third that *organizations are deceptive*, and fourth *organizations are ambiguous* (Bolman & Deal, 2017). What makes organizations complex is that they are open systems and on a day-to-day basis there are ongoing changes, new challenges, and erratic environmental factors (internal and external). In other words, organizations will reflect the society in which they operate, both in historical and cultural dimensions (Scott & Davis, 2007). When there are multiple organizations across systems, as you often see with large healthcare systems that may include inpatient services, outpatient services, long-term care, and home care, it can get "messier" (Bolman & Deal, 2017, p. 32). Leadership approaches that prove to be more adept will be those that focus attention on a systems level approach, while not losing track of the inherent complexity of human behavior.

Burnout

In the wake of the COVID-19 pandemic, nursing leadership is facing an unprecedented crossroad. An intersection where there is mounting pressure to produce results-driven data that meets quality indicator benchmarks as part of pay-for performance-finance models and doing so in a time where there are record numbers of nurses leaving or intending to leave the workforce. Approximately 100,000 nurses left the workforce during the pandemic and by 2027, almost 900,000, or almost one-fifth of the 4.5 million total registered nurses, intend to leave the workforce (National Council of State Boards of Nursing [NCSBN], 2023).

The majority of those leaving the workforce or reporting an intent to leave over the next five years cited stress, burnout, and retirement as the top reasons for their intent to leave. Additionally, 62% of those surveyed by the NCSBN stated they experienced an increase in workload. Survey responses highlighted that nurses were feeling emotionally drained, used up, fatigued, burned out, and at the end of their rope. The report also noted that these feelings and issues were most prevalent among nurses with ten or fewer years of professional experience and this alone has contributed to the declining nursing workforce. Furthermore, nurses entering the profession are exhibiting decreased proficiency in nursing practice and assessment. These findings should not only concern nurse leaders and healthcare organizations, but the greater society at large as the adverse consequences of burnout can include poor patient outcomes, high turnover rates, increased cost, and clinical illness and suicide (NASEM, 2019; 2021).

The early 21st century has thrown a curve ball at those at the helm of healthcare organizations. Nursing leaders in particular whose focus has been on improving patient care through transformational leadership initiatives and strategic plans to reshape the delivery of care have seen their efforts thwarted by the enormous stress the COVID-19 pandemic placed on healthcare systems and the nurses who work in them. Nursing leaders are now contending with the vast number of nursing professionals who are leaving the workforce. Even prior to the COIVD-19 pandemic, the policies and regulations surrounding nursing work hours and workload were already driving the conversation in relationship to patient quality of care and safety (IOM, 2004).

With the growing attention to medical error rates, The Agency for Healthcare Research and Quality asked the IOM to investigate and bring understanding to how factors impacting the nursing workforce, such as nurse-to-bed ratios, mandatory overtime or extended work time, fatigue, poorly designed spaces, lack of support systems and communication channels to promote effective decision-making contributed to the bigger picture of medical errors, adverse events, the quality of patient care, and safety (IOM, 2004). At the time this new and growing exodus of nursing professionals from the healthcare workforce opened questions for new directions in healthcare leadership and the impact of the patient experience, but little has changed to slow the departure of nurses from the workforce or the increasing feelings of burnout.

In order to take care of others, nursing and other healthcare leaders need to similarly take care of nurses. In other words, it is not enough to encourage nurses to put on their face masks first, before taking care of others. Leaders must work to create the conditions to ensure that nurses feel empowered and confident in their ability to put on their face masks first. The snapshot of physical health of American nurses published in the NASEM (2021) Future of Nursing report 2020–2030 shared startling evidence of a less than healthy nursing workforce. Some highlights include a nursing workforce that is struggling with obesity and being overweight, which is in part attributed to a lack of regular exercise and limited access to employer-based exercise facilities and healthy food choices at work. Other issues included lack of sleep and overall health issues faced by shift workers, including an increased risk for cardiovascular disease and work-related injury with nearly 80% of newly licensed nurses working 12-hour shifts.

In addition, newly licensed nurses worked 44% of the nightshifts as well as little over 60% of the mandatory or voluntary overtime (NASEM, 2021, p. 307). Given these reports on the health of the nursing workforce it is not surprising to frequently see reports about nursing burnout. While nurses experiencing burnout on a personal level is in and of itself of great concern, nursing burnout has a compounding effect in that it has a direct impact on patient care. For both of these reasons nursing leadership needs to develop expertise in the prevention of burnout, both for the good of the individual nurses but also to promote improved patient care.

Bullying

Working in a blaming culture and under the conditions predisposing nurses to burnout should be enough to alarm nursing leaders. The ANA has also reported that those in the healthcare professions are experiencing bullying and incivility in multiple types of healthcare settings (Chenot, 2020). It is most certainly for this reason that in a review of top issues that nursing leadership needs to be mindful of, understand, and address workplace violence, bullying, and incivility all make the list.

Evidence of the attention to workplace violence, bullying, and incivility is found across nursing literature and scholarship. The phenomenon is also a concern to organizations concerned with the quality and safety of patient care such as the ANA, the Joint Commission, and National Institute of Health. Considerations for nursing leadership regarding these untoward workplace behaviors include ethical, moral, and legal implications (American Nurses

Association [ANA], 2015). Bullying may be defined as the repeated, unwanted actions intended to humiliate, offend, and cause distress in the recipient and that such actions can harm, undermine, and degrade a person (ANA, 2015). While bullying and incivility can occur between any persons in a healthcare setting, the most frequently reported bullying occurs horizontally between nursing co-workers (Granstra, 2015; Marquis & Huston, 2017)

Incivility on the other hand is defined as rude and discourteous actions, of gossiping and spreading rumors, and of refusing to assist a co-worker (ANA, 2015). Bullying and incivility are not only significant issues in nursing because of their effects on the work environment and the toll on an individual's overall health and well-being, but also because it impacts the patient experience. The distractions and emotional distress caused by workplace violence can cause distractions and put patients at risk (Armstrong, 2018). By endangering the nurse as well as the patient, workplace violence jeopardizes not only the nursing profession, but nursing's contract with society more broadly (Saltzberg, 2011).

Left unchecked, bullying and incivility in the workplace can produce determinantal and harmful effects that are additive and create compounding burdens that can accelerate in intensity (ANA, 2015). For this reason, the ANA has a clear position statement on incivility, bullying, and workplace violence. These issues need to remain front and center in any discussion of nursing leadership and the patient experience. While it would be nice to think that nurses, who are drawn to a profession to provide empathy and care to others, would not be engaging in acts of bullying and incivility toward each other in the workplace, that is unfortunately not the case, and therefore the problem requires the active and ongoing attention of nurse leadership. The ANA's Code of Conduct is clear on the point that all nurses in all practice settings should actively work to establish and maintain a work environment characterized by respect and collaboration and not conducive to and free of incivility, bullying, and workplace violence. (ANA, 2015; Marquis & Huston, 2017)

The *ANA Code of Ethics for Nurses with Interpretive Statements* further advances the position regarding this matter and the role of nurses regarding acts of bullying, incivility, and workplace violence by stating that "The nurse creates an ethical environment and culture of civility and kindness, treating colleagues, coworkers, employees, students, and others with dignity, and respect." Other experts go further to state that bullying needs to be addressed beginning in nursing education programs, and then educational programming needs to continue into the workplace. Teri Chendot, EdD, MS.

MSN, RN, CCCE, FNAP, FAAN, a member of the ANA Center for Ethics and Human Rights Advisory Board, boldly states that "Healthcare systems need to promote positive values and a healthy work environment. Healthcare leadership must develop orientations, onboarding, and residency programs that include procedures for handling bullying and incivility issues" (2020, para. 8).

Moving beyond the Three Bs: Building Resilience and a Learning Culture

In a study conducted by McNicholas et al. (2017), researchers hypothesized that by improving nursing satisfaction there would be a marked improvement in the patient experience. The study, while small but reflective of other studies, focused on measuring change through nursing satisfaction surveys, post-discharge patient telephone debriefing, and patient Press Ganey scores. Through the implementation of additional supportive structures for patients and nursing centered around the discharge process on a 28-bed medical-surgical trauma unit they were able to see an immediate impact as measured through nursing satisfaction scores through the National Database of Nursing Quality Improvement RN satisfaction survey results and improved Press Ganey Results, where scores indicated improved patient satisfaction on nursing related indices but also on physician indices as well.

While every patient care unit or healthcare system will have different areas in need of improvement, this study serves as an example of how important it is to identify where nursing practice impacts patient satisfaction and the importance of setting a goal, applying measurement, implementing changes, and then establishing a process of evaluation. This strategy should be in the toolbox of every nursing leader. It is also the case that oftentimes changes are implemented with direction and measurement strategies, even though everything cannot always be measured. In the case where the metrics do not fully capture the phenomenon of interest, there may be other factors that need to be considered and reflected on, and in these instances, surrogation or the process of focusing strategy on metrics alone can lead down an incorrect path or direct the focus where it should not be (Ford, 2022). Being mindful of both the quantitative metrics available and the qualitative story can enrich the development of meaningful changes.

Resilience in nursing is a key factor influencing nursing satisfaction and thus a positive patient experience (Brown, Wey, & Foland, 2018; Meier et al.,

2019). It is not surprising that "resilience" is noted throughout the Future of Nursing 2020–2023: Charting a Path to Achieve Health Equity. The NASEM (2021) most recent report mentions "resilience" throughout the document. The report recommends that promoting nursing resilience is critical to nursing well-being as well as "ensuring the delivery of high-quality care and improving the health of our communities" (p. 25). Resilience acts as what NASEM refers to as a mediating factor in helping clinicians on the front line avoid burnout and ensure well-being as they work day to day in an environment where the demands of the job are influenced by a number of demands and much change.

Nursing leaders and others in healthcare leadership who can foster an environment supporting a culture of resilience are critical to improving the patient experience. Meier et al. (2019) note that leaders need their attention focused on "holistic learning, respite, and engagement." It is in this way that leaders will be able to provide a culture-fostering resilience in nursing. It follows then that for nurse leaders to promote an environment where nurses can be resilient and thus contribute to positive patient environments, it makes sense that nursing leaders aim to lead with attributes of a resilient leader.

Belasen (2022) provides a framework to understand the attributes of a resilient leader that suggests the attributes of resilient leaders include balancing the four specific attributes of being *adaptive, empathetic, analytical,* and *confident.* By *adaptive,* it means that leaders can adjust their circumstances through innovative ideas and promote supportive communication practices that align the goals of those both internal and external to an organization or any given unit.

The second attribute is of being *empathetic,* a practice well known to nurses when working with patients. In a leadership role being empathetic is about using active listening, asking the right questions, being self-aware, and using emotional intelligence. It is through using these characteristics of empathy that leaders can support and cultivate a collaborative environment and develop relationships. It is also in this way that nurse leaders can retain talent, inspire learning, and promote interprofessional collaboration, an ongoing challenge in any healthcare organization.

Third, being *analytical* as an attribute of a resilient leader includes referring to the ability "to align goals, behaviors, and process to sustain the reliability and efficiency" using critical analysis in an evidenced base manner to make rational choices and doing so with multiple stakeholders.

Fourth is the attribute of *confidence.* Being confident is about working with imperfect information and being able to take bold action (Belasen,

2022). But confidence is also about being "relentless" about pursuing performance targets and ensuring accountability for results. Doing so creates symbolic value and empowers care team members in a way that helps maintain focus on long-term goals using data. Decisive decision-making using rational thinking grounded in goals, data, and in some instances, uncertainly due to imperfective information are all aspects of a confident and informed leader who can efficiently pivot an organization and unit when needed because they are prepared. They did their homework. Healthcare leaders, or more specifically nursing leaders, face a number of daunting issues and moments of decision-making and by honing the attributes of resilient leaders they will be able to cultivate an environment where nurses will be able to thrive and be resilient.

It is important to note that transformational leadership style and strategies situated in an organizational structure defined as a "learning organizations" is the key to improving not only the quality of patient care but also decreasing cost and improving population health (IOM, 2001). Attributes of a *learning organization* go beyond proficiencies associated with day-to-day operational activity and characterize an organization in which leaders work together and with others to facilitate an environment that is collaborative, has core values of continuous growth, and is innovative in its mindset (Maccoby et al. 2013).

Peter Senge, organizational management scholar and founder of the Society for Organizational Learning, introduced the vision of a learning organization in 1990 in his book *The Fifth Discipline: The Art and Practice of the Learning Organization.* Senge purports that organizations such as healthcare organizations that find themselves in rapidly changing environments need a continuous learning mindset that is flexible, adaptive, and productive. There is an element of nurturing a growth mindset that fosters the creative capacities that allow organizations to not just survive but thrive. Importantly, learning organizations require different types of leaders; these include those that can network, who are strategic, creative, and those that that can move a vision to reality (Senge, 2006; Northouse, 2018).

In addition to the ANA and the AANC, the NASEM reinforces the need for and importance of nursing leadership in being central to healthcare reform, and it is for this reason among others that the American Nurses Credentialing Center reinforces nursing leadership in its awarding of Magnet Status. This discussion of Magnet is not meant to endorse the Credentialing Center, as there are many ways in which leadership practices can be embedded in an organization, but it is meant to serve as an example of the ways in which systems are supporting and embedding nursing leadership with healthcare organizations. This is also to say that there is not a "One fit Model" in promoting nursing leadership. The Credentialing Center designated the first Magnet hospitals in the 1990s and served to recognize hospitals for excellent nursing care, highlighting hospitals that both attracted high-quality nurses but also retained them (ANA, n.d.).

Recruitment and retention are closely tied to the practice environment and an organization's practice model. A nursing practice model and a corresponding practice environment that centers its strategy to empower nurses and provide nurses with a work environment where as professionals, nurses can lead patient care initiatives through innovation and leading the change initiatives. Magnet designation is the highest credential for a nursing facility to receive, and it measures factors related to both clinical nurse satisfactions and patient satisfaction. These components of the accreditation standards fall under the Magnet Component of Exemplary Professional Practice and provides language on practice, professional development, and the importance of collaboration in the delivery of patient care and communities (Meier et al., 2019).

The Magnet credentialling process includes a process of organizations meeting what Magnet refers to as empirical outcomes. It is within these outcomes where there is attention to nursing satisfaction and the patient experience. Magnet status is in part grounded in the principles that nurses who can work in an environment enabling them to provide the highest quality of care will be reflective of how nursing and patients report satisfaction. In other words, nursing satisfaction is tied to patient satisfaction which is tied to an environment that provides high-quality care.

Hospitals who seek Magnet status are required to report survey results asking nurses about "autonomy, professional development, leadership access and responsiveness, interprofessional relationships, fundamentals of quality nursing care, adequacy of resources and staffing, RN to RN teamwork and collaboration" (Meier et al., 2019, p. 520). However, organizations that excel in creating and maintaining environments that support best practices in leadership throughout an organization will best be able to adapt to the leadership needed in the dynamic and fluid healthcare sector.

Conclusion

As highlighted in this chapter, the stressors of the COVID-19 pandemic brought to the forefront critical issues related to nursing and more broadly healthcare leadership. Nurse leaders were called upon to make real-time decisions with often limited information and tight timelines. Effective leaders combined a knowledge of the complexities of healthcare systems and decision-making with a humble understanding that even with the best intentions, missteps would happen, and errors would be made. When identified, course correction involved looking at systems and performing versions of a root cause analysis rather than looking for individuals to blame. This type of leadership helps to prevent future problems and enhance patient outcomes and the overall patient experience.

Similarly, an openness to looking at systems will help effective nurse leaders achieve the goal of providing equitable, high-quality healthcare to the patients they care for, an overarching goal of the NASEM Future of Nursing 2020–2030 report. Likewise, effective nursing leaders will continue to make every effort to address the three Bs – blaming, burnout, and bullying. Focusing attention on reducing and eventually eliminating these common concerns must be a key piece of any effective nursing leader's playbook.

Creating resilient teams and installing a learning culture helps to hardwire these efforts and ultimately should lead to the creation of an organization that will consistently produce excellent patient outcomes and a positive patient experience. Magnet status is one example of recognition earned by some hospitals that have taken significant steps toward creating a culture dedicated to the highest levels of nursing care, thus demonstrating real commitment to positive patient outcomes. Ongoing commitment to these principles by leaders across the healthcare spectrum will only serve to enhance the development of the U.S. healthcare system.

References

American Nurses Association (ANA). (n.d.). *About Magnet.* American Nurses Credentialing Center. https://www.nursingworld.org/organizational-programs/magnet/about-magnet/

American Nurses Association (ANA). (2015). *Incivility, Bullying, and Workplace Violence.* American Nurses Position Statement. https://www.nursingworld.org/practice-policy/nursing-excellence/official-position-statements/id/incivility-bullying-and-workplace-violence/

American Psychological Association (APA). (2023). *APA Dictionary of Psychology: Burnout.* https://dictionary.apa.org/burnout

Armstrong, N. (2018). Management of nursing incivility in the health care settings: A systemicReview. *Workplace Health and Safety, 66*(8), 403–410. (https://doi.org/10.1177/2165079918771106)

Belasen, A. (2022). *Resilience in Healthcare Leadership: Practical Strategies and Self-Assessment Tools.* New York, NY: Routledge.Routledge. (https://doi.org/10.1093/intqhc/mzab036)

Belasen, A. T., Oppenlander, J., Belasen, A. R., & Hertelendy, A. (2021). Provider-patient communication and hospital ratings: Perceived gaps and forward thinking about the effects of COVID-19. *International Journal for Quality in Health Care*, 33(1). (https://doi.org/10.1093/intqhc/mzaa140)

Bolman, L. G. & Deal, T. E. (2017). *Reframing Organizations: Artistry, Choice, and Leadership* (6th ed.). Jossey-Bass. Hoboken, New Jersey.

Brown, R., Wey, H., Foland, K. (2018). The relationship among change fatigue, resilience, and job satisfaction of hospital staff nurses. *Journal of Nursing Scholarship*, 50(3), 306–313. https://doi.org/10/1111/jnu.12373

Burns, J. (1978). *Leadership.* Harper Row. New York, NY.

Chenot, T. (2020, May 9). Promoting civility in the workplace. *American Nurse Journal.* https://www.myamericannurse.com/promoting-civility-in-the-workplace/

Cronenwett, L. R., & Barnsteiner, J. (2017). National initiative: Quality and safety education for nurses, in Sherwood, G., & Barnsteaner, J. (Eds.), *Quality and Safety in Nursing: A Competency Approach to Improving Outcomes* (2nd ed., pp. 43–57). Wiley Blackwell.

Doody, O., & Doody, C. M. (2012). Transformational leadership in nursing practice. *British Journal of Nursing*, 21(20), 1212–1214. (https://doi.org/10.12968/bjon.2012.21.20.1212)

Dunton, N., Gajewski, B., Klaus, S., & Pierson, B. (2007, September 3). The relationship of nursing workforce characteristics to patient outcomes. *The Online Journal of Issues in Nursing*, 12(3). (https://doi.org/10.3912/OJIN.Vol12No03Man03)

Ford, E. (2022). You can't manage what you don't measure. *Journal of Healthcare Management*, 67(4), 221–222. (https://doi.org/10:1097/JHM-D-22-00114)

Granstra, K. (2015). Nurse against nurse: Horizontal bullying in the nursing professional. *Journal of Healthcare Management*, 4(6), 249–257.

Institute of Medicine (IOM). (2000). *To Err Is Human: Building a Safer Health System.* National Academies Press. Washington, D.C.

Institute of Medicine (IOM). (2001). *Crossing the Quality Chasm: A New Health System for the 21st Century.* National Academies Press. Washington, D.C.

Institute of Medicine (IOM). (2004). *Keeping Patients Safe: Transforming the Work Environment of Nurses. Committee on the Work Environment for Nurses and Patient Safety.* National Academies Press. Washington, D.C.

Marquis, B. L., & Huston, C. J. (2017). *Leadership Roles and Management Functions in Nursing: Theory and Application* (9th ed.). Woltzers Kluwer. Philadelphia, PA.

Maccoby, M., Norman, C. L., Norman, C. J., & Margolies, R. (2013). *Transforming health care leadership: A systems guide to improve patient care, decrease costs, and improve population health.* Jossey-Bass. San Francisco, CA.

McNicholas, A., McCall, A., Werner, A., Wounderly, R., Marinchak, E., & Jones, P. (2017). Improving patient experience through nursing satisfaction. *Journal of Trauma Nursing*, 24(6), 371–375.

Meier, A., Erikson, J. I., Snow, N., & Kline, M. (2019). Nurse and patient satisfaction: Magnet perspectives. *The Journal of Nursing Administration*, 49(11), S20–S22.

National Academies of Sciences, Engineering, and Medicine (NASEM). (2021). *The Future of Nursing 2020-2030: Charting a Path to Achieve Health Equity.* The National Academies Press. Washington, D.C. (https://doi.org/10.17226/25982)

National Academies of Sciences, Engineering, and Medicine (NASEM). (2019). *Taking action against clinician burnout: A systems approach to professional well-being.* The National Academies Press. Washington, D.C. DOI:10.17226/25521

National Council of State Boards of Nursing (NCSBN). (2023, April 13). *NCSBN Research Projects Significant Nursing Workforce Shortages and Crisis.* https://www.ncsbn.org/news/ncsbn-research-projects-significant-nursing-workforce-shortages-and-crisis

Northouse, P. G. (2013). *Leadership Theory and Practice* (6th ed.). Sage Publishing. Thousand Oaks, CA.

Northouse, P. G. (2018). *Introduction to Leadership: Concepts and Practice.* Sage Publishing. Thousand Oaks, CA.

Penque, S., & Kearney, G. (2015). The effect of nursing presence on patient satisfaction. *Nursing Management*, 46(4), 38–44.

Quality and Safety for Nurses (QSEN). (2022). *QSEN About.* QSEN: Francis Payne Bolton School of Nursing Case Western University. https://qsen.org/about-qsen/

Scott, R. W. & Davis, G. F. (2007), *Organizations and Organizing: rational, natural, and open system perspective.* Pearson Education, Inc. Upper Saddle River, New Jersey.

Senge, P. (2006). *The Fifth Discipline: The Art and Practice of the Learning Organization.* Random House Business. New York, NY.

Shapiro, M. L., Miller, J., White, K. (2006). Community transformation through culturally competent nursing leadership: Application of theory of culture care diversity and universality and tri-dimensional leader effectiveness model. *Journal of Transcultural Nursing*, 17(2). 113–118. (https://doi.org/10.1177/1043659605285413)

U.S. Department of Health and Human Services (n.d.). *What is Bullying.* https://www.stopbullying.gov/bullying/what-is-bullying

Wolters Kluwer. (2014, Sept. 14). *The Three Bs of Med-Surg Nursing.* Wolters Kluwer Expert Insights. https://www.wolterskluwer.com/en/expert-insights/the-three-bs-of-medsurg-nursing

Yellowless, P. & Rea, M. (2022, September 27). *Burnout.* Agency for Healthcare Research and Quality Patient Safety Network. https://psnet.ahrq.gov/primer/burnout

Chapter 7

Engaging Hospital Boards in Patient Safety and Quality of Care

Introduction

Each day, accounts of safety-related incidents in hospitals appear in news reports across the country. The issues are wide-ranging, for example, worker burnout leading to staffing instability, overcrowded conditions in Emergency Departments, cyberattacks threatening the integrity of patient data, dismissals of whistleblowers, and medication errors. If we were to compile the headlines, such a list could be endless, occupying multitudes of volumes. The purpose of this chapter is not to chronicle quality and safety incidents, but rather to (1) examine the underlying forces that have an influence on the work of boards of directors in order to gain insight into how and why such errors, accidents, and even calamities can occur and (2) identify strategies and actions that boards can undertake in order to foster more robust and effective organizational cultures of safety and quality of care.

We may start by asking, are most accidents preventable? Are they merely an inconsequential artifact of the massively high number of patients, 611,000, in hospitals on a given day (Statista, 2019)? Could the explanation be as simple as a certain number of improper or random occurrences due to the sheer volume of patient visits every day? And if so, perhaps we should just accept the notion that since it is impossible to prevent errors in the margins of the vast amount of work performed in healthcare facilities, we need not hand wring over the matter.

DOI: 10.4324/9781003431077-7

The short answer, of course, is an unequivocal "no." Certainly, preventing every single adverse event would be an unachievable endeavor. But the extraordinary number of such events is sobering. Austin and Derk (2016) claim that of the 34,305,620 annual hospital admissions, an estimated 161,250 are avoidable deaths [from safety-related issues] in U.S. hospitals each year. The causes are diverse. According to Dughi (2022), the most prevalent safety-related problems include exposure to bloodborne pathogens, catheter-associated urinary tract infections; diagnosis errors (delayed, wrong, missed); and hacked medical devices such as glucometers, heart rate monitors, MRIs, and pacemakers. This also includes data breaches that have affected millions of patient records; healthcare-associated venous thromboembolism, or blood clots, which the Centers for Disease Control (n.d.) claims accounts for one in ten hospital deaths and that nearly half of all hospital patients do not receive proper preventive measures; hospital-acquired pneumonias; medication errors; methicillin-resistant Staphylococcus aureus (MRSA); and hospital-based sepsis, from which one in three patients die.

The human toll from safety mishaps is, of course, the most significant. While some safety and quality events are minor, many, of course, are serious, even life-threatening. At the same time, the economic cost is staggering, ranging from $33 billion to $63 billion, estimates which reflect direct costs to hospitals without ambulatory services and readmission costs (Adler et al., 2018).

Of course, we should consider even one safety problem, especially one that leads to an undesired outcome, to be one too many. This is not a pie-in-the-sky fantasy, but rather the essence of the bedrock tenet of healthcare, and that is the pursuit of continuous quality improvement (CQI). O'Donnell and Gupta (2023) define this guiding principle of CQI as "a progressive incremental improvement of processes, safety, and patient care. The goal of CQI may include improvement of operations, outcomes, systems processes, improved work environment, or regulatory compliance."

CQI is the healthcare equivalent of striving to form a more perfect union. Above all, it proposes that the status quo must be regarded as more than a snapshot of where things stand but must also be considered foundational for a better tomorrow. That endeavor – to advance, to become more knowledgeable, more skilled, more driven to ensure that outcomes are good and that whatever interferes with that goal can be more capably defined and controlled – is doctrinal in healthcare. And anything that rises to the level of doctrinal, given its apex level of significance, must be viewed as central to the work of the institution's most authoritative body, the board of directors.

Boards of directors have the special obligation of creating a climate in which safety and outcome quality constitute driving forces in institutional policy and organizational culture. We may assume that no board wishes for patients to be at risk, much less harmed. And yet, as the data show, safety and quality risks occur at a more prevalent rate than should be considered acceptable. If intent is not the issue, then what might account for the disturbing data which indicate that too many patients experience an unsafe event during a hospital stay?

Plainly stated, safety and quality may fail to occupy the proper level of the board's attention. Again, this is not to suggest that these critical issues are absent from the board's radar. Quite presumably, they are on every board's radar. The key question is to what degree. And if the degree is not sufficient, what might be crowding it out? What other matters might be absorbing too much of their attention, diluting what might otherwise be a laser-like focus on safety and quality? But even more, we posit that when safety and quality are effectively and extensively integrated into the network of responsibilities addressed by boards – not as distinct or isolated phenomena to be addressed only when seemingly more urgent matters are remedied – the organization's overall effectiveness is strengthened.

A Board's Focus on Safety – What Gets in the Way

Broadly speaking, we may think of five main areas that hold the attention of healthcare organizations' boards: (1) funding and financial management, (2) strategic direction, (3) service orientation and service mix, (4) regulatory constraints, (4) reputation and image management, and (5) high reliability. These are all critical. The failure to attend any can prove problematic, if not perilous, for the organization. Well-functioning boards view these as highly interrelated, with each having an influence on the others. When this dynamic prevails, it is assumed that the organization's performance related to safety and quality will be more favorable than in those circumstances in which the board views these areas as predominantly discrete.

Each area is discussed here as a means of contextualizing the premise that safety and quality can become overshadowed within the board's priority spectrum. Following that, recommendations are offered for advancing the prospect of enhanced board attention to quality and safety. It is important to underscore the notion that an organization's management typically follows the board's lead with respect to priority development. Thus, if quality and safety are not placed in spotlight by the board, free of distraction, it will prove challenging for management to maintain its attention on them as well.

Funding and Financial Management

It goes without saying that financial management will be a primary focus of a hospital's board members, just as it would for board members of any organization. Any hospital board that does not treat financial management as a priority would be engaging in a dereliction of duty. In this regard, two areas of financial management are pertinent. One involves the processes associated with financial management, that the board ensures that record keeping, accounting, reporting, and related policies follow regulatory, legal, and related requirements (Anning et al., 2009).

If the first area of relevance to financial management involves the ability to demonstrate *compliance* with financial reporting, the second relates to the organization's financial *performance*. The metrics that are employed to assess financial performance should be comprehensive, empirically based, rooted in industry standards, and meaningful to goal development. To get a complete financial picture, a hospital would employ a broad range of key performance indicators beyond revenue and expenses, including trends related to patient days, utilization, payer mix, length of stay, productivity, cash on hand, and service volumes, not to mention detailed analyses of Profit & Loss (P&L) data, operating margins, and competitor performance.

The central issue is not whether financial management is important, but whether the economic and financial environment facing hospitals makes it difficult to maintain a laser-like focus on safety and quality. Referencing a comprehensive report by Kaufman Hall, the American Hospital Association (2022) indicated that the financial outlook for hospitals is bleak. They noted that margins are down 37% relative to pre-pandemic levels; and that annual labor and operating costs across the healthcare industry are on the rise.

For the majority of hospitals in the United States, such a grim financial picture is daunting. Strategic plans focus on service line expansion, market growth, and cost containment. It would be imprudent for hospital boards not to devote time and energy to strategy formulation related to opportunities on both sides of the revenue and expense equation. Within that sphere lies safety and quality. Considering the unfavorable outlook, it would not be unexpected for a healthcare organization to succumb to the temptation to pare expenses to the point that standards are minimally met in vital areas like staffing, reporting requirements, training and education, and qualification requirements for staff. In fact, as Gooch (2023) points out, in the period of September 2022 to May 2023 alone, 53 hospital/health systems have trimmed their workforces or jobs due to financial and operational challenges.

As staff levels get close to the minimum requirements, potentially dipping below, the probability of safety and quality mishaps intensifies. In a survey of nurses across 357 hospitals, Aiken et al. (2022) concluded that even pre-pandemic hospital working conditions will not match the level of disruptions in hospital care that have persisted even as the pandemic has subsided.

Over the last 20 years, more than 100 studies by academic researchers have produced evidence confirming the link between inadequate hospital nurse-to-patient staffing levels and poor patient outcomes up to and including unnecessary death… it is not unusual for many hospitals across the country to set nurse-to-patient workloads higher [than recommended standards]. One reason hospital administrators do this is to lower costs by having fewer nurse employees, meanwhile, they can press the remaining nurses to work harder. But this spreads less nursing care across a larger group of patients and can have very serious consequences (Levins, 2023).

Moreover, inadequate staffing can morph into a vicious cycle as stress and burnout among existing staff impose pressures on recruitment, retention, and productivity enhancement initiatives. While the COVID-19 pandemic intensified burnout across wide swaths of the healthcare workforce, high levels of stress had already been prevalent. For example, according to the National Academies of Sciences, Engineering, and Medicine (2019), prior to the pandemic, between 35 and 54% of nurses reported symptoms of burnout. Stress levels are compounded by worker shortages in critical areas, including a shortage of between 54,100 and 139,000 physicians by 2033 (Boyle, 2020).

Boards of directors, therefore, confront an economic landscape with considerable economic challenges – worker shortages, higher stress levels in the workforce, and troubling trends related to escalating expenses unmatched by revenue increase potential. In such a scenario, it may prove challenging for safety and quality to receive a robust level of attention. Compounding the problem is the aging of the population. Long et al. (2013) demonstrate that older patients are at greater risk of a safety event, often significantly so, than younger patients. Contributing factors include heightened levels of frailty, extended stays, cognition and retention diminishment, and polypharmacy complications (Lavan & Gallagher, 2015). Given the aging patient environment, the risks associated with safety and quality have increased, while the resource environment has become more tenuous. It is in this challenging framework of competing forces that boards of directors in healthcare organizations operate. Organizational performance is decidedly dependent on how effectively they can develop strategies that reconcile them.

Strategic Direction

Forty years ago, in the pre-merger and acquisition (M&A) era, strategy was confined to the vision achievement of a single hospital entity. Today, with most hospitals belonging to systems, strategy relates to a broader and more complex set of variables. These include how to build configurations of partners to solidify and grow market share, leverage reimbursement opportunity, achieve economies of scale, and create continuity of care and referral networks. For example, St. Louis-based Ascension Health, which operates 139 hospitals, has targeted billions of dollars of opportunities in cost optimization and service line and revenue growth (Landi, 2023).

Another example involves the recent merger of Aurora Health and Atrium Health, with market coverage across Illinois, Wisconsin, North Carolina, South Carolina, Georgia, and Alabama. It will serve 5.5 million patients, operate more than 1,000 sites of care and 67 hospitals, employ more than 7,600 physicians and nearly 150,000 teammates, and have combined annual revenues of more than $27 billion (Atrium Health News, 2022). These examples are representative of the scope of strategic focus in the healthcare sector today. And considering the challenges associated with unfavorable revenue-expense imbalance, finding ways to achieve financial stability and reinvigorate the budgetary outlook requires dedicated strategic planning.

To devote the proper attention, energy, expertise, and resources to strategic planning, healthcare organizations must assemble boards of directors that bring relevant experience, knowledge, and talent. As discussed elsewhere in the book, it is not surprising that only about 15% of board members have healthcare backgrounds, while over 50% of board members have finance or business backgrounds. Of course, safety and quality may be – and should be – integrated into strategic thinking and planning. But if those who possess the relevant expertise occupy only a few board seats, and if deliberations regarding strategy are too dominated by other perspectives, namely business and finance, then safety and quality may not receive high priority.

Strategy development is central to the work of a board of directors. Strategy can be targeted or encompassing, short-term or long-term, oriented toward cost containment or growth, and driven by evidence or speculation. It is up to each healthcare organization to determine the goals and the scope of strategy, the timeframe for implementation, and the process by which it gathers data and mobilizes stakeholders to participate. But one thing is certain: if the various processes associated with strategic plan development and implementation are not inclusive and fail to balance short- and long-term objectives, and if staff development is viewed as an expense as opposed to an investment, the probability of building a culture of safety and patient satisfaction may be compromised.

Service Orientation and Service Mix

Over the past 50 years, there has been a steady increase in any given board's understanding of who comprises the hospital's patient population, including who they are demographically and how they are treated. There are three underlying reasons for this accelerating focus. First, one would hope that such a trend is grounded in the ethical obligations of hospitals to honor the dignities afforded to patients by the Patient Bill of Rights, among them the right to considerate and respectful care (American Hospital Association, n.d.). Second, the healthcare industry has increasingly factored the patient's perception of care and level of satisfaction into matters of regulatory compliance (Heuer, 2004) as well as reimbursement (Centers for Medicare & Medicaid Services, n.d.).

Third, patient satisfaction has emerged as a significant factor with respect to image maintenance, reputation, marketing strategy, and market development. It is presumed that market development would be hampered to the extent that a hospital is unable to deliver on its commitment to create an organizational culture conducive to patient satisfaction. As such, a strong service orientation, which is an important precondition to securing high levels of patient satisfaction, and service mix, i.e., the clinical and educational offering, are interrelated.

Boards cannot turn a blind eye to patient satisfaction and service offerings. Aside from the ethical imperative, the hospital's financial well-being and strategic disposition are dependent on it. Thus, the potential loss of revenue associated with a poor HCAHPS rating as well as the potential revenue gain from a positive rating has elevated patient satisfaction to a key institutional and, thus, board priority.

> Improving the patient experience can help a hospital improve its financial performance by strengthening customer loyalty, building reputation and brand, and boosting utilization of hospital services through increased referrals to family and friends. Furthermore, research has shown that better patient experience correlates with lower medical malpractice risk for physicians and lower staff turnover ratios." Moreover, Baird also references the finding that "a 10 percentage-point increase in the number of respondents giving a hospital a … 9 or 10 out of 10 rating is associated with an increase in net margin of 1.4%" (Baird, 2019).

Again, this would not automatically crowd out safety and quality as board priorities. In fact, satisfaction is positively linked with safety and security. When they are viewed as interrelated, progress is achievable. When they are viewed as discrete, progress may be made but it may prove transitory. For example, a hospital seeking to make constructive inroads in response to less than desirable patient satisfaction survey results may, understandably, institute interpersonal training programs for staff. But if the core problem is not related to lack of empathy or communication skill deficiencies, the training may not yield positive and sustainable results. If, say, the issue is one of worker burnout, employees may come to feel that the training lacks relevance. If that occurs, not only might extended compliance with the goals of the training fail to materialize, but staff could become resentful if they believe they are being scapegoated for a problem they did not create.

Boards of directors have the special obligation of ensuring that organizational strategy is well-developed. This includes addressing the notion of institutional culture, that is, to work toward ensuring that the climate is hospitable to high levels of patient satisfaction. A hospital not perceived as "employee-centered" by those working there is less likely to be perceived as "patient-centered" by those who come for care. And if the hospital does not promote safety and quality as core institutional prerogatives, with a sincere concern for employee safety and quality of work experience, it is unlikely to achieve consistently high levels of either centeredness.

Regulatory Environment

Healthcare is among the most heavily regulated industries in the world, and certainly in the United States. Regulations cover a virtually endless array of activities. While diagnosis and the provision of care occupy a central domain of regulatory oversight, it is far from the only one. The following is a partial list of functions and activities that are also subject to regulation from a wide variety of bodies, including the Joint Commission and other accrediting organizations, numerous federal agencies, state departments of health, and insurance regulators: patient privacy rules, including medical records retention and HIPAA compliance; hospital and bed licensing and registration; accreditation; medical practice activity and reporting requirements; capital acquisition and new technology development; diagnosis and treatment protocols; licensing of healthcare workers; housekeeping and environment controls; public health policy and application, and end of life and withdrawal of life support (Eisenberg, 2015).

The effort and expense associated with regulatory compliance and reporting are enormous. The American Hospital Association (2017) estimated that an average-sized community hospital (161 beds) spends nearly $7.6 million annually on administrative activities to support compliance with the reviewed federal regulations. This equates to an overall national expense of $39 billion or about $47,000 per hospital bed. Additionally, as the AHA reports, an average hospital dedicates 59 full-time equivalents (FTEs) to regulatory compliance.

A significant number of regulations relate to safety and quality, including, for example, the noteworthy regulatory attention to conditions of participation. CoPs, as they are called, are qualifications developed by CMS that healthcare organizations must meet in order to maintain their participation in federally funded healthcare programs such as Medicaid, Medicare, and children's insurance programs (HealthStream Resources, 2021).

Despite the enormity of the regulation network, three concerns regarding safety and quality persist, specifically that time and attention related to reporting detracts from actual patient care. First, the considerable number of reporting requirements across federal, state, and local agencies create a substantial amount of administrative work for healthcare organizations. According to the American Hospital Association, "Health systems, hospitals and PAC providers [post-acute care] must comply with 629 discrete regulatory requirements across nine domains," which include Hospital CoPs, program integrity, fraud and abuse; privacy and security; billing and coverage; quality reporting; new models of care; meaningful use; and post-acute care (American Hospital Association, 2017).

Second, rules and regulations are updated at a pace that can prove oppressive for organizations to manage. By way of example, healthcare organizations had a narrow window of four months to implement a Centers for Medicare & Medicaid Services (2016) final rule policy on physician fee schedules. The short time between announcement and implementation created a stir since compliance demanded sweeping changes to payment policies, complex IT reprogramming, and substantial education for a broad range of coding, finance, intake, and administrative personnel. The Association of American Medical Colleges (2016) opposed the plan, describing it as a "burdensome and complex data collection process."

Third, the reporting requirements related to quality can be cumbersome, grounded in inefficiencies, and involve duplication of effort, particularly for providers engaged in value-based purchasing (American Hospital Association, 2017). Moreover, because of the complexity and multiple replication of demands, up to 25% of clinical FTEs, including physicians, nurses, and others, are dedicated to report-generating activities and compliance (American Hospital Association, 2017). It is also not uncommon for unplanned demands to be made upon clinical workers to remove themselves from patient care activities to support a compliance project.

Boards of directors are the most authoritatively accountable body for compliance. As such, they are compelled to devote attention to ensuring that the institutional mechanisms for safety and security are well-established and protocols are followed. And yet, as the data have shown, the extent of mishaps, errors, and accidents is higher than desired levels. This should be a clarion call for boards to reimagine priority development, devote time, energy, and resources to be certain they are sufficiently grounded in compliance, and examine their membership composition to be certain that it includes more than token expertise in this very vital area.

Reputation and Image Management

The reputation of a hospital and its performance from an evidence-based perspective are linked. After all, among the factors that contribute to perceptions of reputation are data about outcomes that are publicly available. But the connection between reputation and evidence is hardly fixed, or even strong for that matter. Take the example of the *U.S. News Best Hospitals* report, considered the healthcare equivalent to the *Good Housekeeping* Seal of Approval, which is often touted as "a signal to consumers that a product can be trusted" (Stiehm, 2019). The *U.S. News Best Hospitals* rankings have been employed extensively in marketing and advertising campaigns and have been used in the political arena to advocate for policy positions.

But as much as reputation is influenced by evidence and data, it is also shaped by perception. A clean hospital is more likely to be viewed as a competent hospital. There may be some legitimate basis for drawing such a conclusion since cleanliness does not come about without effort, and if effort is devoted to environmental maintenance, the thinking goes, it may also be devoted to other areas of institutional activity, like patient care. But the leaps required to make such a judgment render it, at best, syllogistically questionable.

An examination of the data underlying the U.S. *News Best Hospitals* rankings demonstrates the point that the rankings are based largely on perception rather than evidence (Sehgal, 2010). The subjective component in the rankings was derived from compiling perceptions of reputation from 250 physicians from around the county. The study correlates such reputation scores with more objective measures of quality, including nurse-to-patient ratios, nurse Magnet hospital designation, availability of key medical technologies, and the degree to which standards were met based on data from the American Hospital Association and American Nursing Association. Moreover, the top-ranked hospitals earned their place on the list primarily from subjective reputation and not the objective measures regarding hospital quality. As Sehgal (2010) points out: "Little relationship exists between reputation and objective measures in the top 50 hospitals."

The report's rankings are reinforced through messaging to the communities served by the honored hospitals. For example, New Jersey's Atlantic Health System announced in a widely distributed press release that the Atlantic Health System's (2022) Morristown Medical Center rated number one hospital in New Jersey for the fifth year in a row by U.S. News & World Report. Such messages are amplified in news reports, other media, and through word-of-mouth. Thus, a positive ranking creates momentum for future positive rankings.

Boards of directors take institutional reputation quite seriously, of course. And they should. But safety and quality problems are conceivably unfavorable, potentially at odds with goals associated with reputation maintenance. And while there are multiple mechanisms required of healthcare organizations to monitor, track, and report on incidents, such mechanisms are not fully employed (Binder, 2021). This could be a function of a patient failing to report an incident, a belief on the part of an employee or a supervisor that the infraction does not warrant reporting, senior management deemphasizing such problems in its reporting, or the board relegating such information as unworthy of considerable attention in its reports. Hospitals reporting of harmful events is quite low, with some estimates as low as 1% (Allen, 2012).

Among the problems associated with underreporting safety or quality incidents is the loss of an opportunity to improve. Thus, such failures are antithetical to the principle of CQI. Boards of directors have a distinct responsibility for creating a climate in which reporting incidents is encouraged. The probability of reporting is strengthened to the extent that CQI is a dominant feature of the organizational culture. Further, boards that recognize that faithfulness to CQI is linked to long-term and ongoing reputational integrity would be expected to oversee organizations that have favorable records with respect to safety and quality.

High Reliability

Healthcare organizations are included in the industry classification known as high-reliability organizations or HROs. Understandably, safety and quality would be central concerns for organizations that are obligated by law, regulation, and ethics to establish and strive for error-free goals. Five characteristics of HROs pertain to safety; three are associated with *anticipating* errors and include having monitoring and warning structures in place; understanding the potentially complex array of factors that contribute to error; and recognizing that errors are generally related to ineffective or inefficient interrelationships among the components of a system. The two characteristics associated with effective *containment* of errors include an organizational willingness to learn, grow, and adapt from errors and ensuring that the necessary expertise to manage error is available and fully consulted (Weick & Sutcliffe, 2007).

In 2010, the American Nurses Association adopted a position statement by the Congress on Nursing Practice and Economics on a *Just Culture* model with the goals of strengthening the probability of a safe environment for those who work in healthcare facilities and those who come for care.

The Just Culture model, which has been widely used in the aviation industry, seeks to create an environment that encourages individuals to report mistakes so that the precursors to errors can be better understood to fix the system issues… [the model] is an ideal fit for healthcare systems, where errors have just as serious consequences. By promoting system improvements over individual punishment, a Just Culture in healthcare does much to improve patient safety, reduce errors, and give nurses and other healthcare workers a major stake in the improvement process (American Nurses Association, 2010).

The lens through which boards of directors view their organizations are most telling with respect to whether initiatives like Just Culture take root and gain traction or are subservient to or obscured by other organizational priorities. While grassroots initiatives can mobilize organizations and invigorate positive change, including, by the way, persuading an organization's leadership and board to embrace and support change, without board support, such initiatives are unlikely to be sustained. The Just Culture policy, like many such policies and programs that seek to construct a climate in which safety is paramount, is most likely to come to fruition when it has the full backing of the board of directors.

Board Initiatives to Achieve a Safety Culture

While it is presumed that all boards would be inclined to support safety-related actions, the difference between lip service and meaningful support lies in the commitment of resources and the active and ongoing encouragement provided to senior management to keep safety and quality at the forefront of priority development. And yet, doing so has been challenging. This is not surprising considering the other imperatives which compete for a board's attention, including the unfavorable economic and financial outlook, pressures from competition, and ever-advancing technologies that test an organization's capacity to remain current. In such an environment, winning or losing depends on high levels of acumen for strategy development.

For safety and quality to achieve the necessary status of sustained priority, boards are encouraged to devote energy and attention to six pursuits: (1) promote a values-driven culture of communication and transparency, (2) integrate board-related priorities, (3) align board composition with a safety and quality priority environment, (4) institute training and development for board members on safety and quality, and (5) ensure that mechanisms for safety management and reporting are well-established and accessible.

Promote a Values-Driven Culture of Communication and Transparency

As part of its commitment to promote high reliability in healthcare, the Joint Commission (2018) urges organizations "to establish a safety culture that fosters trust in reporting unsafe conditions to ensure high-quality patient care". A report by the Institute of Medicine (IOM) underscores the notion that culture is central to a safe healthcare environment, and that absent such a culture even the most effective protocols can prove insufficient in safeguarding the organization from error. This is because even the most highly trained workforce is capable of being fallible. So are even the most seemingly foolproof work processes. Accordingly, promoting patient and workforce safety requires measures that go beyond staff training and the engineering of effective work processes. It requires an organizational dedication to remaining vigilant for error detection, assessment, resolution, follow-up, and learning (Page, 2004). When this cycle is embedded in expectations for how the organization conducts its work, it may be said to have a culture of safety.

The basic notion of culture is that it is a shared sense of norms, customs, and beliefs that manifest in predictable patterns of conduct. But by focusing on the implications and nuances of conduct, we understand that culture is a phenomenon reinforced through the interplay of extrinsic and intrinsic forces, bound by rituals which serve as social bonding agents, and comprised subcultures (Watkins, 2013).

The gap between the importance of organizational culture and a board's understanding of it is perhaps greater than the gaps in other areas of board responsibility. For example, recent studies indicate that more than 80% of directors don't have a firm grasp on the culture that exists in the organizations they serve. Most directors would be hard-pressed to define corporate culture, and those who can don't always know what their role should be in influencing it (Henman, 2019).

The gap should come as no surprise for at least two reasons. First, sensitivity to organizational culture is less likely to be present as the distance between the board and the corporation's organizational members widens. Social science research is clear about the phenomenon that culture can be apprehended most effectively when the researcher adopts a participant-observer perspective. Three activities are fundamental to a participant-observer perspective: (1) locating oneself in the community one wishes to study, (2) creating relationships with members of the community; and (3) devoting sufficient time to obtain relevant data (Guest et al., 2013).

The same would hold for a board of directors. And yet, in healthcare, the very phenomenon of hospital system expansion has moved boards – in this case, the parent or corporate boards – further from an ability to experience firsthand the cultures of the various corporate entities they oversee.

Second, organizational cultures are not monolithic (Watkins, 2013). As the healthcare environment has grown progressively competitive, senior management has had to focus more and more on securing an advantaged position in a market that demands alliance building and competition management. Accordingly, hospital system leadership has come to be increasingly characterized by an entrepreneurial culture, its transformational orientation growing ever more distinct from the transactional work culture demanded of middle management who must attend to the necessities of operational stability. Given the enormity of demands to maintain competitive viability in the high-stakes and big business climate of healthcare, boards of directors at the corporate level may be even more apt than their executives to be significantly predisposed to have fomented a board culture of entrepreneurship.

If it has become more difficult in recent years for boards of directors to become sensitive to the cultures of their organizations' member providers, there are at least three principles they should embrace to close the gap. First, boards are encouraged to place greater emphasis on values, or core beliefs, in managing relationships and communications with employees. Employees seek connections to their organizations and are motivated when they perceive alignment between their personal values and those of the organization. Indeed, it is important for employees to believe that their organization's leadership is dedicated to and capable of achieving organizational success. But it is of equal or greater importance for employees to understand that its leadership and governance are values driven.

The Cleveland Clinic provides a useful example of a statement of values. It is instructive to note that the order in which values are expressed is indicative of their relative importance. With respect to the Cleveland Clinic, the first five relate to caring about people and the commitment to a respectful environment. It is not until the sixth and final value that reference is made to the work or output of the organization.

THE CLEVELAND CLINIC STATEMENT OF VALUES

- Quality and safety – We ensure the highest standards and excellent outcomes through effective interactions, decision-making, and actions.
- Empathy – We imagine what another person is going through, work to alleviate suffering, and create joy whenever possible.
- Inclusion – We intentionally create an environment of compassionate belonging where all are valued and respected.
- Integrity – We adhere to high moral principles and professional standards with a commitment to honesty, confidentiality, trust, respect, and transparency.
- Teamwork – We work together to ensure the best possible care, safety, and well-being of our patients and fellow caregivers.
- Innovation – We drive small and large changes to transform healthcare everywhere.

The Cleveland Clinic (n.d.)

But statements of values are not enough if they are not suitably communicated and if those with the highest authority for safeguarding those values are not viewed as role models. Madonko and April (2020) identify a complementary set of interaction purposes that encompass both relationship and substantive information needs. The former, defined as relational, comprise signals that suggest how the organization and its leadership regard employees. To the extent that employees perceive the communication as two-way, that space in the communication environment is created for their input, that consultation with staff prior to decision-making is honored, and that meaningful engagement with employees constitutes an organizational priority, then the values espoused in publicly stated values statements are likely to be perceived as sincere.

Tactical messages are denotative and include information about specific organizational activity. If relational messages are largely symbolic, that is, they communicate how we perceive the relationship, then tactical messages are about substance, the purpose and work of the organization. These communication dimensions go hand in hand. Leadership that expresses a commitment to seek employee input in decision-making but fails to do so in practice invites frustration or cynicism.

An initiative like *Just Culture* is a case in point. It stipulates: "Traditionally, healthcare's culture has held individuals accountable for all errors or mishaps that befall patients under their care. By contrast, a *Just Culture* recognizes that individual practitioners should not be held accountable for system failings over which they have no control" (American Nurses Association, 2010). Such a policy dignifies the employee relational perspective while alluding to the need for a comprehensive examination of the system's effectiveness from a tactical perspective.

The governance board holds the ultimate authority and responsibility for creating a communication climate in which relational and tactical communication are practiced, but of greater significance, that they are in alignment. When both are present and in sync, trust between the board, senior management, and employees is concomitantly probable. In an era in which distance between the board and rank-and-file has grown – at both proximity and organizational levels – board leadership is strongly encouraged to work diligently to not permit those barriers to encroach on communication goals. The greater the board's transparency and laser-like focus on communication, the more productive and satisfying the culture. And when that occurs, when employees feel respected, their commitment to CQI and safety is sure to be strengthened.

Integration of Priorities

Research on priority formulation in hospitals and hospital systems suggests that priority setting accounts for macro and micro levels of activity, but far less on the "meso" level, that is, the connective tissue comprised of rules and linkages between the panoramic macro and narrow micro views (Martin et al., 2003). The fiduciary obligations of boards and trends in healthcare over the past few decades explain why.

With respect to fiduciary obligations, boards have defensive as well as prosperity achievement functions. The former compels the board to protect the organization, including from harm related to legal, financial, regulatory, and reputational risk. The latter demands that risk be considered. After all, the healthcare environment is not static, demanding that organizations continuously evaluate and strengthen their prospects with respect to ally/competitor networks and resource investments in infrastructure, program development, talent, and market base. It would not be unusual for risk and safety to constitute conflicting parameters. The more conservative the board, the more likely it would be to adopt a risk-averse posture, encouraging seemingly safer choices from within the spectrum of strategic options. A more enterprising board may be inclined to adopt positions with higher probabilities of both the magnitude of the outcome benefit and the uncertainty of achieving it.

Trends in healthcare have contributed to the tendency to compartmentalize priorities. Once the transition from fee-for-service to prospective payment got underway, the nature of the healthcare industry changed. Most especially, the shift injected a considerably heightened competitiveness into the industry, setting off the relatively unabated pursuit of mergers and acquisitions. It is not surprising to learn that corporate boards of hospital systems would be preoccupied with their position in the marketplace and would devote much energy to strategic priorities that focus on the risk side of the equation. In such a market-driven atmosphere, safety could take a back seat to the system's economic welfare.

Thus, it is not surprising that 72% of chairs of boards of directors in England, a nation with a national health program, view safety and quality as the top priority, while only 31% of U.S. board chairs viewed those matters as the paramount priority for board oversight (Jha & Epstein, 2013) The latter were more inclined to reference financial and business performance as the top board priority. This proclivity is reinforced in trends of board meeting agendas: whereas 98% of British hospitals included safety and quality at every meeting, only 68% of hospital board meetings in the U.S. did so.

These findings should not be taken to imply that safety is ignored. However, they would suggest that the decision-making culture has tended to emphasize growth over stability. Growth need not always suggest expansion of the number of institutional entities in the system. It can refer as well to program growth, market share growth, and infrastructure development.

Integrating priorities is a key challenge for leadership. Board leaders who create a deliberation and decision-making culture in which priorities are linked enhance their organization's success potential. For example, safety training may be viewed as a cost or as an investment. If the former, training may be approved only insofar that it satisfies a regulatory requirement but would not be sufficient to make a meaningful difference with respect to elevating the safety capabilities of the organization. Conversely, if safety training is viewed as an investment, it should lead to enhanced awareness and skills in the workplace. Likely, the tangible benefit would exceed the cost of the training by reducing safety-related incidents, strengthening quality of outcomes and thereby for example reducing preventable readmissions, and positively affecting employee satisfaction, retention, productivity, and team spirit. This is borne out by Tsai et al. (2015) who found that "Hospitals with boards that paid greater attention to clinical quality had management that better monitored quality performance. Similarly, hospitals with boards that used clinical quality metrics more effectively had higher performance by hospital management staff on target setting and operations."

By integrating priorities, organizations blur the distinction between risk and safety. It takes wisdom on the part of board leadership to promote a perspective that transcends and unifies those seemingly discrete categories. When such a perspective prevails, safety shifts from being viewed as a *cost* to an *outlay* with an important benefit. The failure to do so would be the assumption of an unwise risk.

Aligning Board Composition with a Safety and Quality Priority Environment

Among the challenges for healthcare organizations boards of directors is determining the proper configuration of expertise. Over the years, compositions, especially those of corporate boards, have significantly favored business and financial expertise over expertise in healthcare, whether in administrative or clinical affairs. For example, among those hospitals that placed high on the *U.S. News & World Reports'* hospitals ranking list, only one in seven board members has a background in healthcare; 44% work in the financial activities sector and over 80% of that group led financial corporations such as private equity firms, wealth management firms and banks; other board members in the financial sector work in real estate and insurance (Gondi et al., 2023).

While business and financial expertise is crucial, the concentration of expertise in those areas has resulted in underrepresentation in other areas. First and foremost, if a board is going to devote more concerted and more effective oversight of safety and quality performance, it is unlikely that success can come about with limited seats assigned to those with expertise in those areas. That includes more individuals with clinical backgrounds, particularly physicians and nurses. Today, however, of the 14.6% of board members who are health professionals, the vast majority of those, 13.3%, are physicians, while less than 1% are nurses (Southwick, 2023).

The lack of front-line employees on nonprofit hospitals' boards raises questions about whose voices are heard, whose experiences inform decision-making, and, above all, who is valued. The near absence of specialists other than physicians on boards is particularly notable, given the critical roles of nurses, therapists, technicians, and other staff.

In Chapter 4, we discussed the importance of committing 20% of a corporate board's seats to members of the boards of the individual healthcare facilities in the hospital system. The goal is to promote a stronger understanding of the communities served by the system as a whole. In the same way, it is proposed that at least 25% of a corporate board should comprise members with healthcare backgrounds. This would be essential to promote a stronger understanding of safety and quality. Today, however, and even though nurses constitute the largest component of the healthcare workforce, many hospital boards do not have even one nurse among their membership (Reinhard, 2023). A 2020 Institute of Medicine Report highlights the significance of a fortified nursing perspective in the boardroom: "The growing attention of hospital boards to quality and safety issues reflects the increased visibility of these issues in recent years. ... This is one area ... in which nurse board members can have a significant impact" (Reinhard, 2023).

Expanding nursing representation holds the dual promise of strengthening sensitivity to the community as well as to safety and quality There are at least three benefits of a nursing presence that addresses both areas of need: (1) proximity to the science of medicine, (2) expertise in safety and quality as well as the relationship between the two, and (3) access to the community by virtue of their firsthand connections with patients and their families (Minemyer, 2016).

Institute Training and Development for Board Members on Safety and Quality

A survey of board leaders found that 95% of respondents indicated that their organizations' safety and quality plans had been shared with them and that 85% said the plan is routinely discussed at board meetings (McGaffigan et al., 2017). On the surface, the substantial percentages would appear reassuring. Upon probing, however, the survey revealed that the promising broad-brush data did not accurately reflect the level of understanding of safety issues, including, for example, the main causes of safety problems or the frequency and extent to which those issues were discussed. While the majority of respondents expressed beliefs about the importance of prioritizing safety, the underlying knowledge base proved to be far more limited.

Strengthening the culture of safety is crucial. But such bolstering cannot occur absent a strengthened knowledge base. The failure of boards to have a robust clinical representation renders discussions on safety challenging. Nurses, physicians, and other clinicians would be more suitably positioned to facilitate discussions and to provide explanations and interpretations of safety and quality data that might be confusing to those with different areas of expertise.

Board members should become acquainted with safety and quality as these concepts pertain to high reliability organizations. The training, which should be conducted by experts, should be mandatory and assume that the participants have a novice-level grounding in the material. Topics should include Joint Commission standards on safety and quality, the board's role as it relates to these standards, and policies and positions on safety from the American Hospital Association, the American Medical Association, the American Nurses Association, and other relevant bodies. Board members should become familiar with the definition of a culture of safety and how they can actively support and lead the way in instituting such a culture in their organizations. Once the broad framework is developed, the board should be encouraged to examine how it can actively create a culture of safety and, of great importance, sustain it.

SIX AREAS FOR TRANSLATING EDUCATION INTO ACTION THAT ALIGN WITH JOINT COMMISSION STANDARDS

1. setting aims – set a specific aim to reduce harm this year; make an explicit, public commitment to measurable quality improvement
2. getting data and hearing stories – select and review progress toward safer care as the first agenda item at every board meeting
3. establishing and monitoring system-level measures
4. changing the environment, policies, and culture – commit to establish and maintain an environment that is respectful, fair, and just for all who experience the pain and loss as a result of avoidable harm and adverse outcomes
5. learning, starting with the board – develop the board's capability and learn about how "best in-the-world" boards work with executive and medical staff leaders to reduce harm
6. establishing executive accountability – oversee the effective execution of a plan to achieve aims to reduce harm, including executive team accountability for clear quality improvement targets (Conway, 2008)

Mechanisms for Safety Management and Reporting Are Well-Established and Accessible

The route from the board of directors to the actual site where safety is practiced is long and can be quite circuitous. Boards may conduct their work in the sanctum of a conference room, while the practices of safety take place on the front lines of patient care. Creating a culture of safety would be virtually impossible without the board's active oversight support because they communicate priorities to senior management, which, in turn, communicates those priorities through the various chains of command in the organization; despite the potentially many layers between the board and staff, those priority messages get through.

The substance of the messages that are communicated about the importance of safety and quality care are, of course, important. But messages alone are insufficient to empower employees to act concertedly to prevent errors and take necessary action if one occurs. For that to occur, policies, tools, and mechanisms must be in place for reporting errors along with the belief that errors are learning opportunities, and unless otherwise warranted because of a personal conduct issue, that reporting is welcomed on a nonpunitive basis. If employees perceive a discrepancy between overt messages from the top about the importance of a "safety-first" culture and tacit messages which appear intended to dissuade speaking up when an error occurs, employees are understandably likely to feel discouraged. A hospital unwilling to bolster staffing and address shortages in a timely way may be implicitly communicating that safety is less of a priority than what is stated in its public pronouncements. Commitments to productivity and quality may decline. Retention may suffer. The failure to effectively attend to safety becomes a vicious cycle as the potential escalates for some staff to leave.

Boards are advised to put themselves into the shoes of their employees when developing a mandate for safety and quality. That means backing up verbal commitments with teeth. Two areas are critical in this regard. The first involves empowering employees to act when a safety issue occurs. Empowerment may be defined as the ability to make independent decisions and do so with access to support, resources, information, and opportunities to learn and grow (Agency for Healthcare Research and Quality, n.d.). An empowered employee, therefore, can take action intended to resolve a problem, and such action is also intended to prevent similar occurrences in the future. The emphasis on the learning experience introduces the benefit of helping future patients by limiting their exposure to risk of a similar error.

Accordingly, this expansive notion of empowerment is characterized by an ethical imperative.

The second way that boards can tangibly promote a culture of safety is by ensuring that comprehensive and easily accessible monitoring and reporting systems are in place and that employees possess the knowledge about how to engage them. With respect to systems, a broad-based framework is provided by the Leapfrog Group (n.d.), self-described as "a nonprofit watchdog organization that serves as a voice for healthcare consumers and purchasers, using their collective influence to foster positive change in U.S. healthcare. Leapfrog is the nation's premier advocate of transparency in healthcare—collecting, analyzing, and disseminating data to inform value-based purchasing and improved decision-making."

As discussed in Chapter 2, Leapfrog provides a well-documented safety metric composite that allows for standardization of evaluation of safety across hospitals (Austin et al., 2014). Its 30 measures of safety are subdivided into two domains: (1) process/structural measures which refer, respectively, to the frequency of providing recommended treatments, and environmental conditions and resources that either facilitate or hinder the quality and responsiveness of caregiving activity; (2) outcome measures identify occurrences to patients, for example, a foreign body retained in body, pressure ulcers, falls and trauma, and postoperative respiratory failure. The use of such systems enables monitoring, tracking of trends, reporting, and comparative analyses. By extension, it allows consumers to review hospital performance.

But the monitoring and evaluation system is only as effective as the input. This is why empowerment and safety policy are so highly interdependent. If the reporting mechanism is inaccessible, or if a supervisor's response to an untoward event is characterized by defensiveness, the matter may go unreported or get diluted. Invariably, it is up to the board of directors to set the tone for how the organization defines and responds to safety. If the supervisor behaves defensively, it may be a function of that person not being correct for the job. But if defensiveness is a more common response, then it is possible that the board failed to create a climate in which safety is dignified with the level of importance that all those going into the facility for care deserve.

If boards of directors devote time and attention to safety, so will the rest of the organization, up and down the chain of command. The board will expect to see reports, which the organization will mobilize to produce; various staff with relevant expertise will be invited to give presentations; board members will become increasingly familiar with specific safety situations, will express interest in anecdotes that breathe life into data, and be motivated to see firsthand the environment in which safety is practiced. To the extent that they understand and value a safety culture, they will demonstrate an interest in learning about the root causes of safety problems so that they can best understand which management proposals to endorse. And they will seek to reassure that while poor conduct is unacceptable, a genuine safety culture can thrive only in a nonpunitive environment.

Conclusion

Patients typically enter hospitals not out of desire, but out of need. Vulnerabilities are heightened and they depend on the skill, care, and attention of a hospital workforce to care for them and remedy their health issues.

Yet, hospitals are highly complex facilities, and the activity that occurs in them is bound up in thousands of rules, all designed to help achieve those patient goals. Keeping patients safe and protecting their welfare is most central to the facility's purposes. But institutional priorities are layered, including in ways in which they compete with one another. Managing within a defined revenue stream means that choices will be made. And boards create the framework in which that choice-making occurs. If the board becomes too distracted from that perspective of the patient, then it is quite possible that safety will fall short of being unwaveringly heralded by the organization.

Keeping their eye on the patient's perspective does not mean sacrificing attention to other matters of importance. In fact, as we have strongly suggested, in all likelihood, keeping their eye on the patient's welfare will translate into overall improved institutional performance. This requires deft leadership on the board. But given the centrality of the board's influence in all aspects of the organization's activity, it is exactly what all stakeholders, particularly patients, deserve.

References

Adler, L., Yi, D., Li, M., McBroom, B., Hauck, L., Sammer, C., Jones, C., Shaw, T., & Classen, D. (2018). Impact of inpatient harms on hospital finances and patient clinical outcomes. *Journal of Patient Safety*, 14(2), 67–73. (https://doi.org/10.1097/PTS.0000000000000171)

Agency for Healthcare Research and Quality (n.d.). *Module 3: staff empowerment.* https://www.ahrq.gov/hai/quality/tools/cauti-ltc/modules/implementation/long-term-modules/module3/mod3-slides.html

Aiken, L., Sloane, D., McHugh, M., Pogue, C., & Lasater, K. (2022). A repeated cross-sectional study of nurses immediately before and during the COVID-19 pandemic: Implications for action. *Nursing Outlook*. https://www.nursingoutlook. org/article/S0029-6554(22)00238-X/fulltext

Allen, M. (2012). Why patients don't report medical errors. *ProPublica*. https:// www.propublica.org/article/why-patients-dont-report-medical-errors

American Hospital Association (n.d.). *AHA Patient's Bill of Rights*. https://www. americanpatient.org/aha-patients-bill-of-rights/

American Hospital Association (2017). *Assessing the regulatory burden on health systems, hospitals and post-acute care providers*. https://www.aha.org/ guidesreports/2017-11-03-regulatory-overload-report

American Hospital Association (2022). *The current state of hospital finances: fall 2022 update*. https://www.aha.org/guidesreports/2022-09-15-current-state-hospital-finances-fall-2022-update

American Nurses Association (2010). *Position statement: Just culture*. https://www. nursingworld.org/~4afe07/globalassets/practiceandpolicy/health-and-safety/ just_culture.pdf

Anning, D., Entin, F., & Totten, M. (2009). *The Guide to Good Governance for Hospital Boards*. Center for Healthcare Governance. https://trustees.aha.org/ sites/default/files/trustees/09-guide-to-good-governance.pdf

Association of American Medical Colleges (2016). *AAMC comments on 2017 PFS proposed rule and global surgical data*. https:// www.aamc.org/advocacy-policy/washington-highlights/ aamc-comments-2017-pfs-proposed-rule-and-global-surgical-data

Atlantic Health System (2022). *Atlantic Health System's Morristown Medical center rated number one hospital in New Jersey for the fifth year in a row by U.S. News & World Report*. https://www.atlantichealth.org/about-us/stay-connected/news/ press-releases/2022/us-news-best-hospitals.htm

Atrium Health News (2022). *Advocate Aurora Health and Atrium Health to combine*. https://atriumhealth.org/about-us/newsroom/news/2022/05/ advocate-aurora-health-and-atrium-health-to-combine

Austin, J., D'Andrea, G., Birkmeyer, J., Leape, L., Milstein, A., Pronovost, P., Romano, P., Singer, S., Vogus, T., & Wachter, R. (2014). Safety in numbers: The development of Leapfrog's composite patient safety score for U.S. hospitals. *Journal of Patient Safety*, 10(1), 64–71. (https://doi.org/10.1097/ PTS.0b013e3182952644)

Austin, M., & Derk, J. (2016). *Lives Lost, Lives Saved: a Comparative Analysis of Avoidable Deaths at Hospitals Graded*. Armstrong Institute for Patient Safety and Quality: Johns Hopkins Medicine. https://www.hospitalsafetygrade.org/ media/file/Lives-Saved-White-Paper-FINAL.pdf

Baird, K. (2019). Stewards of the patient experience: trustees' key role. *Trustee Insights: Performance Improvement*. https://trustees.aha.org/system/files/ media/file/2019/09/TI_0919_trustee_as_steward.pdf

Binder, L. (2021). Holding hospitals accountable for patient safety. *Harvard Business Review*. https://hbr.org/2021/08/holding-hospitals-accountable-for-patient-safety

Boyle, P. (2020). U.S. physician shortage growing. *AAMC News*. https://www.aamc.org/news/us-physician-shortage-growing

Centers for Disease Control (n.d.). *Hospitalization and blood clots*. https://www.cdc.gov/ncbddd/dvt/hospitalization-infographic.html

Centers for Medicare & Medicaid Services (n.d.). *HCAHPS: Patients' perspectives of care survey*. https://www.cms.gov/medicare/quality-initiatives-patient-assessment-instruments/hospitalqualityinits/hospitalhcahps

Centers for Medicare & Medicaid Services (2016). *Medicare program; revisions to payment policies under the physician fee schedule and other revisions to Part B for CY 2017*. https://www.cms.gov/medicare/medicare-fee-for-service-payment/physicianfeesched/pfs-federal-regulation-notices-items/cms-1654-f

Cleveland Clinic (n.d.) *Mission, vision & values*. https://my.clevelandclinic.org/about/overview/who-we-are/mission-vision-values

Conway, J. (2008). Getting boards on board: Engaging governing boards in quality and safety. *Joint Commission Journal on Quality and Patient Safety*, 34(4), 214–220. (https://doi.org/10.1016/s1553-7250(08)34028-8)

Dughi, P. (2022). Can you name the top 10 patient safety risks in your hospital? *Berxi*. https://www.berxi.com/resources/articles/top-10-risks-to-patient-safety-in-hospitals/

Eisenberg, B. (2015). Prone to illness: Corruption in healthcare and the role of leadership. In Prone to Illness. In Belasen, A., & Toma, R. (Eds.). (2015). *Confronting Corruption in Business: Trusted Leadership, Civic Engagement*. Routledge, New York and London.

Eisenberg, B., Belasen, A., & Huppertz, J. (2014). Leading the highly reliable healthcare organization: a competency framework, Annual Meeting of the Association of University Programs in Health Administration, June, San Antonio, TX.

Gondi, S., Kishore, S., & McWilliams, J. M. (2023). Professional backgrounds of board members at top-ranked US hospitals. *Journal of General Internal Medicine*, 10.1007/s11606-023-08056-z. Advance online publication. (https://doi.org/10.1007/s11606-023-08056-z)

Gooch, K. (2023). 53 hospitals, health systems cutting jobs. *Becker's Hospital Review*. https://www.beckershospitalreview.com/finance/17-hospitals-health-systems-cutting-jobs-february-2023.html

Guest, G., Namey, E., & Mitchell, M. (2013). *Participant Observation*. (Vols. 1-0). SAGE Publications, Ltd, (https://doi.org/10.4135/9781506374680)

HealthStream Resources (2021). *What are conditions of participation?* https://www.healthstream.com/resource/blog/what-are-conditions-of-participation-(cops)

Henman, L. (2019). *How boards set the tone for the organization*. Corporate Compliance Insights. https://www.corporatecomplianceinsights.com/the-foundation-of-a-strong-culture

Heuer, A. (2004). Hospital accreditation and patient satisfaction: Testing the relationship. *Journal for Healthcare Quality: National Association for Healthcare Quality*, 26(1), 46–51. (https://doi.org/10.1111/j.1945-1474.2004.tb00471.x)

Jha, A. K., & Epstein, A. M. (2013). A survey of board chairs of English hospitals shows greater attention to quality of care than among their US counterparts. *Health affairs (Project Hope)*, 32(4), 677–685. (https://doi.org/10.1377/hlthaff.2012.1060)

Landi, H. (2023). Ascension Health details $2.5B economic recovery plan to rebound from financial, operational headwinds. *Fierce Healthcare*, January 11, https://www.fiercehealthcare.com/providers/jpm23-ascension-health-details-25b-economic-recovery-plan-rebound-financial-operational

Larson, R. J., Schwartz, L. M., Woloshin, S., & Welch, H. G. (2005). Advertising by academic medical centers. *Archives of Internal Medicine*, 165(6), 645–651. (https://doi.org/10.1001/archinte.165.6.645)

Lavan, A. H., & Gallagher, P. (2015). Predicting risk of adverse drug reactions in older adults. *Therapeutic Advances in Drug Safety*, 7(1), 11–22. (https://doi.org/10.1177/2042098615615472)

Levins, H. (2023). How inadequate hospital staffing continues to burn out nurses and threaten patients. *Penn LDI: Leonard Davis Institute of Healthcare Economics*. https://ldi.upenn.edu/our-work/research-updates/how-inadequate-hospital-staffing-continues-to-burn-out-nurses-and-threaten-patients/

Long, S. J., Brown, K. F., Ames, D., & Vincent, C. (2013). What is known about adverse events in older medical hospital inpatients? A systematic review of the literature. *International Journal for Quality in Health Care: Journal of the International Society for Quality in Health Care*, 25(5), 542–554. (https://doi.org/10.1093/intqhc/mzt056)

Madonko, N., & April, K. A. (2020). The effectiveness of leaders in communicating organizational values. *Effective Executive*, 23(4), 22–38. http://library.esc.edu/login?url=https://www.proquest.com/scholarly-journals/effectiveness-leaders-communicating/docview/2495511961/se-2

Martin, D., Shulman, K., Santiago-Sorrell, P., & Singer, P. (2003). Priority-setting and hospital strategic planning: A qualitative case study. *Journal of Health Services Research & Policy*, 8(4), 197–201. (https://doi.org/10.1258/135581903322403254)

McGaffigan, P., Ullem, B., & Gandhi, T. (2017). Closing the gap and raising the bar: Assessing board competency in quality and safety. *The Joint Commission Journal on Quality and Patient Safety*, 43(8), 267–274.

Minemyer, P. (2016). 4 reasons to add nurses to hospital boards. *Fierce Healthcare*. https://www.fiercehealthcare.com/hospitals/4-reasons-to-add-nurses-to-hospital-boards

National Academies of Sciences, Engineering, and Medicine. (2019). *Taking Action Against Clinician Burnout: A Systems Approach to Professional Well-Being*. Washington, DC: The National Academies Press. (https://doi.org/10.17226/25521)

O'Donnell, B., & Gupta, V. (2023). *Continuous Quality Improvement*. National Library of Medicine. *StatPearls Publishing* (Internet). https://www.ncbi.nlm.nih.gov/books/NBK559239/.

Page, A. (ed.) (2004). *Keeping Patients Safe: Transforming the Work Environment of Nurses*. Washington, DC: *The National Academies Press* https://www.ncbi.nlm.nih.gov/books/NBK216181/

Reinhard, S. (2023). *Getting nurses on board*. AHA Trustee Services. https://trustees. aha.org/articles/1212-getting-nurses-on-the-hospital-board

Sehgal, A. R. (2010). The role of reputation in U.S. News & World Report's rankings of the top 50 American hospitals. *Annal of Internal Medicine*, 152, 521–525. [Epub 20 April 2010]. doi:10.7326/0003-4819-152-8-201004200-00009

Southwick, R. (2023). About 1 in 7 hospital board members works in healthcare. *Chief Healthcare Executive*. https://www.chiefhealthcareexecutive.com/view/ about-1-in-7-hospital-board-members-works-in-healthcare-study

Statista. (2019). *Average daily census in hospitals in the U.S. from 1946 to 2019*. https://www.statista.com/statistics/459736/average-daily-census-in-hospitals-in-the-us/#:~:text=In%202019%2C%20the%20daily%20average,hospitals%20located%20in%20the%20country.

Stiehm, C. (2019). Celebrating 110 years of the good housekeeping seal. *Hearst*. https://www.hearst.com/-/celebrating-110-years-of-the-good-housekeeping-seal

The Joint Commission (2018). Safety culture assessment: Improving the survey process. *The Joint Commission Perspective: The Official Newsletter of the Joint Commission*. (6)38. https://www.jointcommission.org/-/media/tjc/documents/ accred-and-cert/safety_culture_assessment_improving_the_survey_process.pdf

The Leapfrog Group. (n.d.). About us: https://www.hospitalsafetygrade.org/

Tsai, T. C., Jha, A. K., Gawande, A. A., Huckman, R. S., Bloom, N., & Sadun, R. (2015). Hospital board and management practices are strongly related to hospital performance on clinical quality metrics. *Health Affairs (Project Hope)*, 34(8), 1304–1311. (https://doi.org/10.1377/hlthaff.2014.1282)

Watkins, M. (2013). What is organizational culture? And why should we care? *Harvard Business Review*. https://hbr.org/2013/05/what-is-organizational-culture

Weick, K., & Sutcliffe, K. (2007). *Managing the Unexpected: Resilient Performance in an Age of Uncertainty*. San Francisco, CA: Jossey Bass. (https://www. researchgate.net/publication/265106124)

Chapter 8

Shared Leadership and the Patient Experience

Introduction

Shared leadership promotes robust management structures by providing broader competence, continuous learning, and joint responsibility for clinical services. Co-leaders create synergistic work environments that foster trust and interprofessional collaboration with the mutual understanding of when to lead and when to step back and allow peer-leaders to step in. Shared leadership also enables the promotion of women to senior executive positions, accelerates gender parity at the top, and improves the leadership development pipeline and retention of talent. As described in this chapter, shared leadership leverages the combined strengths of the coequal leaders for better outcomes. When clinical and nonclinical staff collaborate effectively, healthcare teams can improve patient outcomes, prevent medical errors, improve efficiency, and increase patient satisfaction over prolonged periods.

The foundation for successful clinical integration (CI) includes shared governance with strong leadership focusing on transforming the hospital culture and achieving clinical outcomes as key drivers of value-based care. This requires a mindset of cross-functional synergy, sharing information, transferring best practices, managing utilization, and providing proactive care. Interprofessional collaboration within multidisciplinary teams in acute care settings involves clinical problem-solving and planning episodes (e.g., such as teamwork during surgical procedures) among physicians, nurses, pharmacists, and caregivers where shared awareness and positive communications are

DOI: 10.4324/9781003431077-8

crucial for the success of care delivery. At the top, successfully sharing leadership draws on clinicians and administrators working closely together in dyad or triad structures to deliver high-quality care.

Self-assessment instruments for identifying strengths and weaknesses of co-leaders and for developing and sustaining the performance of dyad structures are included in this chapter. Assessments of leadership roles are useful because they help managers and organizational leaders target gaps in behaviors and skills and enhance leadership performance. Executives can use these instruments for self-development, but also to evaluate whether gaps in the behavior of aspiring leaders have been addressed and to help make important decisions about their suitability to lead teams, service lines, or organizations.

> Applying a structural approach in the form of leadership dyads, in combination with relational competencies, may provide for a more fruitful path to develop hospital leaders and ameliorate hospital performance. … [D]yad-based leadership relationships result in fewer communication breakdowns and, as such, facilitate the possibility of better care. In this way, leadership dyads may act as a patient outcome pathway. An extended health leadership model that incorporates the dyad (or triad) partnership at multiple levels of the hospital hierarchy has powerful potential in advancing how hospitals organize for patient care and patient safety. Dyadic leadership promotes strong relationships and effective communication between traditional organizational and disciplinary boundaries to achieve organizational and clinical goals…. Practically, our study also shows that… health leaders agree that leadership is key to advancing healthcare quality and patient safety….(Leach et al., 2021)

Diversity and Inclusion at the Top

Building a culture of diversity, inclusion, and collaboration, essential for the success of integrated health networks, begins at the top. However, in addition to racial and ethnic disparity, gender disparity is still prevalent in senior healthcare positions, even as women continue to play critical roles in strengthening the integration of health services. Women drive 80% of consumer purchasing power and decisions in healthcare and constitute 77% of all hospital employees, 92% of nursing students, and 50.5% of students in American medical schools. Yet, women are markedly underrepresented in healthcare executive suites and boardrooms: just 15% of CEOs, 15.8% of CEOs of health insurance companies, 33% of chief financial officers, 23.4% of chief operating officers (COOs), 25% of chief information officers, and 25% of board members.

Women are significantly less likely to be promoted to senior healthcare management positions, even when considering personal and organizational characteristics. Provider organizations with at least 40% of their C-suite positions held by women have also been shown to have 1.5 times larger C-suites than those with only 20% women in the C-suite with the additional roles assumed by women designated primarily technical and lower paid than the core roles (Wyman, 2019). The women have a seat at the table, but they may not be the key players who enjoy high-impact, strategic responsibilities.

Research shows that more diverse and inclusive teams make better decisions up to 87% of the time, are faster 50% of the time, and deliver 60% better results. In industries with a high prevalence of executive overconfidence, gender-diverse boards are also associated with more measured investment policies, better acquisition decisions, reduced negative impact of crises on firm performance, and improved financial outcomes (Chen et al., 2019).

Social and interaction skills are keys to better healthcare outcomes and female CEOs improve the patient experience faster than male CEOs do, particularly in large urban environments with high-volume hospital facilities (Silvera & Clark, 2019). Gender diversity that starts at the top and trickles down to all levels of management can transform healthcare organizations in the direction of patient centeredness, improved financial performance, and it can help to ensure stakeholder alignment.

An important pathway for shifting the healthcare leadership landscape is to replace the entrenched solo leadership model typically headed by a nonclinical administrator with a shared leadership model that casts the net far and wide. At its core, shared leadership is emerging as a vital strategy for integrated health systems faced with increasing complexity. It reflects an executive clinical partnership based on interprofessional cooperation between two or more individuals with complementary strengths and abilities.

One form of shared leadership is the dyad. The dyad management structure is congruent with complex healthcare environments and with the shift to cost-effective, long-term, chronic, acute, and primary health service programs across the continuum of care.

The dyad supports the narrative of interprofessional collaboration and encourages ongoing dialogue with staff and clinicians during the transition and deployment of care teams. This helps to inspire employees to change their way of thinking about patient care and the culture of the organization, avoid confusion during transitions, and facilitate collaborative behaviors. Instituting a dyad management structure imbeds physician and nurse leaders in the leadership structure and creates opportunities for dealing with complexity through effective collaboration and shared experiences. Dyad leaders, who appreciate the value of cooperation, also encourage teams to meet broader, emerging goals through interprofessional collaboration and teamwork.

Interprofessional Collaboration within Multidisciplinary Teams

Diverse teams bring a variety of backgrounds, talents, and experiences that help boost creativity and innovation in figuring out problems and articulating solutions. A common understanding in the business world is that teams perform well when bringing different perspectives and ideas to their shared decision-making. Indeed, reports by McKinsey (Barta et al., 2012) and Deloitte (Bourke & Dillon, 2018) suggest that diverse perspectives among senior leaders create substantial value for firms. Diversity allows teams to leverage the combined strengths and perspectives of team members for better outcomes.

Communication among the healthcare team is essential to providing high-quality patient care. In the hospital, nurses care for multiple patients during their shifts. Physicians or advanced practice clinicians (APCs) visit hospitalized patients daily to update orders, complete assessments, and contribute to care plans. One method to ensure that healthcare providers communicate effectively is interdisciplinary, or dyad, rounding in the hospital. This consists of purposeful rounding on each patient by the nurse and the physician or APC together to review the patient's status and update the care plan. When healthcare providers and nurses round together, it improves communication, patients are more satisfied, and patient safety is increased (Christensen et al., 2020).

Interprofessional collaboration refers to the confluence of multi-disciplinary health professionals from diverse backgrounds working with patients to provide quality care. The Affordable Care Act (ACA) has promoted CI by reducing two of the barriers to delivering high-quality care: information and incentives. Expansion of the use of electronic health records (EHR) facilitates the sharing of data across multiple health organizations, enabling clinicians to better monitor, prevent, and manage diseases. Financial support for providers focuses on bundled payments and incentives for accountable care organizations (ACOs) and patient-centered medical homes (PCMH) for delivering high-quality, cost-effective primary care. ACOs represent a shift from a physician-centered to a *team-*based approach *in which a* primary care provider assumes responsibility for care, with access to a *multi-disciplinary team* to address unique patients' needs. The result is an improvement in the patient experience and clinical outcomes, with a decrease in hospital readmission rates and hospital-acquired infections.

Patients who participate in decisions about their care have better knowledge about conditions, tests, and treatment; have more realistic expectations about options, benefits, and risks; are more likely to follow screening, diagnostic, or treatment plans; and experience decreased decisional conflict and anxiety. Engaged patients are also more likely to effectively manage chronic conditions by asking clinicians questions about their care, practicing healthy behaviors, mitigating any harm from their chronic condition, seeking, and using more health information, following up with their primary care clinician and specialists, or getting needed tests and screenings to monitor their condition, adhering to daily medications, and participating in self-monitoring activities (Krist et al., 2017).

Team collaboration and efficient communication practices are essential across health professions. Sometimes, however, lack of time and training, unclear roles, perceived threats to professional identity, and poor communication tend to limit the success of multidisciplinary teams. For a health system to foster the development of well-functioning teams and interprofessional collaboration, a positive organizational culture, where team members trust one another with open and transparent communication, must exist. The integrated behavioral healthcare model, for example, engages a practicing team of primary care and behavioral health professionals who work jointly with patients and families to address the spectrum of behavioral health concerns and psycho-social factors (Davis et al., 2019). The model relies upon shared decision-making for patient care and close coordination of clinical activities, reduces silos within healthcare, and utilizes scarce resources to the maximum capacity (Brown et al., 2021).

The IOM (2011) identified the following best practices to help develop, foster, and sustain interprofessional collaboration:

■ Put patients first and design systems of care to achieve that end. Putting patients and their families first serves as an equalizer across each team member as patients' interests supersede the potentially competing interests of individual team members and help people "connect the dots" between their role, patient care, and the mission of the organization.
■ Demonstrate leadership commitment to interprofessional collaboration as an organizational priority through words and actions. To be effective, leadership must model collaboration regularly, build trust, and promote respect across the organization.
■ Create a level playing field that enables team members to work at the top of their license, know their roles, and understand the value they contribute. It is critical that each team member understands, values, and respects the complementary nature of contributions of various professions in the team and of their interdependence.
■ Cultivate effective team communication by giving team members shared language and tools. This helps overcome perceptual gaps and barriers associated with different communication styles and expectations.
■ Explore the use of organizational structure to hardwire interprofessional practice and have resources in place to advance interprofessional collaboration.
■ Train different disciplines together so members work together early, break down the professional silos, and help establish joint accountability.

Multidisciplinary teams have the added benefit of lowering patient wait times, resulting in uninterrupted therapy. Clinical information can also be easily shared between in-house providers. This can mitigate patients' anxiety, as the patients can avoid repeating their stories to every specialist they meet. Team-based interventions are also cost-effective. A recent study showed that 91% of surgical multidisciplinary teams reported a reduction in hospital costs with an average of $5,815 saved per patient (Davis et al., 2021). Thus, multidisciplinary teams and interprofessional collaboration help attain the quadruple aim of improving the health of populations, enhancing the patient experience of care, reducing the per capita cost of health, and improving the work life of healthcare providers. Interprofessional collaboration can also help achieve the three pillars of personal health: care anywhere, care networking, and care customization.

Care Delivery and Shared Leadership

Common funding models such as fee for service are fragmented and less compatible with coordinated or collaborative care delivery, as they focus on individual episodes of care and reward the quantity of services offered by providers rather than the quality of care provided. On the other hand, incentive plans that encourage a much more integrated patient experience across the spectrum of care reward physicians' efforts to achieve quality care and reduce cost. A key priority is to develop a risk-based cost model that links patient care costs to interventions and quality outcomes. Bundled payments, which link payments for the multiple services beneficiaries receive during episodes of care, encourage more efficient care delivery by providing incentives for a better patient experience and higher levels of productivity using the same resources. These models align incentives for providers – hospitals, post-acute care providers, physicians, and other practitioners – allowing them to work closely together under the guidance of co-leaders across specialties and settings.

At the executive clinical partnership level, shared leadership can take two forms – *dyad* and *triad* – and both have the potential to transform healthcare organizations. In the dyad, the equal partners bring diverse perspectives to create win-win outcomes. Administrators bring business skills essential for managing productivity and cost-effective delivery of care to populations. Physicians bring medical expertise for determining health initiatives, providing high-value patient care, ensuring quality and patient safety, and assessing clinical outcomes. In triads, nurse managers join the leadership team. The value of nurse management to patient care and improving clinical quality and efficiency is promoted via shared accountability in a physician-nurse-administrator leadership structure.

A survey of 868 Insights Council members by the *New England Journal of Medicine* (Swenson et al., 2018) found that 72% use a dyad leadership model in their organizations and 85% believe that the dyad works effectively. A more recent survey of over 1300 healthcare leaders by the Medical Group Management Association (MGMA, 2019) found that 77% of the respondents indicated that their organizations utilize a physician and administrator (dyad) leadership model. Here are some of the responses about their experience with dyad leadership:

■ "Used at each practice location and works very well for continuity of information and building trust."
■ "Wouldn't do it any other way. Physician leads monthly Board meetings and presents to the Board the agenda items. Practice Administrator

runs the practice and meets weekly with physician leader to discuss operations."

■ "Very good. A necessity in today's physician practice environment."

■ "Successful. The dyad keeps appropriate skills and decision-making separate. Regular and transparent communication is key."

The triad has also been found to be a highly functioning leadership structure with improved patient outcomes. Dyads and triads, action pathways for change, create a clinical leadership pipeline and reach higher performance across many hospital quality indices. Now is the time to benefit from dyads and triads and make sure that they are inclusive with team members who are treated respectfully and fairly, are valued, feel that they belong, and are confident and inspired.

Shared leadership could operate in multiple areas of a healthcare organization, including the C-suite (e.g., CMO, CQO), divisions of care providers (e.g., Regional Primary Care Network, health centers), and service lines (e.g., cardiovascular, orthopedics, cancer care), divisions of care (e.g., health centers). In acute care hospitals, this model could draw on board-level chairs and directors, COOs, and clinical operations officers. In nursing homes, shared leadership could draw on facility owners, administrators, directors of nursing, and managers. These partnerships are relational means for making action pathways into a new era of quality-based, team-driven care.

Shared leadership may help reverse the trend of what is holding women back from assuming leadership roles and accelerate the development of women leaders in healthcare, as a model for other industries as well. In forging action pathways for change, dyads and triads create a clinical leadership pipeline to accelerate the representation of women leaders at the top. The coequal partners must have a high level of emotional intelligence and women's transformational qualities (Belasen & Frank, 2008) add indispensable value to diverse dyads and triads by closing the gender gap of competency perception. After all, the exercise of leadership is about having strong interaction skills, active listening, interpersonal influence, and behavioral flexibility.

Through a common vision, the shared leadership model encourages systems thinking and aligns clinical and operational resources to improve outcomes and efficiency. The model, illustrated in Figure 8.1, includes important leadership roles: value strategist, CI champion, patient advocate,

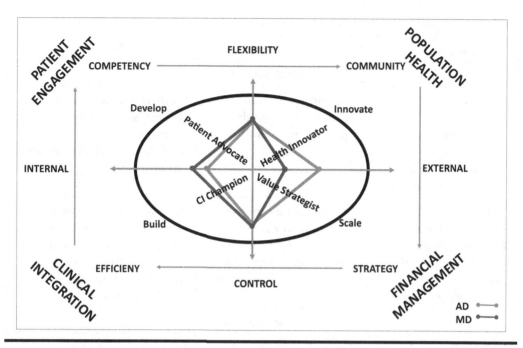

Figure 8.1   Shared leadership.

Source: Adapted from: Belasen, A. (2019). *Dyad Leadership and Clinical Integration: Driving Change, Aligning Strategies,* Chicago, IL: Health Administration Press.

and health innovator. These roles span vital areas of hospital performance: financial management, CI, patient engagement, and population health (Table 8.1). They provide co-leaders with opportunities to receive recognition for their competencies, gain visibility, and move up the career ladder (Belasen, 2019).

The roles and their respective target areas in addition to milestones of hospital growth and development are illustrated in Figure 8.1. The pursuit of a sustained growth strategy (*scale*) depends on the ability of the organization to align its resources and capabilities (*build*), improve communication processes and competencies (develop), and create groundbreaking community-based programs (innovate). When the strengths of the coequal partners are leveraged, they respond well to the requirements in their task environment. Their complementary roles and skills help mitigate their relative weaknesses or blind spots within the stretched area of responsibilities of the dyad. Through learning and further education and development, the combined 'profile' (Figure 8.2) of the dyad can be expanded for optimal performance.

Table 8.1   Dyad Roles and Selected Responsibilities

Administration	Shared	Medical
Health Innovator		
Establishing collaborative partnerships, joint ventures, and affiliations that add expertise and scope	Creating post-acute offerings within the population health management	Improving care quality and patient safety through interfunctional collaboration and innovative solutions
Delivering services across the continuum of care at an affordable cost and appropriate quality to the community	Transforming care from episodic to value-focused and provide meaningful coordination across the continuum of care	Improving care coordination and communication among clinicians, patients, and patients' families; engaging patients in shared decision-making
Value Strategist		
Scaling clinically integrated provider networks and care systems	Expanding market share for ambulatory surgery centers (ASCs) and outpatient procedure	Engaging in the revenue cycle process
Evaluating accounting and information systems and methods; monitoring KPIs	Creating new service lines and revenue streams to increase profitability	Reducing risk and ensuring high-value care is delivered promoting higher rates of utilization
Conducting competitor strategic analysis; evaluating market-share performance	Developing and implementing strategic plans	Recruiting physicians to support growth and patient loyalty
Clinical Integration Champion		
Integrating IT systems and managing health informatics	Optimizing clinical informatics and data analytics systems including design, transparency, patient care and quality, and compliance	Promoting teamwork and improving interprofessional collaboration

(Continued)

Table 8.1 *(Continued)*   **Dyad Roles and Selected Responsibilities**

Administration	Shared	Medical
Improving cost containment and efficiency	Increasing rate of interoperability to improve quality and reduce cost	Providing high-value care by incorporating evidence-based information into patient diagnosis and treatment
Ensuring compliance with medical and legal regulations and internal policies	Using analytics to improve coordination of care optimizing	Keeping physicians informed about EHR implementation and securing physician buy-in to ongoing improvement projects involving clinical and operational integration
Patient Advocate		
Providing resources for training and development	Improving teamwork training and interpersonal skill building	Engaging physicians and patients in lowering clinical variation
Enhancing hospital ratings and reputation	Increasing patient satisfaction and quality outcomes; reducing readmissions	Track physician adherence with evidence-based practices
		Improving provider-patient communications

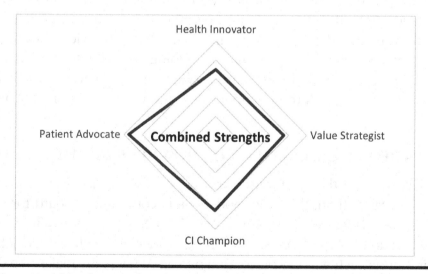

Figure 8.2   Combined strengths of dyad leaders.

The vertical axis (flexibility/control) focuses on leadership roles essential for coordinating activities and improving quality and patient safety across the continuum of care. Medical and nursing leaders promote teamwork, self-direction, interfunctional collaboration, and joint accountability. They encourage teams to meet broad population health objectives and emerging goals. Simultaneously, administrative control is needed to achieve higher levels of coordination and operating efficiencies across allied partners and affiliates. Administrators are tasked with aligning structures and processes, achieving internal consistency, applying proven solutions to problems, setting performance targets, monitoring implementation, and tracking results.

The horizontal axis (internal/external) reflects the need to align socio-technical systems (e.g., care teams, IT capabilities, minimizing clinical variation) with quality metrics and cost-effective thresholds. Simultaneously, it focuses on external stakeholders (e.g., regulators, communities, partners) to ensure hospital profitability and strategic growth by improving ambulatory access, strengthening primary care alignment, and redesigning health system services for population health.

For example, most health systems strive to align clinical practices and services internally to ensure that the system operates reliably (control). The goal of meeting community health needs is achieved through innovative thinking and effective communication practices (flexibility), aligning organizational goals with the values and interests of stakeholders (e.g., patient populations, health plans, employers, and suppliers), complying effectively with laws and regulations, and maintaining robust financial performance. To fulfill its maximum potential, the organization must create sustainable linkages between internal clinical practices, community partners, and external strategic alliances. Doing so facilitates patients' access to preventive and chronic care services and improves overall patient safety and quality across the continuum of care (Belasen et al., 2021).

ADVOCATE HEALTH CARE, DOWNERS GROVE, ILL.

Advocate created the cardiovascular service line and its dyad team five years ago. Since then, the dyad model has become the standard for most service lines. Because the system is transitioning operationally to a more horizontal focus based on service lines, leadership realized the job of administering each was too big for one person. What really makes the dyad approach work is when dyad pairs are transparent with each other and key stakeholders during the decision-making process… the relationship thrives when each partner knows the other's strengths…. One area [the dyad] works tightly on is ensuring the system's approach to cardiovascular medicine is uniform across all facilities. This alignment helps reduce variability in how patients are cared for. For instance, the dyad is establishing standards around disease processes and equipment purchasing.

Mayo Clinic, Jacksonville, Fla.

A dyad relationship results in many benefits, most notably to patient care. "We are able to provide better decision making for the benefit of the patient and organization, and fundamentally we are stronger because of these dyads. So faster, stronger, better…."

Palomar Health, San Diego

Currently, the physician partners in the dyad are responsible for clinical input and physician perspective. They participate in quality and safety initiatives and in enhancing patient throughput. The staff physicians provide insights into how they can work on cost-saving initiatives, especially in physician preference items in the hospital. The physicians are responsible for their own governance. On the nursing and administrative side, the responsibilities are primarily related to operations, strategic planning, budgeting, and finance, and all the other aspects of running a complex healthcare organization are the ways the approach benefits patients and Mayo, and that is why over the years this has proven to be one of the bedrocks of success for Mayo Clinic (Buell, 2017).

The dyad structure leverages the partners' synergy to achieve shared strategic goals and advance the mission of the organization. It goes beyond role clarification and shared accountability as the co-equal partners must understand their unique and complementary roles and responsibilities. These partnerships are relational methods for leading through communication lines. The partners in the dyad are advocates and supporters of each other with open and effective interpersonal communication. Notably, the exercise of shared leadership is about having strong interaction skills and a high degree of emotional intelligence, potential pathways for an increased understanding of interpersonal influence.

Thomas Deering, MD, chief of Clinical Centers of Excellence and the Arrhythmia Center of Excellence at Piedmont Heart Institute, and his partner, Katie Lund, says: "We work together as a team to create a better product that looks at everything from the whole perspective...We learn from each other so that I become more administrative, and my dyad partner becomes more clinical and understands the subtleties a little more".

A productive partnership can help quell another concern sometimes voiced over dyad rule: Who is really in charge? Jennifer Zelensky, executive director at Providence Heart and Vascular Institute in Oregon and a dyad co-leader, maintains that she and her physician partner are "reasonably interchangeable," adding: "He can go to certain meetings, and I can go to others and people know that we're in sync. If an issue arises over medical quality, he's much more the lead, whereas if it is about budget or long-range financial plans, it is clear I am on-point" (Young, 2017).

When diverse strengths are combined, dyad partners can rely on their complementary skills to respond well to their task environment. Furthermore, involving physician leaders in operational and strategic decision-making increases their commitment to the organization's mission and aligns them well with the shared vision. Trust between physician leaders and administrative leaders is based on transparent communication and reciprocal exchanges of information – which are key to a successful collaboration. Shared leadership creates synergistic work environments that promote trust and interprofessional collaboration. The dyad, as an action pathway, can also enable the promotion of women to leadership positions, accelerate gender parity at the top, and improve recruitment and retention of women leaders. It sends a strong signal to health stakeholders that women leaders are indispensable for both the clinical and administrative sides of the business.

Patient-Focused Dyad – Advocacy

Patient advocacy, especially doctor-patient communication, is crucial for establishing trust between patients and doctors, reducing the number of errors, and ultimately increasing patient satisfaction. Advocating for patients is a core value in patient care. The Code of Conduct for the American College of Surgeons (2016) includes it as its first principle (see textbox). In *Speak Up*, the Joint Commission reinforced the imperative to clarify the rights of patients and caregivers about how to be involved in their healthcare. Patients have the rights to the following:

- Be informed about the care you will receive
- Get important information about your care in your preferred language
- Get information in a manner that meets your needs, if you have vision, speech, hearing, or mental issues
- Make decisions about your care
- Refuse care
- Know the names of the caregivers who treat you
- Safe care
- Have your pain addressed

AMERICAN COLLEGE OF SURGEONS, CODE OF PROFESSIONAL CONDUCT

As Fellows of the American College of Surgeons, we treasure the trust that our patients have placed in us because trust is integral to the practice of surgery. During the continuum of pre-, intra-, and postoperative care, we accept the following responsibilities:

- Serve as effective advocates of our patients' needs
- Disclose therapeutic options, including their risks and benefits
- Disclose and resolve any conflict of interest that might influence decisions regarding care
- Be sensitive and respectful of patients, understanding their vulnerability during the
- Perioperative period
- Fully disclose adverse events and medical errors
- Acknowledge patients' psychological, social, cultural, and spiritual needs
- Encompass within our surgical care the special needs of terminally ill patients
- Acknowledge and support the needs of patients' families
- Respect the knowledge, dignity, and perspective of other healthcare professionals

As surgeons, we acknowledge that we interact with our patients when they are most vulnerable. Their trust and the privileges we enjoy depend on our individual and collective participation in efforts to promote the good of both our patients and society. As Fellows of the American College of Surgeons, we commit ourselves and the College to the ideals of professionalism.

Some schools of medicine provide training to medical students to become better patient advocates. The Advocacy Training Program (ATP), at Boston University Medical Campus, for example, trains medical students to advocate for the health and well-being of patients and their communities. About 15% of students in each class participate in the program. Some of them go on to teach in the program, mastering content and resources and acquiring the skills and techniques necessary to teach. They also become mentors to fellow students.

The program comprises a first-year course focused on the social determinants of health, taught by students who have taken the course and faculty engaged in advocacy, and a second-year course with a focus on interdisciplinary learning, taught by medical and law students and physicians and lawyers engaged in advocacy. In the third year, students learn from case-based online modules related to the rotations they are taking that year, and in the fourth year, they choose an advocacy project mentored by a faculty member.

Patient advocates may handle complaints about treatment plans or healthcare providers that potentially obscure or impede optimal patient care. They facilitate medical encounters, which can be stressful and difficult for individuals (even in good health) without a medical background, helping patients make the best decision about their healthcare (Belasen, 2019).

Self-Assessment

To determine the most important areas for improvement, the co-leaders can initiate a review of self-assessment findings, discuss, and compare their individual and overlapping roles, identify weak spots and sweet spots for further development, and agree on improvement efforts to optimize their collaborative efforts. Self-assessment is a powerful medium that helps co-leaders enhance awareness of their individual and combined strengths and weaknesses, develop trust and mutual respect, build stronger relationships, and communicate effectively. Social context is important because women and men in leadership positions look to others for validation of their choices and motivations. When the assessment process is transparent and values and preferences are explicit, it also helps curb unconscious biases, encourages cooperation, and removes hidden barriers to career progression for women (Belasen et al., 2021).

Focused assessments for one role – patient advocate – are illustrated in Figure 8.3, for each of the dyad leaders; and Figure 8.4 for the combined

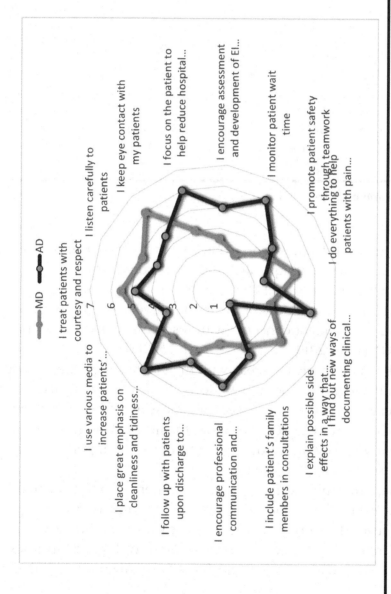

Figure 8.3 Dyad Patient Advocate/Engagement role.

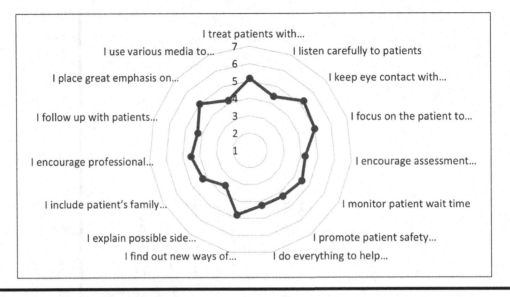

Figure 8.4   Combined strengths.

strengths of the dyad leaders. The behavioral indicators appear in Table 8.2. The assessments involve unique and shared responsibilities of the co-leaders in that role, which span patient communication, safety, care quality, and patient engagement. The 15 questions in the survey reflect typical patient advocacy and engagement concerns with responses based on a 7-point Likert scale (Belasen, 2019).

The dyad can focus on the areas with the greatest gaps and prioritize their own training and development efforts. Their peers may also complete the assessment to provide a more accurate measure of perceived gaps between what the dyad leaders say about themselves and how others evaluate them. Any significant difference can provide important insights about areas that require fine-tuning.

Of course, tailoring the leaders' development plans, skill building, and improvement efforts should match the organization's strategic goals and future directions. Thus, the assessment could serve as an alignment strategy that links the development of leadership roles and competencies with present and future organizational goals and strategies.

A culture of safety is reinforced through leadership's commitment to transparent communications in response to adverse events, near misses, and unhealthy conditions. Good leaders pave the way by rounding for outcomes and giving patients access to timely and relevant information. Administrators

Table 8.2 Patient Advocate/Engagement-Assessment

Next to each statement indicate the response that best matches your situation. Make sure to mark your designated role: Administrator (AD) or Physician (MD) 1. – *Never* 2. – *Rarely, in less than 10% of the chances when I could have* 3. – *Occasionally, in about 30%* 4. – *Sometimes, in about 50%* 5. – *Frequently, in about 70%* 6. – *Usually, in about 90%* 7. – *Every time*	AD	MD
1. I treat patients with courtesy and respect		
2. I listen carefully to patients		
3. I keep eye contact with my patients		
4. I focus on the patient to help reduce hospital readmission		
5. I encourage assessment and development of EI and interpersonal skills of care teams		
6. I monitor patient wait time		
7. I promote patient safety through teamwork		
8. I do everything to help patients with pain management treatment		
9. I find out new ways of documenting clinical encounters and using data		
10. I explain possible side effects in a way that patients understand		
11. I include patient's family members in consultations		
12. I encourage professional communication and spur collaborative team efforts		
13. I follow up with patients upon discharge to improve medication adherence		
14. I place great emphasis on cleanliness and tidiness of hospital rooms		
15. I use various media to increase patients' meaningful participation		

Source: Adapted from: Belasen (2019).

can join interdisciplinary team members in initiatives designed to achieve optimal patient outcomes, support training programs, and incentivize professional growth. Clinicians can engage with patients and their families, checking procedures, learning from errors, and communicating effectively with care teams.

Conclusion

Shared leadership structures are congruent with the growth strategies of team-based, integrated health systems. By adopting an inclusive leadership structure, hospitals and health systems can advance the Quadruple Aim of enhancing the patient's experience of care; reducing the per capita cost of healthcare; improving the health of populations; and fostering employee satisfaction, engagement, and retention. Necessary success factors include the following:

1. Supportive senior clinical leaders who act as change champions and promote shared leadership initiatives for aspiring women and men in healthcare
2. A shared vision and the pursuit of common goals
3. Clear expectations and key performance indicators for aspiring leaders and financial incentives for achieving shared goals
4. Patients placed at the center of all decision-making
5. A culture of mutual respect, transparency, and supportive communication
6. Pipeline opportunities for women clinicians to experience leadership through special projects, board committee assignments, and engagement in hospital integration and alignment strategies

A shift to a shared leadership structure with greater involvement of clinicians and administrators can help prioritize interprofessional collaboration, enhance patient engagement and the quality of care, and ultimately enhance the patient experience. Healthcare organizations that foster a shared leadership model focusing on gender parity in clinical as well as administrative leadership roles also send a strong signal to all stakeholders that women are indispensable to the success of the entire enterprise.

References

American College of Surgeons, Statements on Principles, https://www.facs.org/about-acs/statements/stonprin#code (Approved by Board of Regents June 2003, Revised April 12, 2016)

Barta, T., Kleiner, M., & Neumann, T. (2012). Is there a payoff from top-team diversity? *McKinsey Quarterly* 12: 65–66.

Belasen, A. (2019). *Dyad Leadership and Clinical Integration: Driving Change, Aligning Strategies*. Health Administration Press, Chicago, IL.

Belasen, A. T., Belasen, A. M., Belasen, A. R., & Belasen, A. R. (2021). A win-win for health care: Promoting co-leadership and increasing women's representation at the top, *Gender in Management*, 36(6), 762–781. (https://doi.org/10.1108/GM-06-2020-0176).

Belasen, A., & Frank, N. M. (2008). Competing values leadership: Quadrant roles and personality traits. *Leadership and Organizational Development Journal*, 29(2), 127–143.

Bourke, J., & Dillon, B. (2018). The diversity and inclusion revolution: Eight powerful truths. *Deloitte Review*, 22: 82–95.

Brown, M., Moore, C. A., MacGregor, J., & Lucey, J. R. (2021). Primary care and mental health: Overview of integrated care models. *The Journal for Nurse Practitioners*, 17(1), 10–14. (https://doi.org/10.1016/j.nurpra.2020.07.005)

Buell, J. M. (2017). Dyad leadership model: Four case studies, *Healthcare Executive*, Sept/Oct 2017, https://www.asahq.org/-/media/sites/asahq/files/public/education/other/dyad-leadership-model-healthcareexec.pdf?la=en&hash=A8CF C43CC2940B87EB5C3BA8E01D207A1100CB54

Chen, J., Leung, W. S., Song, W., & Goergen, M. (2019). Why female board representation matters: The role of female directors in reducing male CEO overconfidence. *Journal of Empirical Finance*, 53(C), 70–90.

Christensen, A., Miller, K., Neff, J., Moore, R., Hirschi, S., & Collette-Merrill, K. (2020). The effect of dyad rounding on collaboration and patient experience. *Nursing Management*, 51(1):16–25. DOI: 10.1097/01.NUMA.0000617052.03686.74

Davis, M. M., Gunn, R., Cifuentes, M., Khatri, P., Hall, J., Gilchrist, E., Peek, C. J., Klowden, M., Lazarus, J. A., Miller, B., & Cohen, D. J. (2019). Clinical workflows and the associated tasks and behaviors to support delivery of integrated behavioral health and primary care. *The Journal of Ambulatory Care Management*, 42(1), 51–65. (https://doi.org/10.1097/JAC.0000000000000257)

Davis, M. J., Luu, B. C., Raj, S., Abu-Ghname, A., & Buchanan, E. P. (2021). Multidisciplinary care in surgery: Are team-based interventions cost-effective? *The Surgeon*, 19(1), 49–60. (https://doi.org/10.1016/j.surge.2020.02.005)

Institute of Medicine (IOM) Committee on the Robert Wood Johnson Foundation Initiative on the Future of Nursing, at the Institute of Medicine. (2011). *The Future of Nursing: Leading Change, Advancing Health*. National Academies Press (US). https://pubmed.ncbi.nlm.nih.gov/24983041/

Krist, A. H., Tong, S. T., Aycock, R. A., & Longo, D. R. (2017). Engaging patients in decision-making and behavior change to promote prevention. *Studies In Health Technology and Informatics*, 240, 284–302. (https://doi.org/10.3233/978-1-61499-790-0-284)

Leach, L., Hastings, B., Schwarz, G., Watson, B., Bouckenooghe, D., Seoane, L., & Hewett, D. (2021). Distributed Leadership in healthcare: Leadership dyads and the promise of improved Hospital outcomes, *Leadership in Health Services*, 34(4): 353–374. (https://doi.org/10.1108/LHS-03-2021-0011)

MGMA. (2019). *Better together: Most healthcare leaders report using a dyad leadership model*, October 31, https://www.mgma.com/data/data-stories/better-together-most-healthcare-leaders-report-us

Swenson, S., Shanafelt, T., & Mohta, N. S. (2018). Leadership survey: why physician burnout is endemic, and how health care must respond. https://catalyst.nejm.org/physician-burnout-endemichealthcare-respond. NEJM Catalyst Insights Report. Published December 8, 2016.

Silvera, G. A., & Clark, J. R. (2019, June 6). Women at the helm: Chief executive officer, gender and patient experience in the hospital industry. *Health Care Management Review*. https://www.pubfacts.com/detail/31180934/Women-at-the-helm-Chief-executive-officer-gender-and-patient-experience-in-the-hospital-industry

Wyman, O. (2019), *Women in Healthcare Leadership*, https://www.oliverwyman.com/content/dam/oliverwyman/v2/publications/2019/January/WiHC/Women-In-Healthcare-Leadership-Report-FINAL.pdf

Young, R. (2017), "It takes two: can dyad leadership provide a durable pathway in healthcare's brave new world?", *Cardiovascular Business*, January 30. https://www.cardiovascularbusiness.com/topics/practice-management/it-takes-two-can-dyad-leadership-provide-durable-pathway-healthcares.

Chapter 9

The Nurse Executive Professional Development

Introduction

This chapter focuses on the topic of professional development for nurse executives. Professional development is both a personal endeavor and an organizational culture mindset. In this regard, the responsibility of professional development lies with both the individual and the organization. As discussed in Chapter 1, this book is centered on identifying and reducing gaps between best practice and actual practice that may impede the ability of healthcare organizations to provide the highest quality patient care and on ways to mitigate or change organizational factors that may impede a positive patient experience. Professional development falls under the overarching umbrella of an organizational best practice that should be assessed and evaluated in a formalized, ongoing manner (Poell & Van Der Krogt, 2014).

From an organizational perspective, one of the most important ways for health systems to optimize the quality of care provided to patients and the overall patient care experience is by making sure those in leadership roles, including nurse executives, have the necessary competencies and educational background to meet their day-to-day challenges. This cannot occur without a concerted and ongoing investment in their professional development.

The professional development of those serving as chief nursing officers (CNOs), and in other nursing executive leadership roles as designated by

DOI: 10.4324/9781003431077-9

their healthcare organizations, is an important factor for both organizations and the individuals serving in these roles to consider as a continuous and ongoing endeavor. Professional development for the nurse executive is a broad area, and this chapter is written with an understanding that an individual's professional development is unique and depends on several factors. For example, as discussed in Chapter 5, the specific type of professional development depends on the scope and role of the executive position held. Not all executive positions will have the same roles and responsibilities, particularly when comparing one organization to another. The unique educational and experiential background that each individual brings to the executive leadership position is also an important factor. Determining how best to assist and build on the collective experiences and educational background of each unique executive requires a thoughtful and reflective assessment (American Organization for Nursing Leadership [AONL], 2022a; Godsey & Hayes, 2023).

Rosanne Raso, the Vice President and CNO of New York-Presbyterian/Weill Cornell Medical Campus, writes on the meaning of being a nurse leader in this current healthcare environment, and the concept that "every nurse is a leader" (Raso, 2023). To Raso, the scope of nursing leadership spans across the continuum of care, both domestically and globally. She highlights, as other experts long have, that nursing leadership is found at the point of direct patient care, within communities, in the government sector, and across all areas of healthcare organizations at the micro- and macro-organizational levels. Raso aptly notes that nursing leaders constantly face challenges and "changing headwinds from the bedside to the boardroom."

Educational preparation for these challenges is equally complex and there is no one best way to meet the challenges. Godsey and Hayes (2023) go even further, suggesting that public perception of nurses needs to change or be "rebranded" for nurses to be fully recognized as valuable leaders. They contend that nurses need to advance the public perception that nurses are not solely healthcare workers following physician orders, but rather they are equal partners in leading healthcare systems and driving policy change.

Complicating nursing roles and their transition into executive leadership roles is too often a public misperception that nurses "assist" medicine and other healthcare fields (American Association of Colleges of Nursing [AACN], 2022). Bringing public perception into alignment with the American Association of Colleges of Nursing (AACN) statement regarding the discipline and profession of nursing that "nursing operates independent of, not auxiliary to, medicine and other disciplines" will be, in part, an aspect of the role of nursing leaders and how they approach professional development to maximize their education, training, and skills to influence all sectors of the healthcare system.

Executives with Nursing Backgrounds

It is currently unclear how many executives with nursing backgrounds serve in the role of hospital and health systems CEOs (Bean et al., 2022). There is a reported deficit in the data due to the lack of tracking by agencies such as the American Organization for Nursing Leadership (AONL) or the American College of Healthcare executives (Bean et al., 2022). However, Bean et al. (2022) note that data acquired from federal records report that 87% of the nursing workforce identifies as female and only 15% of all industry CEOs are females; this could suggest that the estimated number of CEOs with nursing backgrounds is low.

As discussed in Chapters 7 and 8, and as reported by the American Hospital Association in 2017, the number of individuals with nursing backgrounds or who are woman serving as a trustee or member of a hospital board is also low, with estimates as low as 5% (Bean et al., 2022). While the number of those with nursing backgrounds serving as trustee or on boards is particularly low, Godsey and Hayes (2023) are confident that as more nurses "understand and adopt the professional identity of nurse leaders, they can and should also proactively seek leadership positions on healthcare boards and regional/national committees to allow greater influence and focus on the essential contributions of professional nursing" (2023, p. 191).

A few recent examples of nurse leaders who are increasingly moving into complex government and system-wide healthcare leadership positions include the aforementioned Rosa Rosanne DNP, RN, NEA-BC, FAAN, FAONL; James Ballinghoff, DNP, MBA, RN, who was appointed the University of Pennsylvania Health System Chief Nurse Executive in 2022, Illinois' current Congresswoman Lauren Underwood; and Johnese Spisso, MPA, RN who was appointed the President of University of California at Los Angeles (UCLA) Health and CEO of UCLA Hospital Systems in 2016. These executives in government and industry provide profound examples of those with nursing backgrounds who are leading organizations and government at the highest levels. Both the University of Pennsylvania (UPenn) and UCLA are large and complex academic health systems providing care to patients across multiple inpatient hospitals (six in the case of the University of Pennsylvania), ambulatory care sites, and home care services (Penn Medicine News, 2022). As of 2020, the Illinois 14th Congressional District is home to almost 750,000 people – no small responsibility for Congresswoman Underwood!

In addition to fully understanding the core competencies outlined by the AACN and the AONL, learning from nurse executives can add further context regarding what skills, training, and education are needed to serve in these positions. These include all of the attributes Ballinghoff brings to the executive leadership position at UPenn, which include "clinical processes and outcomes, patient and family experience, quality metrics, nursing professional development" as well as experience in redesigning efforts, ensuring safe environments of care, equitable care, and improving outcomes (Penn Medicine News, 2022).

Lauren Underwood has served in an elected position since 2019, in the 14th Congressional District of Illinois, and in so doing became the youngest Black woman to serve in the United States House of Representatives. Underwood, a registered nurse, has a long and distinguished background in using evidence-based data to advise and influence change, particularly related to reducing disparities. She co-founded the Black Maternal Health Caucus to address needs for improved maternal health outcomes related to identifying and addressing disparities. Prior to her elected leadership position, Underwood served as a Senior Advisor at the U.S. Department of Health and Human Services, where her expertise was to advise in areas ranging from bioterrorism and public health emergencies to broadening Medicare access, reforming private insurance, and development of the Affordable Care Act (University of Michigan School of Nursing, 2022).

Spisso, who oversees all the operations at UCLA's hospitals and in 2020 was named by the LA Business Journal as one of the top 500 Most Influential Leaders in Los Angeles, has had a long career working in a number of different areas in healthcare (UCLA Health, 2023). Beginning her career as a critical care nurse and a director of trauma and emergency services at UC Davis Medical Center, Spisso is lauded for a number of collaborative endeavors as she moved through chief officer positions. Her ability to contribute and play a major role in integrating regional hospitals into larger academic medical centers and leading the development of a statewide trauma systems highlights this collaborative mindset (UCLA Health, 2023). This collaborative mindset shines as an example of a key executive leadership skill. Upon reflecting on the positions held by these leaders and the seemingly vast responsibilities managed and led by them, it becomes clear that there are a number of considerations for areas of professional development along the continuum of a nursing executive's career.

Executive Toolbox

The collective experiences and educational background that contribute to the success of the nurse executive role can be considered the *nurse executive's toolbox.* How this toolbox gets filled should be purposeful, data driven, and a reflection of current outcomes with the mindful intent of ongoing continuous improvement. The concept of a toolbox allows for a flexible and adaptable approach to nurse executive professional development. A toolbox can travel from job to job and many of the tools are transferable in their use and application. Tools can be traded out for new or updated tools. The tools required in any given box can be tailored to specific needs unique to positions, roles, and responsibilities.

The U.S. Department of Education introduced the groundbreaking concept of a *toolbox* for educational leaders in 1988. At the time there was a growing awareness, much like there is in healthcare today, that the quality of education and outcomes of high school students in the U.S. was less than optimal. High school graduation rates, as measured by the U.S. Department of Education, were identified as being low and contributing to poor-quality lifelong outcomes for too many (Adelman, 2006). The impact of poor-quality educational outcomes as measured by high school graduation rates are not only significant for an individual, but they also have lasting intergenerational and intragenerational effects (Murnane, 2013).

The most recent U.S. Department of Education's *Toolbox Revisited Paths to Degree Completion from High School,* first introduced in 1988 and continuously updated since that time, serves as a collection of data designed to provide practitioners with *tools* to close the gaps and improve high school graduation rates across the United States. The toolbox report is based on an evidence-driven data analysis from a longitudinal study tracking trends over time. The report examines what is and what is not working. Its results-oriented assessment focuses on themes, highlights, and implications. Using historical analysis, current data, and a review of stories the toolbox provides direction and recommendations for educational leaders in practice and policy.

It is in this vein that a *toolbox* approach should be considered for nurse executive professional development with the aim to optimize preparing nurses in leaderships and policy positions to reduce the occurrence of poor-quality outcomes in healthcare. In addition, this approach can prepare nurse executives to contribute to the design of better systems using a toolbox filled with science-driven data. Questions for current and aspiring nurse executives to consider include: What do you have in your toolbox already? What needs to be added for a more complete collection of tools? Are there tools that are too old and do not work anymore, or some that just need to be sharpened or adjusted?

This type of self-assessment requires a thoughtful, reflective, and purposeful review of an individual's toolbox. Another consideration is the type of organization a nurse executive works for as different healthcare organization environments have different structures and thus different needs. This can also be a useful approach or exercise for a healthcare organization. When a healthcare organization opens its collective professional development toolbox, does it serve in ways that enhance quality patient care? Does it have the tools to facilitate improvements in health outcomes? And does it provide the necessary tools to aid in fixing and maintaining a healthy well-being across the workforce?

The toolbox or toolkit reference can be found across a number of nursing resource sites. The idea of a toolbox or a toolkit is not a new concept, as it is frequently used as a term to reference a collection of important things needed. The analogy has been used to address knowledge needed by nursing students, nurse educators, and nursing management. The University of Washington Health Sciences Library (2023) has an entire website titled "Nurse Toolkit" that provides a resource for a number of areas such as patient care management, medications, patient education, cross-cultural issues, and evidence-based practices.

The terms toolbox and toolkit seem to be used interchangeably across the literature with little definition included when they are used. However, a toolbox often implies, as the term suggests, that there is a case or a box in which a collection of different tools can be stored and organized, while a toolkit often implies a collection of a specific tool for a specific purpose. They can also be thought of as one and the same or possessing characteristics in their respective uses that are really distinctions without a difference. For the purposes of this chapter, the term *toolbox* will be used to identify the concept of the "organization and storage" of a collection of tools. A nurse executive will need an expansive knowledge set or collection tools and in any given situation the nurse executive will need to pull from their toolbox vastly different tools, so their toolbox needs plenty of storage and it needs to be highly organized.

Building the Toolbox

While there are some consistent leadership attributes that all nurse executives should possess and demonstrate regardless of work environment, including working with an ethical leadership mindset and other core competencies outlined by professional organizations such as the AONL, their specific leadership role within an organization can influence the type of ongoing professional development needed. Nurse executives work across a broad spectrum of organizational types, and these organizational types span the continuum of care across the U.S. health systems. They include healthcare organizations such as small rural community hospitals, large comprehensive academic medical centers, long-term nursing facilities, primary care and urgent care centers, the Veterans Administration, active military bases, Indian Health Services, departments of public health, hospice, and home care organizations. There are also a mix of for-profit and not-for-profit entities.

The need for a tailored perspective in terms of professional development makes sense when considering that there are different regulations and policies in each of these organizations and that healthcare organizations are situated within the larger ecosystem of federal, state, and local government entities. There is considerable variation in local and state-specific laws, regulations, and policies. The ideological root of the U.S. approach to governance rests on the fundamental tension of individual rights and the role of the state government versus the federal government and it is within this tension that many health regulations, laws, and policies are designed (Cohen, 2016).

It is incumbent on nurse executives to purposely focus on overarching professional development principles related to effective leadership styles, but also professional development that is encompassing the specific skills needed to make fully informed executive-level decisions within the context of the type of organization the nurse executive works in, the community in which they work, and the larger laws, regulations, and policies driven by government entities and society at large.

The nurse executive toolbox should be conceptualized as a box that is continuingly filling and refilling with tools that allow nurse executives to perform in the most impactful and dynamic ways. The question of how to fill the nurse executive professional development toolbox is not a new conversation. As far back as the late 1990s, the Harvard Nursing Research Institute assembled nursing leaders from academic medical centers to discuss nursing leadership (Buerhaus et al., 1997). The late 1990s was a critical time in the healthcare industry as there was expanding enrollment in managed care plans and a setting-off of growing economic competition in the healthcare sector, forcing many healthcare organizations to examine cost containment initiatives for the first time (Buerhaus et al., 1997).

Just a little more than ten years ago, Frederickson and Nickitas (2011) asked the question as to whether CNO development was a crisis or challenge. They noted, as Buerhaus et al. (1997) did decades prior, that with the growing roles and responsibilities of nurse executives there was a growing need for executive development education and training. In their review they identified that while there have been a number of nursing organizations that have aimed to improve training and education for executive leadership for nurses, there was a lack of clear and concise information on what specific academic preparation was needed (Frederickson & Nickitas, 2011).

This appears to be a theme that has been carried forward since the assembly of key nursing leadership at the Harvard Nursing Research Center in 1996. However, Frederickson and Nickitas (2011) stated that it is crucial that nurses develop the knowledge and competencies needed to be successful in executive leadership positions as their background positions nurses well to provide strategic insight and influence on shaping the healthcare system.

With an ever-growing focus on the need for an organized and concise means of direction on professional development for nurse leaders and nurse executives, there are a number of professional nursing organizations that are invested in providing a framework and opportunity for professional development. These include, but are not limited to, the AACN, American Nurses Association (ANA), AONL, and the Sigma Theta Tau International Honor Society of Nursing. Interestingly, and to be discussed further in this chapter, are the resounding conclusions drawn at the time from the Harvard Research Nursing Institute meeting all those years ago by Beverly Henry, PhD, RN, FAAN. At the time, Dr. Henry was the editor of the Journal of Nursing Scholarship, Associate Dean at the University of Illinois Chicago (UIC), and Director of Clinical Practice Development at UIC, and the conclusions she drew at the time in many ways still resonate today. These include the need to (1) focus on populations and their healthcare needs, (2) develop more collaborative relationships between nurses and physicians, (3) strengthen collaboration between clinical nursing practice and nursing education entities, (4) pursue more research agendas aimed at improving quality and controlling cost, (5) gain a better understanding of how best to use information systems in the delivery of care, and overall, (6) "increase every aspect of service effectiveness and continuity of care from hospital to home" (Buerhaus et al., 1997, p. 19).

The healthcare sector has not been the only industry asking the fundamental questions about what is needed to prepare executive leaders. Thornton (2023), a Senior Principal of Daggerwing, a global consulting group, noted that the past few years encompassing the COVID-19 global pandemic has placed leaders in a "let's just get through this moment in time" mindset. The type of mindset that Thornton describes as focusing on short-term solutions to meet immediate needs while placing bigger and longer term strategic issues on the backburner. As organizations have been moving through the post-pandemic phase, the pressing issues for any organization aiming for long-term sustainability include identifying new business models, new technologies, and productivity gaps.

The focus is very much back on many of the issues shunted to the side during the height of the COVID-19 pandemic. In addition, what Thornton refers to as issues in organizations related to "environmental, social, and governance" clearly need attention. Using a sports analogy, Thornton argues "that the bench of up-and-coming leaders lack the skills, knowledge, and capabilities to lead their companies into the future." He further argues that "what's needed now is nothing short of a total overhaul of how organizations develop and prepare their leaders to move their company into the future." He claims that to do this, what has been a trend referred to as "upskilling" and as a practice has been a "nice to have" is now a "business-critical priority." The focus on upskilling is not an unfamiliar concept across many global companies, particularly those that have been challenged competitively by the fast-growing technology-driven economy (Friedman, 2016).

Upskilling and Reskilling as a Tool

From an organizational or systems perspective, upskilling and reskilling have long been a popular means used by companies as they have adjusted to the rapid 21st-century growing technology economy. Upskilling and reskilling have been a significant focus of not only national strategic planning to reduce unemployment and to remain globally completive, it has also been a popular lifelong learning tool in the toolbox used by the private corporate sector to educate and provide new training to the currently employed workforce (Borgos et al., 2023). Upskilling and reskilling employees helps companies stay competitive and more able to adapt to idea-to-product-time. To illustrate the point, Friedman (2016), describes the story of AT&T, or what he calls the "big whale," as a result of its innovative strategies in pathway development for its employees, as it created a "huge wake" or sweeping change in how to think about educational opportunities from an industry perspective (p. 233).

AT&T is one of the largest telecommunications companies in the world and is known as being a global leader in investing in the upskilling and reskilling of its employees to help their employees remain relevant in their skill set (Friedman, 2016). AT&T, while a tech company, has similar traits to the healthcare sector. There are employees of all educational levels who are in high demand. The industry itself, like healthcare, changes rapidly in terms of new knowledge and attention to customer service is a significant part of keeping and drawing in new customers. AT&T invested in academic partnerships by pursuing opportunities for their employees to upskill, reskill, and remain relevant (Friedman, 2016). The concept of academic-practice partnerships is not new to the healthcare sector or nursing. Initiating academic-practice partnerships for upskilling and reskilling professional nursing development has also been highly recommended by the AACN-AONL Task Force on Academic-Partnerships and highlighted in the 2021 AACN Essentials Competencies for Professional Nursing Education (AACN, 2016; AACN, 2021; Kiss & Smith, 2020, p. 100).

To maintain relevance, AT&T, which is situated in the fast-growing and changing telecommunication market, needed to ask the big questions: "what direction do we want the company to go in? What skills do we need to go in that direction, and how do we reskill our employees to get us to where we want to go?" (Friedman, 2016). This allowed the company to explore and strengthen its understanding of the ways professional development could contribute to keeping their employees relevant but also connecting this concept of "professional development" or "upskilling and reskilling" to the long-term goals of the company. In keeping with the toolbox analogy, comparatively a short-sighted focus would be akin to filling the toolbox once, not being purposeful in what is in the toolbox to complete the job at hand, and then not ever returning to the toolbox to make sure it is updated and not taking the time to sharpen the tools occasionally. Using this line of thought and thinking about nurse executives – if assuming a healthcare organization wants to move in the direction of producing quality outcomes and providing high-quality patient experiences, then key questions to follow include: what skills or tools do nurse executives need to help the organization go in that direction? And how does the organization upskill or reskill nurse leaders to help get the organization to where they want to go?

For AT&T, after the "what direction" and "what skills" questions were addressed, the company developed partnerships to address the "how" question (Friedman, 2016). They partnered with higher education entities and online platforms. The partnerships included relationships with universities such as the Georgia Institute of Technology and the University of Oklahoma and platforms such as Udacity and Coursera (Friedman, 2016, p. 231). These relationships allowed AT&T to better target and align their specific educational needs through online degrees and certificates to support the professional development needed for employees who worked as intelligence specialists and predictive analytics specialists (Friedman, 2016).

Large academic healthcare systems, typically associated with large universities and having an abundance of educational resources, such as the University of Michigan Health System, the University of Pittsburgh Medical System, and the University of Virginia Health System, may in many ways find it easier to align the long-term goals of the organization with educational upskilling and reskilling opportunities. However, for health systems operating in a space away from higher education systems, reskilling and upskilling may be more difficult, and implementing these strategies may require new, innovative, collaborative, and creative partnership to support these types of professional development.

While AT&T and Telecom in general are distinctly different from the healthcare industry, the AT&T experience still serves as a prime example of what can be achieved when intentions and outcomes are aligned with professional development. Importantly, regardless of how the academic-practice partnerships are established to advance the professional development of nurses, the AACN notes that any partnership arrangement needs to be "predicated on respect, relationships, reciprocity, and co-design" (2021, p. 8).

The Executive Role

One of the challenges for nursing professionals and other healthcare professionals who move into leadership roles, as discussed in Chapter 5, is moving through the process of adapting from a more exclusive focus on patient care and into the mindset of an executive (Frederickson & Nickitas, 2011; Smith & Johnson, 2018; Dempsey, 2022). While both clinical nursing practice and nursing executive leadership require a significant amount of multitasking and an ability to interact with a vast number of both professional colleagues and customers (patients and their families), the executive role specifically encompasses the organizational perspective where there is tremendous complexity, ambiguity, and uncertainty. The mindset shift needs to move from the nursing-patient interaction of assessment, planning, implementation, and nursing diagnosis and care to the executive mindset of assessment, planning, implementation, evaluation, and diagnosis of the organization and all the theatre that goes with it (Bolman & Deal, 2017).

The assessment of an organization requires specific skills, training, and education that is different than that often learned in a STEM or clinical education. Bolman and Deal (2017), characterize the executive leadership of an organization as the art of understanding the differences of simple to complex firms, their power structures, human resources issues, political dynamics within and outside the organization, and the symbolic and cultural nuances inherent to any organization. Frederickson and Nickitas (2011) further the discussion and note the core knowledge areas required by nurse executives which include understanding the healthcare marketplace, healthcare policy, and the greater needs of society. There are additional considerations for gaining knowledge in the areas of finance, accounting, data analytics, and economics. It is through this lens, with the fundamental needs of an organization being placed front and center, that the choice of skills, training, and education required for any given person moving into an executive role should be viewed.

As noted in the introduction to this chapter, professional development should start with a couple of key questions. What is already in the toolbox in terms of executive knowledge tools? And then what needs to be added to be effective in the role of a nurse or healthcare executive? An honest self-assessment of the knowledge, skills, and abilities that a nurse executive brings to the job is critical, because as Frederickson and Nickitas (2011) suggest that without the "prerequisite knowledge, skills, and abilities" required to make executive decisions, a "chief nurse executive can easily be rendered ineffective and powerless" (p. 347).

Collins (2001) found something very interesting when studying what made organizations great, and it was not that they were led by "larger than life charismatics leaders" but rather that they were led by leaders whose interest was not focused on their own reputation, but rather the focus was on building their organization. His work also suggested that there is an element of discipline that great leaders possess. Collins' work is reminiscent of Maslow's *Hierarchy of Needs* which highlights how humans are motivated to meet their needs starting from a base tier such as food and shelter and moving through the level of the pyramid toward the top of the pyramid of self-actualization. *Maslow's Hierarchy of Needs* is one of the first and fundamental frameworks nursing students are exposed to during their undergraduate studies as they learn about human motivation grounded in physiological and psychological needs.

Collins' pyramid of leadership hierarchy, like Maslow's Hierarchy of Needs, has five tiers and begins with a base and moves toward a point where a leader exhibits characteristics of a more fully formed executive leader, demonstrating self-actualization as a leader. The base of Collins' pyramid or level 1 is where the leader, from a professional development perspective, needs to have the *essential knowledge* and skills to do the job, or what Collins calls a highly capable leader who can contribute due to good work habits. The pyramid then moves up in levels, highlighting a level 2 leader as someone who can contribute as a team member and works effectively with others. A level 3 leader is highly organized and can maximize resources aligned with objectives, while a level 4 leader catalyzes commitment and a vigorous pursuit of a vision with high-performance standards.

Like Maslow's top pyramid tier, where a person can reach their full potential, this is what Collins refers to as a level 5 executive, in which a sense of self-actualization in their leadership role is achieved (TandemSpring, 2017). Collins states that level 5 leaders "build enduring greatness through a paradoxical blend of humility and professional will" (2001, p. 20). Importantly, level 5 leaders are less focused on their ego and self-interest and fully focused on the success of the institutions they lead in a manner that balances being modest, willful, humble, and fearless (2001, p. 22).

For executives, this pyramid concept can potentially be helpful in developing their plan for organizational development, clarifying their professional development priorities, and designing the layout and components of their toolboxes. Unlike Maslow's Hierarchy of Needs that suggests an individual must satisfy one level before being able to move onto the next level, Collins notes that an executive leader may fall into different levels at different points in time or in a varying sequence, but level 5 is the point that Collins specifically attributes to a leader who "fully embodies all the layers of the pyramid" (2001, p. 21).

Current Challenges of Nurse Executives

One of the most well-known organizations that focuses solely on the development of nurse leaders and executives is the AONL. The AONL is a national professional organization that advances the professional development of nurse leaders and executives. Its central aim is rooted in promoting the educational development of nurse leaders, supporting advocacy efforts in collaboration with the American Hospital Association, and it serves as a community for its members to provide networking opportunities (AONL, 2023). AONL competencies are anchored by five overlapping domains that have been established as a foundation, to guide with depth, areas of need in executive leadership. These areas include communication and relationship management, professionalism, knowledge of the healthcare environment, business skills & principles, and leadership (AONL, 2022, p. 1). The AONL is guided by the mission that nursing leaders "transform healthcare through expert and influential leadership" (AONL, 2023). To support AONL's mission, the AONL outlines the following five strategic priorities for 2022–2024:

- Lead, influence and support the healthcare workforce
- Improve Health through advocacy
- Advance nursing leadership
- Advance and promote value-informed healthcare
- Unite nurses to achieve health equity

These strategic objectives are grounded in a number of principles that focus on advancing and optimizing health outcomes but specifically focus on the active ways in which nursing can optimize their contributions to advancing health outcomes and the profession of nursing as a whole (AONL, 2023).

In addition to establishing strategic priorities and stated objectives, the AONL is working to further advance the current state of nursing executive leadership throughout the U.S. healthcare system through the recent 2022 Longitudinal Nursing Leadership Insight Study (Insight, 2022, AONL, 2022b). The study provides a revealing and opportune glimpse of the current state of nursing leadership and its challenges. The opportunity of this study is that it gives a reference point to how nursing leaders are elevating the current state of healthcare, with particular attention to the way in which it has been impacted by the COVID-19 pandemic.

The AONL's current 2022 study is keenly focused on understanding how healthcare has changed over time since July 2020, or pre-COVID-19 from the perspective of CNOs, nurse directors, and nurse managers across the care continuum. The survey attempted to capture information on the top challenges, intent to leave, and preparedness for future infectious events and more. The AONL report notes that the majority of the most recent

2,336 responses in the August 2021 survey were submitted by CNOs, nurse directors, and nurse managers who were white or Caucasian, over the age of 45, and from urban acute care hospitals. Many fewer responses (3%) came from those that work in the long-term acute care sector (AONL, 2022b, p. 1).

The top overall challenges included *"emotional health and well-being of staff,"* staff *"retention, furloughs, layoffs,"* and *"travelers, contingent workforce"* (AONL, 2022b, p. 2). When asked about their ability to respond to these respective challenges, the two most common responses included concerns with financial resource availability and how to manage traveler and contingent workforce, followed by staff retention, health equity, workplace violence, bullying, and incivility. These findings on workplace violence, bullying, and incivility being identified as significant issues impacting the nursing workforce by nurse executives in this AONL survey mirrors the data discussed in Chapter 6 addressing nursing leadership and the impact on patient outcomes.

One noteworthy point about the survey was the slight variation in how managers, directors, and CNO/CNE rated their top perceived challenges. For managers and directors, it was financial resource availability. For CNO/CNEs their top-rated challenge was workplace violence, with financial resource availability second. The AONL, recognizing that bullying was reportedly becoming more prevalent in the workplace, recently added the question about workplace bullying to its surveys. The results are not surprising given the prior surveys administered by the ANA.

Similar to The National Council of State Boards of Nursing (2023) survey which was administered to registered nurses, the AONL longitudinal survey also asked nurse executives about their "intent to leave." The AONL (2023) survey of nurse leaders found that 13% of responders intended to leave their position within six months from the time of the survey administration, and 25% selected that they were considering leaving. The reasons for "considering leaving" or "intent to leave" in the aggregated results for managers, directors, and CNO/CNE were most closely tied to wanting a "better work life balance" (44%) and feelings associated with "burnout, exhaustion" (43%).

Burnout, one of the three B's discussed in Chapter 6, continues as a prominent trend for nurse executives. Nurse executives working in the role or capacity of nurse manager were more likely to report "considering leaving," with burnout as the reported reason, as compared to those in the director or CNO/CNE positions. Burnout becomes less of a reported reason for "considering leaving" as nurse leaders move into higher level executive leadership positions. For example, 59% of nurse managers responding to the survey were considering leaving, while 44% of the nurse director respondents were considering leaving and only 29% of the responding CNO/CNE were considering leaving. This may suggest that those in nursing leadership roles closest to patient care and those directly overseeing those nurses working in direct patient care were more susceptible to burnout. As discussed in Chapter 7, both burnout and exhaustion have also been reported as causative factors for costly and damaging medical errors (Garrett, 2008; Agency for Healthcare Research and Quality (AHRQ), 2016; Phillips et al., 2021). This raises several questions about the factors that need to change to reverse this trend.

The aim of achieving work-life balance also appears to resonate across all nursing leadership roles when it comes to the response rating associated with "intent to leave" or "considering leaving." Work-life balance is reported as the overall top reason for wanting to leave although the survey did not capture whether the actual reason for leaving was associated with "work-life balance" (AONL, 2023, p. 8). It is clear, however, that there are several trends that those in nursing leadership and executive positions should focus their attention on or at least consider assessing closely in their organization and personal work circumstances. These include work-life balance, emotional health, and burnout (AONL, 2023). Given the evidence, building a plan for professional development that includes understanding and managing these trending issues should be considered and included in a nurse executive's professional development toolbox.

Professional Development as Opportunity

Personal or purposeful organizational professional development is about opportunity. Professional development of nursing leaders or those working in executive positions can be considered both an opportunity for the individual and an opportunity for the greater good of the organization. Put another way, the investment made by the individual and by an organization in professional development benefits both. There are both formalized and informal approaches to professional development, and as previously noted, the way in which executives feel and organize their professional development toolbox is unique to each individual, the organization they work within, and the scope of their responsibilities.

These professional development opportunities, or upskilling and reskilling activities, can be achieved through both formal and informal education and training, keeping in mind that training and education are slightly different in their meaning. Providing clarification on the differences, Marquis and Huston (2017) highlight training "as organized methods of ensuring that people have knowledge and skills for a specific purpose to perform their job duties" while education "is more formal and broader in scope than training." Education on the other hand is designed to develop individuals in a broader sense (p. 411). A combination of training and education is often needed to achieve ongoing, lifelong professional development.

There are several degree programs and organizations advancing the pathway for nurses to gain executive leadership in the form of both training and educational opportunities. The Commission on Collegiate Nursing Education (CCNE) accredits nursing master's programs with specific leadership competencies and these programs serve as one of the most obvious formal educational development pathways for nursing professionals who are in the role or hope to move into the role of a nurse executive to gain additional education in leadership. CCNE accredited nursing master's and undergraduate bachelor's programs are expected to have curricula embedded throughout their programs with the AACN Essentials: *Competencies for Professional Nursing Education* which includes leadership development.

The new 2021 AACN Essentials are in part aimed at preparing nurses for executive roles and Domain 10 specifically speaks to the importance of ongoing professional development. Domain 10, titled "Personal, Professional, and Leadership Development," addresses professional development expectations, stating in its descriptor that "participation in activities and self-reflection that foster personal health, resilience, and well-being; contribute to lifelong learning; and support the acquisition of nursing expertise and the assertion of leadership" (2021, p. 53). The focus of Domain 10 resonates with AONL's Longitudinal Nursing Leadership Insight Study 2022 (Insight, 2022, AONL, 2022b) and states that attention to well-being and resilience for self and others are important aspects of executive leadership and thus need to be included in the nurse executive professional development toolbox as part of ongoing professional development.

Degree-granting nursing programs are not the only formal educational pathways for those wanting to advance their careers in executive leadership. Nursing executives can earn advanced degrees in several different master's and doctoral programs in the areas of health administration, public administration, public health, public policy, business education, leadership, and organizational behavior (Frederickson & Nickitas, 2011). It goes to the point stated at the beginning of the chapter that there is no one size fits all and that unique perspectives and backgrounds bring an important diversity of ideas to helping advance health outcomes, health policy, the mitigation of health disparities and the patient experience. Smith and Johnson (2018) support the diversity of options for professional development by documenting several professional development opportunities for nurse executives outside the formal degree pathways. Examples of such opportunities include the previously mentioned AONL, the AACN Leadership Development Programs, the ANA Leadership Institute, the National League of Nursing, the Robert Wood Johnson Foundation, and Sigma Theta Tau International (pp. 159–160). While not exhaustive, this list of professional organizations offers a multitude of pathways for nurses to acquire tools for their executive professional development toolbox.

Conclusion

The building of an executive professional development toolbox can appear overwhelming but taking a strategy from Steven Covey's seminal work *The 7 Habits of Highly Effective People*, particularly Habit 2, may provide some direction. Covey's Habit 2 is about embracing the beginning with the end in mind (Covey, 2020). Those in the field of education know that the concept of beginning with the end in mind is not unlike a best practice of curriculum design. In the development of a course, best educational practices ask at the beginning what in the end someone should learn and why. After defining what goals and outcomes should be achieved, the next step is often asking which objectives need to be met to achieve these goals or outcomes.

What often follows is a selection of exercises to advance learning and an assortment of formative assessments to evaluate that learning. Beginning with the end in mind can be an effective strategy to assess how to best manage filling the executive professional toolbox, by asking which goals need to be achieved personally and for the organization.

Returning to the U.S. Department of Education's *Toolbox Revisited Paths to Degree Completion from High School* introduced earlier in this chapter, the toolbox was designed to close a gap, a gap in achievement and educational attainment of high school students. The end goal was to improve the rates of achievement and the *Toolbox Revisited Paths to Degree Completion from High School* served as a collection of evidence-based strategies to close the gap and achieve the goal of increasing high school graduation rates.

It is with this same intent that nurse executives can embrace Covey's Habit 2, beginning with the end in mind, to identify goals, ultimately identify gaps in knowledge that are impeding the ability to reach these goals, and then organizing a plan to acquire the education, training, and skills to close the gaps in knowledge that may be preventing achievement of the end goals. For each person this will be different. Some executives will need more knowledge in the areas of finance and accounting, for others it may be in communication strategies, data analytics, human resources management, or in the regulatory environment and policy development. Regardless of the gaps, a strategic and planned approach to professional development is a leadership strategy that needs to be exercised to advance best practices, health outcomes, and ultimately optimize patient experiences across the continuum of the healthcare system.

References

Adelman, C. (2006). *The ToolBox Revisited: Paths to Degree Completion From High School Through College.* U.S. Department of Education. Washington, D.C.

Agency for Healthcare Research and Quality (AHRQ). (2016). *Estimating the Additional Hospital Inpatient Cost and Mortality Associated with Selected Hospital-Acquired Conditions.* https://www.ahrq.gov/hai/pfp/haccost2017.html

American Association of Colleges of Nursing (AACN). (2016). *Advancing Healthcare Transformation: A New Era for Academic.* American Association of College of Nursing. Washington, D.C.

American Association of Colleges of Nursing (AACN). (2021, April 6). *The Essentials: Core Competencies for Professional Nursing Education.* American Association of the Colleges of Nursing. Washington, D.C.

American Association of Colleges of Nursing (AACN). (2022, September). *Nursing Fact Sheet.* AACN. https://www.aacnnursing.org/news-data/fact-sheets/nursing-fact-sheet

American Organization for Nursing Leadership (AONL). (2022a). *AONL Nurse Leader Core Competencies.* American Organization of Nurse Executives. Chicago, IL. www.aonl.org/competencies

American Organization for Nursing Leadership (AONL). (2022b). *Longitudinal Nursing Leadership Insight Survey Part Four: Nurse Leader's Top Challenges and Areas for Needed Support, July 2020 to August 2022.* American Organization for Nursing Leadership Foundation. Chicago, IL.

American Organization for Nursing Leadership (AONL). (2023). *American Organization for Nursing Leadership: About.* American Hospital Association. Chicago, IL. https://www.aonl.org/about/overview

Bean, M., Carbajal, E., & Gleeson, C. (2022, March 31). *Is It Time for More Nurse CEOs? Becker's Healthcare.* https://www.beckershospitalreview.com/nursing/is-it-time-for-more-nurse-ceos.html

Bolman, L. G. & Deal, T. E. (2017). *Reframing Organizations: Artistry, Choice, and Leadership.* (6th ed). Jossey-Bass. Hoboken, NJ.

Borgos, J., Kinser, K., & Kline, L. (2023). The borderless market for open, distance, and digital education, in Zawawcki, O., & Jung, I. (Eds.), *Handbook of Open, Distance, and Digital Education* (pp. 355–369). Springer Nature. London, UK. https://link.springer.com/referenceworkentry/10.1007/978-981-19-2080-6_22

Buerhaus, P. I., Clifford, J., Erickson, J. I., Fay, M. S., Miller, J. R., Sporing, E. M., & Weissman, G. K. (1997). Executive nursing leadership. Summary of the Harvard Nursing Research Institute's follow-up conference. *The Journal of Nursing Administration,* 24 (4), 12–20.

Cohen, S. (2016). A primer on political philosophy, in Mason, D. J., Gardner, D. B., Outlaw, F. H., & O'Grady, E. T. (Eds.), *Policy & Politics in Nursing and Health Care* (7th ed., pp. 52–60). Elsevier Saunders. St. Louis, MO.

Collins, J. (2001). *Good to Great: Why Some Companies Make the Leap and Others Don't.* HarperCollins. New York, NY.

Covey, S. R. (2020). *The 7 Habits of Highly Effective People.* Simon & Schuster. New York, NY.

Dempsey, C. (2022). Nursing leadership across the continuum the nurse leader in industry. *Nursing Administration Quarterly,* 46(4), 283–290.

Frederickson, K., & Nickitas, D. (2011). Chief nursing officer executive development: A crisis or a challenge. *Nursing Administration Quarterly,* 35(4), 344–353.

Friedman, T. L. (2016). *Thank You for Being Late: An Optimist's Guide To Thriving In the Age of Accelerations.* Picador. New York, NY.

Godsey, J. A., & Hayes, T. (2023, April). All nurses are leaders: 5 steps to reconstruct the professional identity and brand image of nursing. *Nurse Leader,* 21(2), 188–194.

Health Sciences Library. (2023). *Nurse Toolkit.* University of Washington University Library. Seattle, WA. https://hsl.uw.edu/toolkits/nurse-toolkit/

Insight, J. (2022). *Longitudinal Nursing Leadership Insight Study.* American Organization for Nursing Leadership. Chicago, IL. https://www.aonl.org/resources/nursing-leadership-covid-19-survey

Kiss, E., Simpson, A., & Smith, C. M. (2020). Nursing professional development practitioners in leadership roles: Leading academic-practice partnerships. *Journal for Nurses in Professional Development,* 36(2), 99–103.

Marquis, B. L., & Huston, C. J. (2017). *Leadership Roles and Management Functions in Nursing: Theory and Application* (9th ed.). Woltzers Kluwer. Philadelphia, PA.

Murnane, R. J. (2013, June). U.S. High school graduation rates: Patterns and explanations. *Journal of Economic Literature,* 51(2), 370–422. (https://doi.org/10.1257/jel.51.2.370)

National Council of State Boards of Nursing. (2023, April 13). *NCSBN Research Projects Significant Nursing Workforce Shortages and Crisis.* https://www.ncsbn.org/news/ncsbn-research-projects-significant-nursing-workforce-shortages-and-crisis

Penn Medicine News. (2022, November 3). *Longtime Penn Presbyterian Medical Center Chief Nursing Officer Names University Pennsylvania Health System Chief Nurse Executive.* https://www.pennmedicine.org/news/news-releases/2022/november/ppmc-chief-nursing-officer-named-uphs-chief-nurse-executive

Phillips, J., Malliaris, A. P., & Bakerjian, D. (2021, April 21). *Nursing and Patient Safety. Agency for Healthcare Improvement and Quality: Patient Safety Network.* https://psnet.ahrq.gov/primer/nursing-and-patient-safety

Poell, R. F., & Van Der Krogt, F. J. (2014, January). The role of human resource development in organizational change: Professional development strategies of employee, managers and HRD practitioners, in: Billett, S., Harteis, C., & Gruber, H. (Eds.), *International Handbook of Research in Professional and Practice-Based Learning* (pp. 1043–1070). Springer. New York, NY.

Raso, R. (2023, June). Is every nurse a leader? *Nursing Management*, 54(6), 5.

Smith, C. M., & Johnson, C. S. (2018, May/June). Preparing nurse leaders in nurse leaders in professional development: leadership programs, *Journal of Nursing Professional Development*, 34(3), 158–161.

TandemSpring. (2017, July 24). *Level 5 Leadership: HBR Must Reads on Leadership Review # 7.* https://www.tandemspring.com/level-5-leadershi-hbr-must-reads-on-leadership-review-7/

Thornton, C. (2023, May 30). *Are You Failing to Prepare the Next Generations of C-Suite Leaders?* Harvard Business Publishing. Boston, MA.

UCLA Health. (2023). *UCLA Leadership.* https://www.uclahealth.org/discover-ucla-health/about/leadership/johnese-spisso-mpa

University of Michigan School of Nursing. (2022, April 5). *Congresswoman Lauren Underwood Named Keynote Speaker for U-M School of Nursing 2022 Spring Commencement.* https://nursing.umich.edu/about/news-portal/202204-congresswoman-lauren-underwood-named-keynote-speaker-u-m-school-nursing

Chapter 10

Conclusion: Leadership Practices to Improve the Patient Experience

---

This book began by highlighting a disconnect between how well healthcare leaders believe their organizations perform relative to the patient experience and what their patients report in surveys. We also sought to explain why this gap occurs and create a framework to help leaders narrow it. We have explored how the highest levels of leadership – including governance, senior management, and nursing executives – must assemble priorities within a highly layered landscape of stakeholder agendas with overlapping or even competing values.

The purpose of this final chapter is to demonstrate how the overlap component can prevail and most importantly, why. It is noteworthy that the stakeholder interests that overlap can become easily diminished by parochial interests, and the louder those are expressed, the more that the overlapping interests can shrink into obscurity. Leadership has the special obligation to create a climate in which intersecting needs are given prominence. It doesn't mean that leaders have, or even should have, all the answers. Quite the contrary, in fact, the most effective leaders set a tone for the best answers to emerge from what could otherwise be a cacophonous Tower of Babel message environment in which important priorities cannot be sufficiently heard, let alone addressed.

This goal – promoting an understanding of the common ground among organizational stakeholders and employing that common ground as the basis of a decision-making culture – is far from easy. If it was, all the issues

DOI: 10.4324/9781003431077-10

discussed in this book, such as excessive staff burnout, misalignments of the standards and practice of safety, and a failure to address health disparities effectively and consistently, would be easily remedied.

We cannot develop solutions that fail to account for the premise that today's leaders face formidable challenges in an exceedingly complex healthcare industry environment. Consider that with hospital-based system expansion, both horizontally and vertically, leadership is increasingly separated from front-line employees by ever more layers of senior and middle management. And yet, regulatory, financial, and policy trends demand that the patient experience occupies a central focus in the leadership decision-making culture. We need to look at only one trend for insight – the transition from volume- to value-based care models, which underscores the growing significance of quality of care and patient outcomes as key measures of institutional performance. Yet, it is the very leader who is organizationally furthest from those on the front line who must inspire and mobilize employees to ensure that quality goals are realized.

The world of healthcare is not going to simplify. It is an industry with expenditures and a workforce size that dwarfs every other industry, including that of energy and the military. Hospitals are high reliability organizations that must place a premium on performing flawlessly. At the same time, they are bound by forces that test even the highest functioning organization from achieving that. Leadership success in such a labyrinth, in a sea of competing forces, is contingent on communication practices that engender trust, clarify the information environment and make it accessible, and show respect for all across the continuum of care.

In demonstrating where leadership needs to head with respect to using the patient experience as the organizing principle for its communication culture and decision-making orientation, we need to see where we have come from. This is no simple academic exercise, but rather a necessity; we can either be held hostage by the past or learn from it. As such, we may conceive of leadership in healthcare as occurring largely in three stages over the past 75 years, give or take. We may label the stages as *fiduciary*, *strategic*, and *generative* (Chait et al., 2005; Jiménez-Seminario, 2022). It is posited that healthcare leaders are transitioning from the strategic to the generative and, thus, we are quite early in the latter. As we will discuss, it is the generative phase that holds promise for ushering in a communication atmosphere more encompassing to facilitate stakeholder mobilization on the centrality of patient care.

Stages of Leadership Orientation

As has been discussed throughout this book, leadership style and the choices leaders make are profoundly intertwined. And no decision of organizational significance fails to influence the experience of patients who come for care. But leadership does not occur in a vacuum. While individuals in leadership positions have a great bearing on their organizations' culture and directions, they are influenced quite considerably by the norms and trends of the times.

For much of the 20th century, leadership concerns rested largely with financial and legal compliance. In the early 1980s, healthcare costs escalated out of control with many hospitals, no longer viewed as a function of "community service" being corporatized, giving rise to Healthcare Management Organizations (HMOs). As the new modalities of managed care emerged to mitigate healthcare costs to the patient through capitation, risk pools, and withholds, leadership turned more of its attention to developing strategy and engaging in planning.

As the 21st century got underway, and most particularly in the period following the implementation of the Affordable Care Act, the leaders of healthcare organizations began examining how to reframe the financial relationship between patients and healthcare systems and how to gain input into problem definition. By examining the three stages – fiduciary, strategic, and generative – we can ascertain what had been serviceable in each, and thus should be retained, as well as what should be shed to succeed in a new era of health delivery.

Fiduciary Leadership Stage

The hospital building boom of the 1940s and 1950s was spurred largely by two phenomena: (1) the migration of large swaths of the population from urban to suburban communities, and (2) legislation such as the 1946 Burton-Hill Act that supported the construction and modernization of hospitals and nursing homes through loans and grants (Johnson et al., 2023). At the same time, regulations regarding administrative and clinical protocols were becoming fortified. For example, the Joint Commission for the Accreditation of Hospitals (now "Joint Commission") was formed in the period of 1950–1952, and because of its independent and nonprofit status, it quickly emerged as the gold standard for quality. Accreditation status offered reassurance not only to the public but also to physicians who preferred to provide their services in hospitals with the then-JCAH accredited designation.

Boards of governors, overseers, trustees, or directors – titles notwithstanding – oversaw assets that included not just the physical building in which the hospital was housed but increasingly expensive technology and other materials. At the same time, the need to demonstrate that quality was a central feature of the hospital and to protect against risk, boards and hospital leadership adopted a fiduciary outlook for their role. In this regard, as discussed in Chapter 4, fiduciary obligations placed an emphasis on asset management and safeguarding the institution from untoward incidents. For example, quality would largely be a function of error rates. Accrediting bodies, such as the then-JCAH, set minimum compliance levels, at or above which a hospital would be seen as having satisfied the criteria for recognition.

At the time, there was less focus on two important and related issues that would take on increasing importance in the coming decades. First, the relatively exclusive regulatory focus at the time was on data aggregations, not work processes; as such, more emphasis was placed on the net result, not the protocols and activities related to achieving those results. For example, hospitals would be accountable for reporting error rates, not necessarily what was learned or changed as a result of such information. Second, and related, the failure to place an emphasis on improvement plans, the less able an organization would be to take what it learned and translate that into enhanced efficiencies and greater effectiveness, that is, into improvements in quality.

The fiduciary era, with a predominantly defensive and protective orientation, would understandably flourish in a period of fee for service. The reason is twofold. First, since operational inefficiencies could be passed along to third-party payers, the notion of how hospital services such as health promotion, disease prevention, diagnosis and treatment, and rehabilitation were accomplished would, by extension, take a back seat to ensuring that the hospital and its assets were safe from instability. But second, and more critically, hospitals were not yet under pressure to achieve economies of scale; thus, they were not compelled to merge or affiliate with one another or engage in acquisition behavior. Leadership could concentrate more fully on what was occurring *within* the hospital rather than having to consider *external* relationship management to the same extent.

Again, the prevailing leadership model in a fiduciary-dominated leadership culture involves concerns regarding the integrity of the hospital. Board members and executives would want to ensure that tasks are completed in a way that limits exposure to problematic occurrences. Thus, in a fiduciary-dominant environment, monitoring systems are set up to detect errors. Interpretations of what went wrong would tend to focus on mistakes (e.g., communication breakdowns) and less on broader systems-oriented analyses of interlocking components and processes.

Fiduciary thinking has not lost its importance or relevance. Protecting the organization, whether it be from legal, compliance, or financial risk, is a vital function of leadership at all levels. But as the last quarter of the 20th century got underway, its shortcomings as the dominant or relatively exclusive model would become apparent. As such, it was destined to cede its centrality in the domain of leadership as the 1980s gave way to reform efforts in the 1990s.

Strategic Leadership Stage

The 1970s, particularly the latter part of the decade, was a period of considerable inflation in healthcare and it ran significantly higher than the general consumer price index (CPI). By the time the 1980s rolled around, the national CPI was approximately 6%, while healthcare inflation, at over 11% in some years, was roughly double (US Inflation Calculator, n.d.). Not surprisingly, this produced pressure to control costs. In the period of 1982–1983, the federal government initiated the first substantial effort to implement prospective payment through the Medicare initiative, diagnostic related groups (DRG). Managed care followed suit, exacting limits on reimbursement flow into hospitals. The business of healthcare was changing. Among other undertakings to manage in the aftermath of fee-for-service reimbursement, hospitals began to coalesce into larger health systems to achieve economies of scale. As noted in Chapter 4, the majority of hospitals today are not standalone but rather are members of hospital systems.

As hospitals began contending with payers playing a larger role in defining reimbursement limits, they had to look outward, now seeing other providers who shared their geographic or service menu space as either potential competitors or allies. Key questions guided their assessment of provider organizations in their region or specialty area: with whom did their interests align? With whom would they compete over market share? Build mutually advantageous partnerships with medical staff? Align with insurance companies, HMOs, and other payers? What alliances would position them most favorably in a market in flux – flux as it pertained to health policy, reimbursement prospects, technological and clinical advances, and an aging population?

Fiduciary leadership continued to be, and always will be, a necessary model of leadership. However, in an era of competition and hospital system formation, this type of leadership became insufficient and strategic leadership became more and more essential. The relationship between fiduciary and strategic leadership would prove complex and, in fact, could even be in conflict. After all, and as discussed in Chapter 7, wearing the fiduciary hat evoked protective instincts, while the strategic model was critical not only to evaluate risks but also to take some. At the very least, the strategic model could mean adapting and adjusting. Whereas fiduciary equates with *stability*, strategic equates with *change*. And change during this period was taking place on a significant level of magnitude – merging, acquiring, being acquired, downsizing, upsizing, adding services, curtailing others – all at a rapid rate.

This new era unsettled established norms and, in a relatively short period, undermined the prevailing notion of hospitals as independent enterprises. We might recall that up through the 1960s and into the 1970s, small businesses like hardware stores and even banks were largely standalone entities. But over the course of, say, 20 or 30 years, these have largely been bundled into corporations like Lowe's and Home Depot and national bank corporations with local branches scattered throughout the country. In short order, the same would occur with hospitals, and we can point to events of the early 1980s as the starting point. Once out of the gate, such trends are hard to slow down.

If the era was disruptive to the status quo, it would naturally require leadership skilled in managing disruption (Brennan, 2022). Leaders would now be expected to craft a vision and break prevailing norms and rules to effectively bridge the mission and vision. We may call that *bridge strategy*. Effective leaders could develop a strategic direction through the mobilization of stakeholders and through a participative approach to decision-making. But no matter how it would occur, an industry transformation from independent entities to hospital-based systems could not successfully come to fruition from fiduciary orientation alone.

Disruptive Leadership Factor	Challenges for Today's Leaders
Brainiac	• Lifelong learning takes a lot of time • Because you may not know a priori what information will be useful, lifelong learning can be inefficient • Experimentation is expensive and time-consuming, when is it enough? Will it lead you to paralysis or action?
Disrupt own frame of reference	• Pressing daily concerns makes it hard to find the time to really think and thoroughly analyze • Cognitive myopia – to see new threats, you need to step completely out of your current context • Do you have the required high-level abstract/conceptual thinking ability? • Do you have high openness to new experience (a Big Five personality trait)?
Prioritize long term over short term	• There is no certainty that you will achieve long-term gain, while short-term pain is a (near) given • Financial markets will react adversely if quarterly expectations are not met – can you weather that storm pressure? • You need the resources to pay for short-term pain
High tolerance of uncertainty	• Humans are not wired to embrace uncertainty • Be willing to risk failure by having either a golden parachute or a very strong organizational commitment
Passion for the organization	• True passion for one's organization is rare • Disruptive leadership soaks up time, which conflicts with desire for work-life balance • If necessary, are you willing to prioritize company success over your own? • Are you ready to take the risk that if you lose your protectors in the C-suite, you may be fatally exposed?
Develop effective disruptive networks (Steenkamp, 2021)	• Finding pockets of people with the right mindset. Can you identify your Fishpond? • Creating a culture that encourages openness to change, risk-taking, and tolerance for failure • Disruptive networks are especially difficult to establish in bureaucratic, hierarchical organizations.

The risk of strategic thinking is that it holds the potential to manifest in two institutional cultures that hold the appearance of incompatibility – a leadership class focused on adaptation, and a middle management and staff class focused on steadiness. This would be expected considering the different incentives that reward different types of behavior. Simply, leadership exists in an ever-changing universe of economic challenge, policy ambiguity, corporate realignment, and concerns about market share, particularly as it relates to other providers who may vie for part of that share. In other words, the world of leadership is *change*. Middle management and staff have existed in a more anchored universe bound by compliance, task repetition, and adherence to protocol. In other words, *stability*. When leaders can bring these universes into harmony, middle management and staff are more willing and capable of adapting. But integrating change and stability mentalities is not without challenge as the pressures in both areas have been pronounced in the past decades.

We have seen this in our own work in hospitals. In one recent project, one of the authors was consulting with a hospital system that was about to commence a strategic planning process. The senior management team expressed concern that efforts to obtain input from employees would be for naught and would likely invite complaints about the organization going through too much change. When asked why they believed that staff would resist, senior management offered the following comments about hospital staff:

- "Our employees lack the ability to see the long term"
- "Seems pointless to try, after all, human nature makes people resistant to change"
- "Staff don't understand the challenges and threats we face"
- "They can't see the forest for the trees"
- "They get stuck in doing things the same way over and over"
- "Tunnel vision"
- "They have to look past their own daily work to see what's going on out there"
- "They don't understand the real world of the healthcare industry"

A month later, a focus group was held with employees from various departments around the hospital. The participants were asked how they view the role of management in relation to their own work in the hospital. Representative comments include the following:

- "They don't know what it's like to work in the trenches"
- "Management has no ability or interest to stay focused on today's problems"
- "Change, change, change...it's always change"
- "Working here is not all about the 'big picture,' it's the day-to-day things we do for our jobs and patients"

- "Worrying about tomorrow is fine for them [senior management], but I don't have that luxury with a full caseload of patients today"
- "I've been here 25 years, administrators come and go, each with a new vision that mostly goes nowhere"
- "If they would spend a day in my shoes, they would understand how this place really works"
- "They don't understand the real world of patient care"

It is the disconnect represented in the sampling of statements that can help to explain why disruptive leadership in healthcare can prove so challenging. And perhaps most telling are the final quotes from each, suggesting that leadership and those below it on the organization chart operate in different worlds, the former in the "healthcare industry" and the latter in "patient care."

Among the earliest uses of the term "disruptive" was in the 1990s when the internet was gaining widespread, indeed ubiquitous, application (Dan & Chieh, 2008). The internet introduced change on a profound order of magnitude, forcing companies to question how they can sustain their operation in a rapidly changing information technology environment. New entrants into key sectors were replacing longer-standing companies that had been well established. In short order, Netflix undid Blockbuster, Amazon undid Borders, and e-commerce upended a host of brick-and-mortar department stores (Donahue, 2023).

But healthcare, especially the provider side of the sector, doesn't face quite the same issues as other industries, at least in the sense of threats from new entrants into the system. This is because entering the industry as a large provider, particularly a hospital, is not easy. After all, there are considerable startup costs, a slew of regulatory and legal barriers, and, as discussed in Chapter 4, a return-on-investment opportunity that is limited by rules on reimbursement. These obstacles account for Harzlinger's (2008) contention that innovation in healthcare lags and even though "medical treatment has made astonishing advances over the years ... the packaging and delivery of that treatment are often inefficient, ineffective, and consumer unfriendly."

Thus, while other industries would embrace disruption, in part out of necessity, but also because their employees understood the stakes, disruption in healthcare was at least as much or more a matter of corporate realignment than of innovation. Unlike other industries, hospitals typically did not have R&D divisions which employees could look at and recognize that innovation was as much a part of the enterprise as updating medical records and reports on utilization.

Taking the unique features of healthcare into account, we might think of the industry as experiencing a particular kind of disruption, and that is, dislocation. While there have been far-ranging developments with respect to how patients are directed through hospital systems along with surges in ambulatory care and community health, "none of these 'disruptive' forces represent the fundamental strategic concern facing community hospital systems across the country today: How do healthcare leaders navigate and plan for technological change that is exceeding society's ability to absorb it? It's not disruption that you should be worried about; it's dislocation, the radical reshaping of entire industries, economies, and systems" (Donahue, 2023).

The disconnect between corporate leadership – the boardroom and the C-suite – and the management and staff of individual provider hospitals in a system would indicate the need for a next stage in leadership, one that builds on the assets of the fiduciary and strategic models. In so doing, it would transcend those models to integrate stability and change more fully in vision setting and goal development and implementation. Most especially, it is offered that such a leadership model would embrace the patient experience as the intersection at which all stakeholder interests can come together. The generative model of leadership offers such promise.

Generative Leadership Stage

Albert Einstein reportedly said, "If I had only one hour to save the world, I would spend fifty-five minutes defining the problem, and only five minutes finding the solution" (Calaprice, 2010). If the fiduciary mindset focuses on what would compromise the status of the organization, and the strategic mindset on what would influence the organization's competitiveness, the generative mindset focuses on the mission and its relationship to those served by the organization. If the goal is to understand and frame the situation, as is intended with the generative model, leadership must step back and consider the multiple perspectives essential for comprehensive analysis. It is what Einstein would presumably do in those 55 minutes.

A generative leadership model may be thought of as encompassing three characteristics: (1) a focus on systems, context, and expectations; (2) leadership skill development in the American College of Healthcare Executives (ACHE) competencies of communication and relationship management; and (3) employing mission and quality of patient experience as driving forces of leadership development.

A Focus on Systems, Context, and Expectations

To start with an example, one of our authors recently consulted with a hospital that had experienced an unexpected decline in patient satisfaction scores. A comprehensive examination was undertaken to get to the root of the problem. Satisfaction with the medical and nursing staff remained strong, as did ratings on cleanliness, food, and overall friendliness of staff.

Then they examined the discharge processes. About a year earlier, as part of an effort to increase patient satisfaction, the hospital instituted a practice by which patients would be discharged between 10:00 AM and 11:00 AM. The hospital enthusiastically publicized this new policy, and patients were pleased to hear they would not have to endure a lengthy discharge or spend much of their final day in the hospital just waiting to leave.

The problem was that the discharge staff was typically too overworked to meet the deadline. Despite the new policy, many patients were actually discharged after lunch. Since they were under the impression that the discharge would occur mid-morning, patients would sit in their rooms, dressed, and ready to leave by 10:00 AM, often with a loved one or friend who came to pick them up. As noon approached, the patients would see meal carts being wheeled into patient rooms. But they would not be provided with a meal since their discharge was to have taken place prior to lunch. In their haste to discharge patients as quickly as possible, the discharge staff would often feel harried and would communicate – even unwittingly – their stress in their interactions with patients.

Within a few days of being discharged, patients would receive their satisfaction survey in the mail or through email. An analysis of the responses indicated significant correlations between their discharge experience and their overall satisfaction with care and service at the hospital. All the other aspects of their experience – including, as mentioned, the medical and nursing care, the food, the diagnostic and treatment activities, the therapies, most of which were rated generally positively – did not correlate as well with the overall satisfaction score, as well as the score for "would you recommend this hospital to someone."

Part of the correlation could be explained by the fact that since discharge was the final experience it was freshest in patients' minds when they completed the survey. Another reason is that the hospital created an expectation that went unfulfilled. It would have been more advantageous to indicate a more realistic discharge time, say, 1:30 or 2:00 PM, provided the hospital could feel confident that 2:00 PM was the absolute latest that a discharge would take place. Or, as in the Disneyland wait-time model, it is better to set the expected time later than the actual time patients are more likely to be discharged (Mendoza et al., 2019). Research on compliance gaining and attitude formation suggests that when expectations are not met in one area of an experience, we tend to associate that element of the experience more fully with our perceptions of the whole experience (Gass & Seiter, 2022).

The unfulfilled expectations at the hospital proved problematic for all involved: patients who were left feeling stranded in a situation over which they had no control; friends or relatives who came to take the patient home; discharge staff who had to perform their work on a frenetic basis; the hospital whose ratings on vital measures of patient satisfaction were drifting downward; other patients who may have not gotten the proper attention in the frenzied rush to discharge patients scheduled to leave; other hospital functions and departments which had to factor ill-advised discharge timing into their schedules and routines.

In its eagerness to please patients by "assuring" they would be released from the hospital in the morning, the hospital actually evoked the very opposite reaction it sought to achieve. Through its discharge policy, the hospital intended to communicate to patients that it had their best interests in mind. But communicating expectations involves a powerful risk if the expectations cannot be met. Communication and expectations cannot be separate from operational capability, but very much aligned with it.

A generative model would start with two foundational assumptions: first, from a systems perspective, the components within the system would be viewed as interacting, interrelating, and mutually influencing one another. Failing to view it in this way would render it difficult if not impossible to link goals with operational capacity and consumer interests (Wheatley, 2006). For example, segmenting the discharge staff and reassigning their priorities without considering the broader impact intensified a problem rather than alleviating it. This principle applies to organizations of any size, scope, and purpose.

Second, establishing expectations requires careful forethought and input from the full spectrum of stakeholders who are affected or potentially affected. To paraphrase Einstein, a harried and incomplete approach to defining a problem can create a new problem which may be more serious than the one it originally sought to correct. In a generative model, it is the expectations of those served by the organization that constitute the basis of goal formation; absent a process of facilitating a discussion and listening, leadership could only speculate about those expectations.

Leadership Skill Development in the ACHE Competency Framework

The ACHE advances five domains of leadership skill. The domain entitled "Communication and Relationship Management" is defined as "The ability to communicate clearly and concisely with internal and external customers, establish and maintain relationships and facilitate constructive interactions with individuals and groups" (The American College of Healthcare Executives' Healthcare Executive Competencies Assessment Tool, 2021).

At its core, generative leadership facilitates and ensures communication flow. One cannot engage with others in defining problems without building the relationship, creating a relational climate of trust so that the other party will be forthcoming with information pertinent to the matter at hand, and managing the relationship in a way that motivates others to appreciate the integrity of the leader's intent. In the example of the ill-fated discharge policy presented above, the hospital's goals might have been achieved had it sought input from patients about their preferences for discharge protocols and from staff who would be directly or indirectly involved or affected.

As discussed throughout this book, it is not uncommon for stakeholders to bring differing agendas to decision-making contexts. In fact, this is to be expected. Leadership has multiple avenues to resolve differences that are brought to them. In the generative model, leadership would seek to work with those involved to frame and define the decision options by establishing their connection to the greater good of the organization, namely the quality of the patient experience. This is why the skills of team building, negotiation, conflict resolution, and, notably, emphasis on shared values, are so critical, especially in an era in which the combination of stakeholder diversity and complexity, high stakes, challenging economic conditions, and policy uncertainty can easily create decision-making circumstances in which different agendas appear mutually exclusive. Those relationship management skills are necessary to find common ground. It doesn't mean the definition of the problem will be universally accepted or acceptable, but those skills will go a long way in leading stakeholders to the belief that they were heard.

ACHE HEALTHCARE EXECUTIVE COMPETENCIES ASSESSMENT TOOL: COMMUNICATION AND RELATIONSHIP MANAGEMENT SKILLS ASSESSMENT TOOL (2021)

A. **Relationship Management**
   Organizational structure and relationships
   Build collaborative relationships
   Demonstrate effective interpersonal relations
   Develop and maintain medical staff relationships
   Develop and maintain supplier relationships
   Identify stakeholder needs/expectations
   Provide internal customer service
   Practice and value shared decision making
   Other professional norms and standards
   Creating an ethical culture in an organization

B. **Communication Skills**
   Public relations
   Principles of communication and their specific applications
   Sensitivity to what is correct behavior when communicating with diverse cultures, internal and external
   Communicate organizational mission, vision, objectives, and priorities
   Identify and use human and technical resources to develop and deliver communications
   Prepare and deliver business communications
   Present results of data analysis to decision makers
   Provide and receive constructive feedback
   Use factual data to produce and deliver credible and understandable reports

C. **Facilitation and Negotiation**
   Mediation, negotiation, and dispute resolution techniques
   Team building techniques
   Labor relations strategies
   Build effective physician and administrator leadership teams
   Create, participate in, and lead teams
   Facilitate conflict and alternative dispute resolution
   Facilitate group dynamics, processes, meetings, and discussions

Employing Mission and Quality of Patient Experience as Driving Forces of Leadership Development

Every organization faces challenges, including some of their own making as illustrated by the hospital that modified its discharge policy. By trying to implement a convenience, it created a problem larger than the one it was trying to solve. The lesson lies in how the problem was defined. In that case, hospital leadership assumed responsibility for defining the problem as well as the solution. We have discussed the generative leadership role of facilitator in framing challenges. The question is, what frame is most suitable?

The most effective lens through which to examine any issue, whether a problem or an opportunity, is the one shared by all stakeholders in all hospitals, and that is the quality of the patient experience. Every healthcare organization touts its commitment to the patient. And by and large, we may assume they are all well-meaning. But as we have discussed, there is enough of a disconnect between that desire and the data on quality, revealing that things get in the way. That can include any number of constraining factors such as limited resources or a market with a demographic undergoing change unfavorable to the viability of the hospital's base of services. But we cannot ignore that a disconnect is also a function of leadership.

Leadership is the vehicle through which a common perspective on the organization is established and promoted. It takes hard work daily to do this well. And it involves continuous reminders – through word and deed – that the patient comes first. Consider a billing clerk who works off-campus. How can that person remain motivated to think of the patient's best interest? How can the IT specialist who works with system software issues find meaningfulness in serving the patient? How can the benefits coordinator feel connected to the work of the clinical staff? And how can the physical therapist understand that the billing clerk and the IT specialist also contribute in a valuable way to serving the patient? The route from their boxes on the organization chart to the most senior levels of governance at the corporate level is a long and layered trail. But it is the perspective of the billing clerk, the IT specialist, the benefits coordinator, and the physical therapist that is likely to be more revealing about whether "putting the patient first" is a nice sounding corporate slogan or the authentic central feature of the organization's culture.

In a highly functioning generative leadership environment, this is what those staff members are likely to experience: they would be invited to participate in forums soliciting their views of working conditions and how that relates to their ability to serve patients, and feedback about their contributions would be provided. They will believe that they can freely and comfortably speak to their supervisors and managers about concerns related to their ability to serve the patient effectively. They will receive training on the necessities of doing their jobs but will also gain an understanding of why the new skills are necessary and how they pertain to trends in healthcare and institutional direction. They will be kept apprised of organizational strategy and asked for ideas. They may not readily know the names of those in corporate management or on the corporate board, but they will be aware that its composition and agenda are built around quality of patient experience goals; they will receive regular updates about that and will be invited to participate in forums at which those issues are discussed. They will be asked to participate in multidisciplinary teams and, in so doing, will have a better idea of how their work is connected to the whole. They will see that social justice initiatives like diversity are not just lip service but in keeping with core institutional values. And while their requests may not always be met with "yes," they will feel heard and respected.

Pie in the Sky? Too Costly to Do All these Things?

Given the pace of change in the healthcare industry and the economic challenges that weaken operating margin opportunities, a generative step-back approach may seem like a luxury leader of healthcare organizations can ill afford. Anyone who believes that should consider this: according to NSI Nursing Solutions (2023), over the five-year period from 2017 to 2022, the average hospital experienced a turnover of 105% of its workforce, with 95% being voluntary. Moreover, according to the report: "The average cost of turnover for a bedside Registered Nurse is more than $52,350, costing the average hospital between $6.6 million and $10.5 million per year. With each percentage point increase or decrease in the Registered Nurse turnover rate, hospitals will lose or save $380,600 per year." That final statistic is worth emphasizing: if leading from a generative model can result in just a 1% point improvement in retention, the average hospital may save more than $380,000 per year.

A generative model places an emphasis on employee engagement, which is positively associated with employee and organizational performance. For example, the greater the level of engagement, the less turnover there is, along with up to 41% reduced absenteeism, fewer safety incidents with some organizations improving their records by 70%; additionally, some organizations have experienced profitability increases of over 20% (Nink & Robison, 2016).

THE GENERATIVE APPROACH TO LEADERSHIP

This approach fosters organizational fitness by maintaining flexibility to accommodate changing conditions. This dynamic stability is maintained by focusing collective attention on the intangible and symbolic layers of reality (e.g., values, mission, patterns, processes, learning, and relationships). This enables an organization to both adapt and sustain its identity over time. A generative approach also fosters interdependence. Whereas technical-rational management seeks to isolate variables and reduce analysis to individual components, process structures provide paths for feedback loops that accommodate recursive influences and reflexive causation, promoting information flow between internal and external boundaries at multiple scales (Castillo & Trinh, 2019).

Generative leadership in a healthcare environment begins with the premise that employee motivation should not be taken for granted, and that it is a precious commodity. And such motivation is grounded in two foundational imperatives: respect for the integrity of the patient experience and respect for employees. These are highly interrelated.

When employees understand the importance of their contribution to the patient, they also see their connection to one another and that they are part of a community all oriented around the same broad objective. Generative leadership, when practiced effectively, invests in helping every employee recognize that they add value to the quality of the patient's encounter with the organization, even if their work is remote from direct patient care. Janitors who feel that their work is valued not from occasional patronizing platitudes, but because the organization has committed to helping them understand its importance through training, seeking their opinions, and inviting them to contribute ideas for environmental improvements will have an Environmental Services staff that is more reliable, productive, stable, and capable. Under those circumstances, employees are more likely to be motivated to seek sustained employability as well as advancement opportunities.

The principle is not confined to rank-and-file employees. If the CEO and senior leadership of a hospital in a system believe that the parent board is first and foremost committed – *genuinely* committed – to quality and to the patient experience, they too will perform more capably and productively. Their professional identity and pride are more likely to be linked to the performance of the organization and there will be greater interest in seeing initiatives through to their completion. Absent that, their ambition may be more linked to career climbing best accomplished through opportunities external to the organization.

Ultimately, a focus on quality does not diminish, undermine, or replace leadership priorities related to financial management, strategic initiatives as they relate to partnership opportunity and market-share development, capital improvement, or service line development. In a generative framework, quality is less likely to be buried in the priority matrix and will also be seen as inextricably interwoven among all those areas that can easily come to dominate leadership's attention. It starts with the board, including and perhaps especially, who sits on it. In addition to expanding membership to those who, by virtue of their expertise and role in the organization, can give voice to quality of care, the symbolism of their presence speaks volumes to all stakeholders about what the organization holds near and dear.

Quality and Communication Are Inseparable

As we have sought to demonstrate, quality is more than a collection of standards, metrics, and statistics. All of these, of course, are vital to the evidence-based necessities of any healthcare organization that has the sacred responsibility to care for people whose lives are in their hands. We have shown what quality looks like from an empirical perspective and what accounts for the healthcare organizations falling short in the quest to ensure that high standards are consistently met. We have also sought to establish what leadership of healthcare organizations can do to bring their organizations closer to achieving quality-related goals. In so doing, we focused on the triad of the board, senior management, and physician and nursing leadership. We concentrated on those because, while quality is the responsibility of every stakeholder, certainly every employee, that triad holds great responsibility for setting the tone for a culture of quality and culture of safety in the organization.

In the strictly technical-rational scenario, as highlighted by Castillo and Trinh (2019), quality may be viewed as a function of analysis of system components in a relatively isolated manner. We are best advised to think of the spirit of quality as residing in the realm of communication. Thus, we close by re-examining the aims and scope of effective internal and external communications. We may think of communication as the "process of creating shared meaning." Simple, for sure, but profound in its implications. According to this definition, communication does not require the parties to agree or coalesce around the same conclusion. Nor does it require the parties to forge a closer relationship. However, it does mean that the parties seek a common understanding, that is, they strive to have the other party feel seen, heard, and understood. This cannot occur without active listening. And, by extension, the term "shared" implies that communication is not one-way but rather a dynamic process in which all parties are engaged. Moreover, as a process, communication is shaped by context, history, culture, and motives.

While as an industry, it is important to endeavor to create coherence and fairness, organizational leaders can use tools of communication and relationship management to bring continuous improvement to their organizations, build institutional cultures of quality, promote transparency, and aim for higher levels of stakeholder input and satisfaction. If that is the framework they adopt, they will navigate their organizations so that the experience of the patient is the single most significant determinant of organizational success.

The CEO who believes that communication is a matter exclusively of informing others may be satisfying one condition of communication, but they may miss the complexity, not to mention, the spirit, of the definition. Furthermore, trust is inextricably linked to communication effectiveness. It needs to be initiated and sustained. Establishing trust between patients and providers creates a partnership that helps sustain patient engagement. When trust is present, employees feel empowered to devote more energy, adapt to shifting circumstances and thereby exercise more resilience, and take pride in serving those for whom the organization exists – the patient.

References

Brennan, N. (2022, February). Disruptive leadership: Making waves, thriving when it is hard to be a leader. *Journal of Nursing Administration*, 20(1), 52–55.

Calaprice, A. (2010). *The Ultimate Quotable Einstein*. Princeton, NJ: Princeton University Press.

Castillo, E. A., & Trinh, M. P. (2019). Catalyzing capacity: Absorptive, adaptive, and generative leadership. [Absorptive, adaptive, and generative leadership] *Journal of Organizational Change Management*, 32(3), 356–376. (https://doi.org/10.1108/JOCM-04-2017-0100)

Chait, R., Ryan, W., & Taylor, B. (2005). *Governance as Leadership: Reframing the Work of Nonprofit Boards.* Hoboken, NJ: John Wiley & Sons. John Wiley & Sons. (https://doi.org/10.1093/intqhc/mzab036)

Dan, Y., & Chieh, H. (2008). A reflective review of disruptive innovation theory, in *PICMET '08 – 2008 Portland International Conference on Management of Engineering & Technology,* Cape Town, South Africa, pp. 402–414. (https://doi.org/10.1109/PICMET.2008.4599648)

Donahue, A. (2023). *Why the Idea of Disruption Is So Hard for Healthcare Leaders to Understand.* Healthcare Financial Management Association: Finance and Business Strategy. https://www.hfma.org/finance-and-business-strategy/why-the-idea-of-disruption-is-so-hard-for-healthcare-leaders-to-understand/

Gass, R., & Seiter, J. (2022). *Persuasion, Social Influence, and Compliance Gaining* (7th ed.). Routledge, New York.

Harzlinger, R. (2008, May). Why innovation in health care is so hard. *Harvard Business Review.* https://hbr.org/2006/05/why-innovation-in-health-care-is-so-hard

Jiménez-Seminario, G. (2022, June). Three modes of corporate governance: A call to reflection & effective action-a note. *Corporate Governance Insight,* 4(1), eISSN: 2582–0834. https://grfcg.in/wp-content/uploads/journal/published_paper/volume-4/issue-1/j8ERRjpO.pdf

Johnson, J., Davey, K., & Greenhill, R. (2023). *Sultz and Young's Health Care USA: Understanding Its Organization and Delivery* (10th ed.). Burlington, MA: Jones & Bartlett Learning.

Mendoza, D., Wu, W. & Leung, M. (2019). Predicting the expected waiting time of popular attractions in Walt Disney World. *Journal of Undergraduate Research & Scholarly Work.* 6. https://rrpress.utsa.edu/handle/20.500.12588/99?show=full

Nink, M., & Robison, M. (2016, December 20). The damage inflicted by poor managers. *Gallup Business Journal.*

NSI Nursing Solutions. (2023). *2023 NSI National Health Care Retention & RN Staffing Report.* https://www.nsinursingsolutions.com/Documents/Library/NSI_National_Health_Care_Retention_Report.pdf

Steenkamp, J. (2021, Spring). Admiral Jacky Fisher and the art of disruptive leadership. *Management and Business Review,* 1(2). https://mbrjournal.com/2021/11/02/admiral-jacky-fisher-and-the-art-of-disruptive-leadership/

The American College of Healthcare Executives' Healthcare Executive Competencies Assessment Tool (2021). *The American College of Healthcare Executives.* https://www.ache.org/-/media/ache/career-resource-center/cat_2021.pdf#:~:text=Within%20the%20ACHE%20Healthcare%20Executive%20Competencies%20Assessment%20Tool%2Cthe,the%20Healthcare%20Environment%20and%20Business%20Skills%20and%20Knowledge

US Inflation Calculator. (n.d.). *Health Care Inflation in the United States (1948–2021).* https://www.usinflationcalculator.com/inflation/health-care-inflation-in-the-unitedstates/

Wheatley, M. J. (2006). *Leadership and the new science: Discovering order in a chaotic world.* Berrett-Koehler Publishers, Oakland, CA.

Index

Note: Locators in *italics* represent figures and **bold** indicate tables in the text.

Printed in the United States
by Baker & Taylor Publisher Services